DEREGULATION, BANK FAILURES AND NEW TECHNOLOGY

DEREGULATION, BANK FAILURES AND NEW TECHNOLOGY

Prem Nagpal

CYBER TECH PUBLICATIONS
4264/3, Ansari Road, Daryaganj, New Delhi-110002 (India)
Ph.: 011-23244078, 011-43559448 Fax: 011-23280028
E-Mail: cyberpublicationsdelhi@yahoo.com
Website: www.cybertechpublications.com

DEREGULATION, BANK FAILURES AND NEW TECHNOLOGY

Prem Nagpal

First Edition 2010

Published by :

G.S. Rawat for **Cyber Tech Publications**
4264/3, Ansari Road, Daryaganj, New Delhi-110002 (India)
Ph.: 011-23244078, 011-43559448 Fax: 011-23280028
E-Mail: cyberpublicationsdelhi@yahoo.com
Website: www.cybertechpublications.com

Printed at: Asian Offset Printers, Delhi-53

Preface

Bank failures, crises, global banking, megamergers, changes in technology--the effect of these world events is to weaken existing methods of regulating bank safety and soundness, and even to make some methods ineffective. Federal regulators are evaluating new ways to solve them.

The world's banking system collapsed last fall, was placed on life support at a cost of some trillions of dollars, and remains comatose. We may be too close to the event to grasp its enormity. A vocabulary rich only in euphemisms calls what has happened to the economy a "recession." We are well beyond that. We are in the midst of the biggest economic crisis since the Great Depression of the 1930s.

The search now underway for new methods that are global in scope. Inevitably, they will involve cross-border supervision and international cooperation. Covering a wide range of topics, from the rationale of banking regulation to optimal banking regulation in the new world environments, this book examines the innovative tools needed to cope with these problems. Greater reliance on market discipline; the use of internal controls based on statistical models, such as Value-at-Risk; and subordinated debt are discussed.

This timely, probing analysis of one of the hottest topics in bank regulation today, is an important resource for professionals and their academic colleagues in the fields of banking, finance, investment, and world trade.

—Author

Preface

CONTENTS

CONTENTS

Chapter

1

Introduction

A system of trading in money which involved safeguarding deposits and making funds available for borrowers, banking developed in the Middle Ages in response to the growing need for credit in commerce. The lending functions of banks were undertaken in England by money- lenders. Until their expulsion by Edward I in 1291, the most important money-lenders were Jews. They were replaced by Italian merchants who had papal dispensations to lend money at interest. In the 13th cent. credit was essential to finance commerce and major projects. The most important was the wool trade but other examples included large buildings such as Edward's castles in north Wales. When Italians had their activities in England curtailed in the early 14th cent., they were replaced by English merchants and goldsmiths, whose rates of interest were sufficiently low to avoid the usury laws.

Monarchs had borrowed from merchants and landowners for centuries. By the late 17th cent., the growth of parliamentary power over government expenditures required more regulation. The Bank of England, founded in 1694, gave the government and other users of credit access to English funds. Similar developments occurred in Scotland and Ireland. These banks remained without serious competition until the later 18th cent., when expanding commercial activities gave scope to merchants, brewers, and landowners to establish banks based on their own cash reserves. Errors of judgement sometimes occurred and 'runs on the bank' took place when depositors, fearing for the security of their money, demanded its return.

Fluctuations in the value of money because of the return to a gold-based currency after the end of the Napoleonic wars (1815) precipitated a series of crises. To stabilize the currency the government eventually introduced the 1844 Bank Charter Act, which gave the Bank of England the functions of supervising the note issue and of monitoring the activities of the banking system. Regulatory powers were put in place in 1845 to control banking in Scotland and Ireland.

In the 19th cent., overseas trade and the expanding British empire reinforced the place of London as a centre of merchant banking. The skills of these specialist bankers attracted business from foreign firms and governments Seeking loans. These arrangements made possible the rapid development of railways, heavy engineering, mines, and large commercial developments. Many of these merchant banks survive, including Rothschilds, Lazard Brothers, Kleinwort Benson, and Schroders. Internal trade was funded mainly by a larger number of local banks which, after the middle of the 19th cent., became consolidated into a much smaller number of banks. Numbers continued to diminish so that by 1980 banking was dominated by four companies: Barclays, Lloyds, Midland, and National Westminster.

Banking has been characterized, largely because of technological innovation, by anincreasingly sophisticated provision ofbanking services and an expansion of consumer credit. The business of safeguarding and lending money is often arranged through machine-readable cards and continuous access by telephone.

Savings and Loan Crisis

The savings and loan crisis of the 1980s and 1990s (commonly referred to as the S&L crisis) was the failure of 745 savings and loan associations (S&Ls aka *thrifts*). An S&L association is a financial institution in the United States that accepts savings deposits and makes mortgage loans. The ultimate cost of the crisis is estimated to have totaled around $160.1 billion, about $124.6 billion of which was directly paid for by the U.S. government—that is, the U.S. taxpayer, either directly or through charges on their savings and loan accounts—which contributed to the large budget deficits of the early 1990s.

The concomitant slowdown in the finance industry and the real estate market may have been a contributing cause of the 1990–1991 economic recession. Between 1986 and 1991, the number of new homes constructed per year dropped from 1.8 million to 1 million, the lowest rate since World War II.

Background

The thrift industry traces its origins to the British building society movement that emerged in the late eighteenth century. American thrifts (known then as "building and loans" or "B&Ls") shared many of the same basic goals: to help working-class men and women save for the future and purchase homes. Thrifts were not-for-profit cooperative organizations that were typically managed by the membership and local institutions that served well-defined groups of aspiring homeowners. While banks offered a wide array of products to individuals and businesses, thrifts often made only home mortgages primarily to working-class men and women. Thrift leaders believed they were part of a broader social reform effort and not a financial industry. According to thrift leaders, B&Ls not only helped people become better citizens by making it easier to buy a home, they also taught the habits of systematic savings and mutual cooperation which strengthened personal morals.

For the first forty years following the formation of the first thrift in 1831, B&Ls were few in number and found in only a handful of Midwestern and Eastern states. This situation changed in the late nineteenth century as urban growth and the demand for housing related to the Second Industrial Revolution caused the number of thrifts to explode. The popularity of B&Ls led to the creation of a new type of thrift in the 1880s called the "national" B&L. The "nationals" were often for-profit businesses formed by bankers or industrialists that employed promoters to form local branches to sell shares to prospective members. The "nationals" promised to pay savings rates up to four times greater than any other financial institution.

When the effects of the Depression of 1893 (known as Panic of 1893) resulted in a decline in members, the "nationals" experienced a sudden reversal of fortunes. Because a steady stream of new members was critical for a "national" to pay both the interest on savings and the hefty salaries for the organizers, the falloff in payments caused dozens of "nationals" to fail, and by the end of the nineteenth century nearly all the "nationals" were out of business (National Building and Loans Crisis). This led to the creation of the first state regulations governing B&Ls, to make thrift operations more uniform, and the formation of a national trade association to not only protect B&L interests, but also promote business growth. The trade association led efforts to create more uniform accounting, appraisal, and lending procedures. It also spearheaded the drive to have all thrifts refer to themselves as "savings and loans" not B&Ls, and to convince managers of the need to assume more professional roles as financiers.

In the twentieth century, the two decades that followed the end of World War II were the most successful period in the history of the thrift industry. The return of millions of servicemen eager to take up their prewar lives led to a dramatic increase in new families, and this "baby boom" caused a surge in new mostly suburban home construction. By the 1940s S&Ls (the name change occurred in the late 1930s) provided the majority of the financing for this expansion. The result was strong industry expansion that lasted through the early 1960s.

An important trend involved raising rates paid on savings to lure deposits, a practice that resulted in periodic rate wars between thrifts and even commercial banks. These wars became so severe that in 1966 Congress took the highly unusual move of setting limits on savings rates for both commercial banks and S&Ls. From 1966 to 1979 the enactment of rate controls presented thrifts with a number of unprecedented challenges, chief of which was finding ways to continue to expand in an economy characterized by slow growth, high interest rates and inflation. These conditions, which came to be known as stagflation, wrecked havoc with thrift finances for a variety of reasons. Because regulators controlled the rates thrifts could pay on savings, when interest rates rose depositors often withdrew their funds and placed them in accounts that earned market rates, a process known as disintermediation. At the same time, rising rates and a slow growth economy made it harder for people to qualify for mortgages that in turn limited the ability to generate income.

In response to these complex economic conditions, thrift managers came up with several innovations, such as alternative mortgage instruments and interest-bearing checking accounts, as a way to retain funds and generate lending business. Such actions allowed the industry to continue to record steady asset growth and profitability during the 1970s even though the actual number of thrifts was falling. Despite such growth, there were still clear signs that the industry was chafing under the constraints of regulation. This was especially true with the large S&Ls in the western United States that yearned for additional lending powers to ensure continued growth. Despite several efforts to modernize these laws in the 1970s, few substantive changes were enacted.

In 1979 the financial health of the thrift industry was again challenged by a return of high interest rates and inflation, sparked this time by a doubling of oil prices. Because the sudden nature of these changes threatened to cause hundreds of S&L failures, Congress finally acted on deregulating the thrift industry. It passed two laws, the Depository Institutions Deregulation and Monetary Control Act of 1980 and the Garn-St. Germain Depository Institutions Act of 1982. The deregulation not only allowed thrifts to offer a wider array of savings products, but also significantly expanded their lending authority. These changes were intended to allow S&Ls to "grow" out of their problems, and as such represented the first time that the government explicitly sought to increase S&L profits as opposed to promoting housing and homeownership. Other changes in thrift oversight included authorizing the use of more lenient accounting rules to report their financial condition, and the elimination of restrictions on the minimum numbers of S&L stockholders. Such policies, combined with an overall decline in regulatory oversight (known as forbearance), would later be cited as factors in the later collapse of the thrift industry.

CAUSES

Tax Reform Act of 1986

By enacting 26 U.S.C. § 469 (relating to limitations on deductions for passive activity losses and limitations on passive activity credits) to remove many tax shelters, especially for real estate investments, the Tax Reform Act of 1986 significantly decreased the value of many such investments which had been held more for their tax-advantaged status than for their inherent profitability. This contributed to the end of the real estate boom of the early to mid '80s and facilitated the Savings and Loan crisis. Prior to 1986, much real estate investment was done by passive investors. It was common for syndicates of investors to pool their resources in order to invest in property, commercial or residential. They would then hire management companies to run the operation. TRA 86 reduced the value of these investments by limiting the extent to which losses associated with them could be deducted from the investor's gross income. This, in turn, encouraged the holders of loss-generating properties to try and unload them, which contributed further to the problem of sinking real estate values. This turmoil and repositioning in real estate markets was caused not by changes in market conditions.

Deregulation

The deregulation of S&Ls gave them many of the capabilities of banks, without the same regulations as banks. Savings and loan associations could choose to be under either a state or a federal charter. Immediately after deregulation of the federally chartered thrifts, state-chartered thrifts rushed to become federally chartered, because of the advantages associated with a federal charter. In response, states such as California and Texas changed their regulations so to be similar to federal regulations.

IMPRUDENT REAL ESTATE LENDING

In an effort to take advantage of the real estate boom (outstanding US mortgage loans: 1976 $700 billion; 1980 $1.5 trillion) and high interest rates of the late 1970s and early 1980s, many S&Ls lent far more money than was prudent, and too-risky ventures which many S&Ls were not qualified to assess. L. William Seidman, former chairman of both the Federal Deposit Insurance Corporation (FDIC) and the Resolution Trust Corporation, stated, "The banking problems of the '80s and '90s came primarily, but not exclusively, from unsound real estate lending."

Brokered Deposits

One of the most important contributors to the problem was deposit brokerage. Deposit brokers, somewhat like stockbrokers, are paid a commission by the customer to find the best certificate of deposit (CD) rates and place their customers' money in those CDs. These CDs, however, are usually short-term $100,000 CDs. Previously, banks and thrifts could only have five percent of their deposits be brokered deposits; the race to the bottom caused this limit to be lifted. A small one-branch thrift could then attract a large number of deposits simply by offering the highest rate. To make money off this expensive money, it had to lend at even higher rates, meaning that it had to make more, riskier investments. This system was made even more damaging when certain deposit brokers instituted a scam known as "linked financing." In "linked financing", a deposit broker would approach a thrift and say he would steer a large amount of deposits to that thrift if the thrift would lend certain people money (the people, however, were paid a fee to apply for the loans and told to give the loan proceeds to the deposit broker). This caused the thrifts to be tricked into taking on bad loans. Michael Milken of Drexel, Burnham and Lambert packaged brokered funds for several

S&Ls on the condition that the institutions would invest in the junk bonds of his clients.

End of Inflation

Another factor was the efforts of the federal reserve to wring inflation out of the economy, marked by Paul Volcker's speech of October 6, 1979, with a series of rises in short-term interest rates. This led to increases in the short-term cost of funding to be higher than the return on portfolios of mortgage loans, a large proportion of which may have been fixed rate mortgages (a problem that is known as an asset-liability mismatch). This effort failed and interest rates continued to skyrocket, placing even more pressure on S&Ls as the 1980s dawned and led to increased focus on high interest-rate transactions. Zvi Bodie, professor of finance and economics at Boston University School of Management, writing in the St. Louis Federal Reserve *Review* wrote, "asset-liability mismatch was a principal cause of the Savings and Loan Crisis".

Major Causes According to United States League of Savings Institutions

The following is a detailed summary of the major causes for losses that hurt the savings and loan business in the 1980s:

1. Lack of net worth for many institutions as they entered the '80s, and a wholly inadequate net worth regulation.
2. Decline in the effectiveness of Regulation Q in preserving the spread between the cost of money and the rate of return on assets, basically stemming from inflation and the accompanying increase in market interest rates.
3. Absence of an ability to vary the return on assets with increases in the rate of interest required to be paid for deposits.
4. Increased competition on the deposit gathering and mortgage origination sides of the business, with a sudden burst of new technology making possible a whole new way of

conducting financial institutions generally and the mortgage business specifically.

5. Savings and Loans gained a wide range of new investment powers with the passage of the Depository Institutions Deregulation and Monetary Control Act and the Garn-St. Germain Depository Institutions Act. A number of states also passed legislation that similarly increased investment options. These introduced new risks and speculative opportunities which were difficult to administer. In many instances management lacked the ability or experience to evaluate them, or to administer large volumes of nonresidential construction loans.
6. Elimination of regulations initially designed to prevent lending excesses and minimize failures. Regulatory relaxation permitted lending, directly and through participations, in distant loan markets on the promise of high returns. Lenders, however, were not familiar with these distant markets. It also permitted associations to participate extensively in speculative construction activities with builders and developers who had little or no financial stake in the projects.
7. Fraud and insider transaction abuses were the principal cause for some 20% of savings and loan failures the past three years and a greater percentage of the dollar losses borne by the Federal Savings and Loan Insurance Corporation (FSLIC).
8. A new type and generation of opportunistic savings and loan executives and owners—some of whom operated in a fraudulent manner — whose takeover of many institutions was facilitated by a change in FSLIC rules reducing the minimum number of stockholders of an insured association from 400 to one.
9. Dereliction of duty on the part of the board of directors of some savings associations. This permitted management to make uncontrolled use of some new operating authority, while directors failed to control expenses and prohibit obvious conflict of interest situations.

10. A virtual end of inflation in the American economy, together with overbuilding in multifamily, condominium type residences and in commercial real estate in many cities. In addition, real estate values collapsed in the energy states — Texas, Louisiana, Oklahoma particularly due to falling oil prices — and weakness occurred in the mining and agricultural sectors of the economy.
11. Pressures felt by the management of many associations to restore net worth ratios. Anxious to improve earnings, they departed from their traditional lending practices into credits and markets involving higher risks, but with which they had little experience.
12. The lack of appropriate, accurate, and effective evaluations of the savings and loan business by public accounting firms, security analysts, and the financial community.
13. Organizational structure and supervisory laws, adequate for policing and controlling the business in the protected environment of the 1960s and 1970s, resulted in fatal delays and indecision in the examination/supervision process in the 1980s.
14. Federal and state examination and supervisory staffs insufficient in number, experience, or ability to deal with the new world of savings and loan operations.
15. The inability or unwillingness of the Bank Board and its legal and supervisory staff to deal with problem institutions in a timely manner. Many institutions, which ultimately closed with big losses, were known problem cases for a year or more. Often, it appeared, political considerations delayed necessary supervisory action.

Failures

The United States Congress granted all thrifts in 1980, including savings and loan associations, the power to make consumer and commercial loans and to issue transaction accounts. Designed to help the thrift industry retain its deposit base and to improve its profitability, the Depository Institutions Deregulation and Monetary Control Act (DIDMCA) of 1980 allowed thrifts to make consumer loans up to 20 percent of their assets, issue credit cards, accept negotiable order of withdrawal (NOW) accounts from individuals and nonprofit organizations, and invest up to 20 percent of their assets in commercial real estate loans.

The damage to S&L operations led Congress to act, passing a bill in September 1981 allowing S&Ls to sell their mortgage loans and use the cash generated to seek better returns; the losses created by the sales were to be amortized over the life of the loan, and any losses could also be offset against taxes paid over the preceding 10 years. This all made S&Ls eager to sell their loans. The buyers – major Wall Street firms – were quick to take advantage of the S&Ls' lack of expertise, buying at 60%-90% of value and then transforming the loans by bundling them as, effectively, government-backed bonds (by virtue of Ginnie Mae, Freddie Mac, or Fannie Mae guarantees). S&Ls were one group buying these bonds, holding $150 billion by 1986, and being charged substantial fees for the transactions.

In 1982, the Garn-St Germain Depository Institutions Act was passed and increased the proportion of assets that thrifts could hold in consumer and commercial real estate loans and allowed thrifts to invest 5 percent of their assets in commercial loans until January 1, 1984, when this percentage increased to 10 percent.

A large number of S&L customers' defaults and bankruptcies ensued, and the S&Ls that had overextended themselves were forced into insolvency proceedings themselves.

The U.S. government agency FSLIC, which at the time insured S&L accounts in the same way the Federal Deposit Insurance Corporation insures commercial bank accounts, then had to repay all the depositors whose money was lost. From 1986 to 1989, FSLIC closed or otherwise resolved 296 institutions with total assets of $125 billion. An even more traumatic period followed, with the creation of the Resolution Trust Corporation in 1989 and that agency's resolution by mid-1995 of an additional 747 thrifts. A Federal Reserve Bank panel stated the resulting taxpayer bailout ended up being even larger than it would have been because moral hazard and adverse selection incentives that compounded the system's losses.

There also were state-chartered S&Ls that failed. Some state insurance funds failed, requiring state taxpayer bailouts.

HOME STATE SAVINGS BANK OF CINCINNATI

In March 1985, it came to public knowledge that the large Cincinnati, Ohio-based Home State Savings Bank was about to collapse. Ohio Gov. Dick Celeste declared a bank holiday in the state as Home State depositors lined up in a "run" on the bank's branches to withdraw their deposits. Celeste ordered the closure of all the state's S&Ls. Only those that were able to qualify for membership in the Federal Deposit Insurance Corporation were allowed to reopen. Claims by Ohio S&L depositors drained the state's deposit insurance funds. A similar event took place in Maryland.

Midwest Federal Savings & Loan of Minneapolis, Minnesota

Midwest Federal Savings & Loan was a federally chartered savings and loan based in Minneapolis, Minnesota until its failure in 1990. The St. Paul Pioneer Press called the bank's failure the "largest financial disaster in Minnesota history."

The chairman, Hal Greenwood Jr., his daughter, Susan Greenwood Olson, and two former executives, Robert A. Mampel, and Charlotte E. Masica, were convicted of racketeering that lead to the institution's collapse. The failure cost taxpayers $1.2 billion.

Lincoln Savings and Loan

The Lincoln Savings led to the Keating five political scandal, in which five U.S. senators were implicated in an influence-peddling scheme. It was named for Charles Keating, who headed Lincoln Savings and made $300,000 as political contributions to them in the

1980s. Three of those senators – Alan Cranston (D-CA), Don Riegle (D-MI), and Dennis DeConcini (D-AZ) – found their political careers cut short as a result. Two others – John Glenn (D-OH) and John McCain (R-AZ) – were rebuked by the Senate Ethics Committee for exercising "poor judgment" for intervening with the federal regulators on behalf of Keating.

Silverado Savings and Loan

Silverado Savings and Loan collapsed in 1988, costing taxpayers $1.3 billion. Neil Bush, son of then Vice President of the United States George H. W. Bush, was Director of Silverado at the time. Neil Bush was accused of giving himself a loan from Silverado, but he denied all wrongdoing.

The US Office of Thrift Supervision investigated Silverado's failure and determined that Neil Bush had engaged in numerous "breaches of his fiduciary duties involving multiple conflicts of interest." Although Bush was not indicted on criminal charges, a civil action was brought against him and the other Silverado directors by the Federal Deposit Insurance Corporation; it was eventually settled out of court, with Bush paying $50,000 as part of the settlement, the *Washington Post* reported.

As a director of a failing thrift, Bush voted to approve $100 million in what were ultimately bad loans to two of his business partners. And in voting for the loans, he failed to inform fellow board members at Silverado Savings & Loan that the loan applicants were his business partners.

Neil Bush paid a $50,000 fine and was banned from banking activities for his role in taking down Silverado, which cost taxpayers $1.3 billion. A Resolution Trust Corporation Suit against Bush and other officers of Silverado was settled in 1991 for $26.5 million.

Financial Institutions Reform, Recovery, and Enforcement Act of 1989

As a result, the Financial Institutions Reform, Recovery, and Enforcement Act of 1989 (FIRREA) dramatically changed the savings and loan industry and its federal regulation. The highlights of the legislation, signed into law August 9, 1989, were:

1. The Federal Home Loan Bank Board (FHLBB) and the Federal Savings and Loan Insurance Corporation (FSLIC) were abolished.
2. The Office of Thrift Supervision (OTS), a bureau of the Treasury Department, was created to charter, regulate, examine, and supervise savings institutions.
3. The Federal Housing Finance Board (FHFB) was created as an independent agency to oversee the 12 federal home loan banks (also called district banks).
4. The Savings Association Insurance Fund (SAIF) replaced the FSLIC as an ongoing insurance fund for thrift institutions (like the FDIC, the FSLIC was a permanent corporation that insured savings and loan accounts up to $100,000). SAIF is administered by the Federal Deposit Insurance Corp.
5. The Resolution Trust Corporation (RTC) was established to dispose of failed thrift institutions taken over by regulators after January 1, 1989. The RTC will make insured deposits at those institutions available to their customers.
6. FIRREA gives both Freddie Mac and Fannie Mae additional responsibility to support mortgages for low- and moderate-income families.

Consequences

While not part of the savings and loan crisis, many other banks failed. Between 1980 and 1994 more than 1,600 banks insured by the Federal Deposit Insurance Corporation (FDIC) were closed or received FDIC financial assistance.

From 1986 to 1995, the number of US federally insured savings and loans in the United States declined from 3,234 to 1,645. This was primarily, but not exclusively, due to unsound real estate lending.

The market share of S&Ls for single family mortgage loans went from 53% in 1975 to 30% in 1990. U.S. General Accounting

Office estimated cost of the crisis to around USD $160.1 billion, about $124.6 billion of which was directly paid for by the U.S. government from 1986 to 1996. That figure does not include thrift insurance funds used before 1986 or after 1996. It also does not include state run thrift insurance funds or state bailouts.

The U.S. government ultimately appropriated 105 billion dollars to resolve the crisis. After banks repaid loans through various procedures, there was a net loss to taxpayers of approximately $124 billion dollars by the end of 1999.

The concomitant slowdown in the finance industry and the real estate market may have been a contributing cause of the 1990–1991 economic recession. Between 1986 and 1991, the number of new homes constructed dropped from 1.8 to 1 million, the lowest rate since World War II.

Some commentators believe that a taxpayer-funded government bailout related to mortgages during the savings and loan crisis may have created a moral hazard and acted as encouragement to lenders to make similar higher risk loans during the 2007 subprime mortgage financial crisis.

Chapter

2

Depression-era Bank Failures: The Great Contagion

Deposit insurance was created, at least in part, to prevent unfounded bank failures caused by contagion. The legislation that created the Federal Deposit Insurance Corporation (FDIC) was driven by the widespread bank failures of the Great Depression. In the years immediately before the 1934, when the FDIC began insuring bank deposits, over onethird of all extant banks failed. Many observers argue that these failures occurred because the banking industry is inherently fragile since it is subject to contagion-induced runs. Fragility arises because banks gather a large portion of their funding through the issuance of liabilities that are redeemable on demand at par, while investing in illiquid assets. Specifically, loans, which on average account for 56 percent of bank assets, tend to be made based on information that is costly to convey to outsiders. As a result, if a significant segment of bank customers run, that is, quickly require the repayment of their deposits, the bank is unlikely to be able to sell its assets except at a steep discount. Bank failure can result.

But do Depression-era bank failures imply the need for government provided deposit insurance, or is there another explanation of the failures other than contagion and inherent fragility? Some observers question the view that banks are inherently fragile. They argue instead that the banking industry developed various market-based means of addressing runs such that the danger of failure was reduced. They also argue that the banks that failed in response to runs were weak and likely to fail regardless of runs (Calomiris and Mason 1997; Benston and Kaufman 1995).

If not fragility, what might explain the widespread failures before 1934? One possible explanation is that the banking industry was experiencing a shakeout, not unusual in industries that have previously enjoyed significant growth. The number of banks had grown briskly from the mid-1880s until 1921. Beginning in 1921, bank failures increased significantly, such that the number of banks began a precipitous decline that continued until 1934. There are reasons to think that the industry had become overbuilt and that macroeconomic shocks, in conjunction with overbuilding, produced a retrenchment in the industry that lasted for the next 12 years. Indeed, many authors point to the relationship between bank failures and weakening economic conditions1. This article suggests that overbuilding could have made the banking industry all the more sensitive to macroeconomic shocks.

A number of other industries provide examples of growth followed by shakeouts, the most recent of which is the telecom industry. If a large portion of Depression-era banking failures were the result of a shakeout rather than contagion, an important argument for deposit insurance is undercut. Though the termination of bank failures and the creation of the FDIC in 1934 occurred simultaneously, implying that contagion must have been at work, other explanations are just as credible. First, deposit insurance augmented the profits of risky banks, protecting them from failure. Second, the creation of deposit insurance undercut a market process that caused supervisors to close troubled banks quickly.

GROWTH IN THE NUMBER OF BANKS

The number of U.S. banks grew rapidly from 1887 until 1921. Much of the increase coincided with improving economic conditions. Yet, commentators also claim that a good portion of the increase resulted from a statutory change that lowered the minimum capital required to form a newbank as well as careless application of entry standards by regulators. Many of the newbanks were viewed by commentators as being ill-prepared for the business of banking. In other words, too many banks were formed without adequate financial or managerial resources. The banking market was overbanked. As shown in Figure 1, the number of banks began growing rapidly in the late 1880s. The initial run-up in the number of banks followed an economic recovery occurring in 1885 and 1886. The increase in the number of banks was rapid enough, and the size of new banks small enough, to drive down the U.S. average bank size fairly significantly. The average size bank shrank from $1.04 million in 1886 to a low of $660,000 in 1896 and did not return to its 1886 level until 1916. The growth in number of banks was much faster than the pace of economic growth, so that the increase in the number of banks is still quite apparent even when the number of banks is deflated by the level of real GDP.

Most commentators focus on the increase in the number of banks, especially of very small banks, after the beginning of the 20th century. Figure 1 shows that the growth in the number of banks was indeed rapid from 1900 until 1921. An important explanation for the growth in the number of banks during these two decadeswas the reduction in the minimum capital required to form a bank (Mengle 1990; Wheelock 1993). Specifically, the Currency Act of 1900 lowered from $50,000 to $25,000 the minimum capital needed from investors to start a national bank. In turn, over the next ten years, two-thirds of newly formed banks were quite small, averaging capital of only slightly more than the minimum $25,000 (Mengle 1990, 6). Beyond this reduction in minimum capital, regulatory laxity was also thought to have contributed to the rapid increase in the number of banks. For example, Federal Reserve analysts concluded that during the first two decades of the 20th century "insufficient attentionwas paid to the qualifications of those to whom charters were granted" (Federal Reserve Board 1933, 63–65). These observers saw the banking industry as overbuilt by 1920 (Federal Reserve Board 1933, 67).

Most of these new small banks were formed in small towns and rural communities—especially in the corn and cotton belts of the country. Rising prices of farm commodities along with rising farm real estate values may have played a significant role in the attractiveness of rural banking to new investors (Federal Reserve Board 1933, 65). More generally, economic growth was strong between 1887 and 1920, with the annual rate of growth of GDP averaging over 6 percent for the period. GDP growth was especially strong during 1916, and in the two years of the U.S. participation in World War I, 1917 and 1918.

The formation of state deposit insurance systems in a number of states may also have contributed to a perception of safety and allowed the rapid growth of new small banks. Following the banking panic of 1907, eight states adopted such programs for state-chartered banks (Wheelock 1993, 860). Using regression analysis, Wheelock (1993, 865) finds that the presence of deposit insurance systems encouraged bank formation.

An important trend associated with rapid entry was gradually declining banking profitability. Contemporary writers blamed declining returns on increased competition from new banks. For example, a 1933 Federal Reserve study claimed that "the overbanked condition, which reached its peak shortly after 1920, caused units struggling for existence to increase services to their clients, thus adding to expenses. It served to introduce into many banks high risk and marginal business" (Federal Reserve Board 1933, 67). Net profits relative to assets for the industry fell fairly consistently from 1900 through 1920, from about 2.55 percent to about 1.70 percent (Federal Reserve Board 1933, 67).2 Bank regulators also noted declining loan standards as rapid entry occurred (Federal Reserve Board 1933, 4).

By several measures the banking industry appears to have become overbuilt. As noted earlier, the numbers grew faster than did overall economic growth. Additionally, as shown in Figure 3, the number of banks increased much more rapidly than did U.S. population. The expansion in the number of competitors may also have been driving down bank profitability and loan standards beginning as early as 1900. This declining profitability implies that even without the agricultural shocks of the 1920s, and the macroeconomic shocks of the Depression, the banking industry would have experienced some retrenchment.

1921–1933 BANKING FAILURES

Banking failures, which began growing in number in the early 1920s, coincide with regional agricultural problems, and later with broader economic problems of the Great Depression. Analysts argue that contagion and branching restrictions account for a significant portion of the failures. The number of U.S. banks peaked in 1921 at about 31,000 banks. The year also produced the beginning of a period of rapid annual rates of bank failure. In 1921 there were 505 failures. As shown in Figure 4, during most of the next eight years failures remained between 500 and 1,000 per year. From 1930 through 1933 failure rates were in the thousands. The shift in banking failures in 1921 was precipitated by widespread crop failures of that year. Farm problems were evident in falling farm real estate values in corn- and cotton-producing regions. Real estate values fell each year from 1921 through 1930 (White 1984, 126). The bank failures of the 1920s were heaviest in states with the most rapid growth prior to the 1920s (Wicker 1996, 7). Difficulties suffered by farmers in the Midwest seem to have driven much of the failure.

Between 1921 and 1930, half of all small banks in agricultural regions failed. Larger banks, however, suffered much less. For example, on average between 1926 and 1930, 74 percent of the smallest banks, those with assets less than $150,000, had weak profits. Here, weak profits are defined as return on equity of less than 6 percent. In contrast, only 21 percent of those banks in the largest size category, with assets greater than $50 million, produced profit rates averaging below 6 percent between 1926 and 1930.

A regulatory shift may also account for the disappearance of some small banks. In the early 1920s the Comptroller of the Currency, the agency that regulates national banks, dropped its branching prohibitions (Mengle 1990, 6). In turn, the number of bank branches grew from 1,400 to 3,500 between 1921 and 1930 (Calomiris and White 2000, 170). These new branches would have brought fresh competition to banking markets, and since branch banks probably had advantages in diversity and scale over small unit banks, unit banks would have been imperiled. Therefore, this liberalization of branching restrictions acted as a shock to small bank profitability, occurring in the 1920s. Some contemporary commentators claim that improving transportation technology accounts for the decline of small banks, which were once protected from competition by the costs their customers faced to travel to other towns and cities to conduct banking business. These small banks were suddenly faced with new competition once customers' travel costs fell. The growing availability of the car opened the opportunity to purchase services, including banking services, in central cities (Wheelock 1993).

While the number of banking failures (and therefore the decline in the number of banks) grew rapidly in the 1920s, it grew even more rapidly after the onset of the Depression. Between 1930 and 1932, the number of failures per year averaged 1,700. In 1933, slightly more than 4,000 banks failed. Contagion is often cited to explain the rapid pace of failures between 1930 and 1933. Contagion could work as follows. A prominent bank fails, and because there is no federal deposit insurance protection, depositors of the failed bank suffer losses.3 Customers of other banks learn of the failure, believe that their bank might suffer the same fate, and run their banks—i.e., demand cash repayment of their deposits. Since bank assets are typically tied up in loans and securities, to meet these demands for cash, banks must liquidate these assets. If many banks attempt to sell their securities, prices will fall, and banks will suffer losses on the sales. Further, because outsiders have difficulty determining theworth of bank loans, they will sell at a steep discount, i.e., at firesale prices. Therefore runs of otherwise healthy banks could cause such banks to suffer losses large enough that they would be unable to meet all depositor demands, creating failures of the banks experiencing the runs. The process would become a cycle, spreading widely.

Friedman and Schwartz (1963) identify three banking crises during the Depression involving widespread runs. During these crises, they, along with others, argue that waves of widespread runs created by a "contagion of fear" produced bank illiquidity and the failure of otherwise healthy banks. They hold that much of the bank failure was the result of such contagion and that healthy banks failed as a result.

Branching restrictions are also viewed as an important explanation of bank failures (Mengle 1990, 7–8). While in the 1920s branching restrictions were liberalized for national banks, most states placed severe restrictions on branching, or banned it altogether. As of 1929, 22 states prohibited branching and another ten states restricted it somewhat (Mengle 1990, 6). Branching restrictions prevented banks from diversifying their lending, forcing them to concentrate their lending in one geographic area. The lack of diversity made banks more susceptible to failure caused by localized economic weaknesses. Therefore, oddly enough, both branching restrictions and the branching liberalization, discussed earlier, could have contributed to bank failures.

CONTAGION IS AN INCOMPLETE EXPLANATION OF FAILURES

Contagion is an incomplete explanation of banking failures for two reasons. First, contagion was not a factor in the failures that occurred in the 1920s. The bank failures of the 1920s were not caused by and did not create banking panics, that is, banking runs or heavy withdrawals of currency. There was no increase in currency in circulation during the period (Wicker 1996, 1). If factors other than contagion were important in the 1920s, it seems likely that these same factors would also be at work in the 1930s as well. Therefore, contagion is unlikely to account for at least some of the failures in the Depression years of the 1930s.

Second, in their influential work on U.S. banking and monetary history, Friedman and Schwartz (1963) maintain that the bank failures of the 1930s were contagion-induced. Later reviews, however, cast doubt on the contagion explanation. Using regression analysis to identify factors that accounted for individual bank failures during the 1930 crisis, which occurred in November and December of that year, White (1984) finds that these failures were no different from those occurring in the 1920s. In other words, he finds no evidence that these failures were driven by contagion-sparked illiquidity. Instead, these failures were the result of bad loans. Friedman and Schwartz (1963) give special emphasis to the failure of the Bank of the United States in December 1930 as a cause of contagion-induced bank failures. Wicker (1996, 36–38) questions this view, concluding that the bank's failure did not lead to major deposit withdrawals and could not have accounted for the failures of other banks. Further, of the bank failures that took place between 1930 and 1932, more than 60 percent occurred outside of panic months (Wicker 1996, 1).

While some of these failures might have been the residual effect of runs, it seems likely that most of the failed banks had financial problems unrelated to runs. If an otherwise healthy bank survived a panic, it would have survived the aftermath. Last, Calomiris and Mason (1997) examined the financial condition of Chicago banks during the 1932 banking panic in that city. They found that "while depositors did confuse panic survivors with panic failures, the failure of solvent banks did not result from that confusion." Calomiris and Mason note that the Chicago situation may have been special since Chicago banks met the panic by joining forces to protect banks the group viewed as solvent. Such combined efforts would have been more difficult for the many far-flung banks outside of major cities. Nevertheless, through correspondent relationships, support of banks could have transpired even in a sprawling banking system. Still, one might wonder: if contagion was not the cause of bank failures, then why did bank failures largely come to a halt with the creation of federal deposit insurance in 1934? If, as I argue, a portion of the bank failures of the 1920s and 1930s were the result of a typical shakeout, there is no reason to expect the shakeout to have ended with the creation of the FDIC. One would only expect failures to be ended by the FDIC's creation if they were caused by contagion, a problem overcome by the creation of federal deposit insurance.

Part of the reason for the cessation of failures, and one that is not dependent on the existence of contagion, is the shifting economic backdrop. Those inherently low-profit banks that were created during the rapid growth of the banking industry would have been the first to be driven to insolvency by the extreme macroeconomic problems of the early 1930s. In other words, economic difficulties concentrated the shakeout in the early 1930s. As a result, low-profit banks created during the growth of the industry—banks which might have continued to fail over a number of years after 1933—were quickly expunged by the severe economic times. The severity of the macroeconomic problems is shown by the declines in economic output, which fell by 8.61 percent in 1930, and by 6.42 percent, 13.00 percent, and 1.27 percent in 1931, 1932, and 1933, respectively. But then in 1934 economic output began growing rapidly, increasing by 10.81 percent, and averaged 7.08 percent from 1934 through 1939 so that banks were strong enough to weather the early 1930s the following years.

An additional reason exists—not dependent on contagion—as to why failures ended at the same time the FDICwas formed: Prior to the FDIC's creation, depositors had strong incentive to monitor their banks' health and, in the case of signs of weakness, withdraw deposits. When depositors withdrew funds, government supervisors were forced to review the state of the bank and either close it or allow it to reopen if shown healthy. Once deposits gained FDIC protection, this disciplining mechanism was removed. Without the mechanism, the opportunity for supervisors to forbear arose. Certainly, in the years immediately after the widespread bank failures of the 1920s and early 1930s, it seems that supervisors would tend to err on the side of stability and be reticent to close banks unless the evidence of a bank's problems was quite strong. Consequently, that failures largely ceased at the same time the FDIC was created is not necessarily evidence that contagion was the cause of most bank failures.

Further, FDIC insurance provided a significant profit-boosting subsidy to the riskiest banks. With the government backing their deposits, in 1934 all banks could suddenly gather deposits at the risk-free interest rate. Those banks that might have failed in the near future—the riskiest banks—benefited most. Unless depositors were completely oblivious to their bank's health, in the absence of deposit insurance, such banks would have had to pay depositors high interest rates. Had the FDIC charged risk-adjusted deposit insurance premia, the riskiest banks would have enjoyed no benefit. But premia were calculated as a simple percentage of deposits. Therefore, troubled banks enjoyed a sudden boost in their profits due to the introduction of FDIC insurance. Failures would naturally be minimized, not because contagion was halted, but instead because FDIC insurance provided a subsidy to those banks most likely to fail.

SHAKEOUTS IN OTHER INDUSTRIES

Rapid increase in the number of producers followed by an equally rapid decline is a pattern not only evident in banking, but also in a number of industries. Examples include automobiles, tires, televisions, penicillin, and most recently, telecommunications. While the banking industry failures are blamed on heavy reliance on liabilities that are redeemable upon demand, other factors must have been at work to produce rapid failures in these other industries since they are not reliant upon demand liabilities. Perhaps many of the failures in banking were simply the result of a typical shakeout, driven by factors other than contagion, as in these other industries.

The growth pattern in banking—a significant increase in the number of banks, followed by a rapid decline—is similar to the growth and shakeout that a number of industries experienced, industries for which there are no claims of inherent fragility or contagion-driven runs. Klepper (2002, 37) notes that "After their commercial introduction, the number of producers of automobiles, tires, televisions, and penicillin initially grew and then experienced a sharp decline or shakeout."

More recently, the same pattern was displayed in the telecommunications sector. In the mid-1990s, three factors together implied great opportunities for growth in the industry. First, rapidly growing use of the Internet generated an expanded demand for data transmission services over phone, cable, and long-haul fiber networks. Observers claimed that Internet use was doubling every year, or even several times a year. Second, an important regulatory change was brought to the telecommunications industry by the Telecommunications Act of 1996. The goal of the Act was to introduce new competition to local telephone service, which was largely monopolized by the regional Bells. It opened local telephone service to competition, for example, by requiring incumbent local service providers to sell entrants access to the networks that reach homes and businesses. It was thought that entrants would provide local phone service and that selling accesswould avoid duplication of existing telephone lines to individual homes and businesses. The entrants, known as competitive local exchange carriers (CLECs), rapidly increased in number and earnings. From 30 CLECs in 1996, their number had grown to 711 in 2000. At the same time, revenues of the CLECs rose from $5 billion to $43 billion (Couper et al., 15).

Third, advances in fiber optic technology were occurring rapidly in the mid-1990s, lowering the cost of providing data and voice services to households and businesses. Existing firms, as well as founders of new firms, expected these factors to open huge new markets and responded by rapidly increasing investment in telecommunications equipment and communications lines.

However, as it turned out, by 2000 the promise of the 1996 Act had not been borne out, long-haul fiber communications lines were significantly overbuilt, and the overall economy began to slow. The Act did not lead to nearly as much growth for competitors in local service. The Act's pricing ambiguities meant that rules that would allow entrants to buy access into homes and businesses were slow to be developed by regulatory agencies and were held up by lawsuits. Overcapacity in fiber lines was the result of rapid improvement in the technology for transmitting data over these lines, meaning that fewer were needed than expected. Further, the growth in demand for data communications, while rapid, was not as rapid as expected (Couper et al., 13 and 19). Beginning in mid-

2000, the telecom industry began a rapid retrenchment that involved huge numbers of failures of new firms that had only recently appeared to have bright futures. For example, the number of CLECs declined by about 80 percent from 1999 to 2001 (Grossi, 4).

EXPLANATION OF THE BANKING SHAKEOUT

Several important industries displayed a pattern of rapid growth followed by widespread failure, similar to that in the banking industry. Yet failures in these industries cannot be blamed on contagion resulting from a reliance on demandable liabilities, implying that something else may also have been at work during the similar boom and bust in banking. Still, these industries differed from banking: Automobiles, tires, televisions, and penicillin were all new industries, and the telecommunications industry was experiencing rapid technological change. Therefore a good bit of instability can be expected as the efficient industrial structure evolved. In contrast, the banking industry of the late 19th and early 20th centuries was not new. While not new, the banking industry was undergoing rapid change. The industry was a primary source of capital to a nation undergoing rapid technological and industrial change. The expansion of railroads drove down transportation costs. The spread of electronic communication, the telegraph and telephone, rapidly lowered communications costs. As noted earlier, the popularity of the automobile meant that communities were less isolated from one another, and commercewas better able to flowacross local communities. Also, the growth of the corporation as a business structure and the issue of debt by corporations radically changed the financial structure of the business world. Further, branching and capital regulations in banking were being significantly modified.

In an environment of wide-ranging industrial, technological, and regulatory change, it should not be surprising that the banking industry would struggle in ways similar to a new industry. Bank organizers perceived profit opportunities in the changing setting and rapidly formed banks to take advantage of such opportunities. In doing so, they drove down bank size and profitability, as noted earlier. Ultimately they caused the industry to become overbuilt, and failures ensued. Were bank organizers acting irrationally? Not according to theories economists have advanced to explain the fairly common phenomenon of industry shakeout. Such theories argue that firms can often be expected to expand new investment too far. One such theoretical explanation argues that shakeouts are a result of investments in research and development (R&D) (Klepper 2002, 38).5 Under this explanation, firms invest in R&D to lower their costs, but the cost advantage grows with size, such that large firms benefit more from R&D. Further, some firms are better at R&D than others. Firms enter and make R&D investments to acquire the high margins that are expected to accrue from such actions. Instead, rapid entry drives down profit margins. Eventually entry stops, and smaller firms, which have higher per-unit R&D costs, fail. Firms that make less productive use of R&D expenditures also fail, since their costs will be relatively high. In this environment, entry seems to progress too far, since many of the firms that were initially profitable fail when profit margins are driven down. Unanticipated increases in costs or decreases in earnings can also cause failure.

More broadly, overinvestment works as follows. A technological or business process innovation occurs, and firms make investments to take advantage of the new technology. Firms are uncertain concerning how much their output might increase as they implement the new technology but must invest before knowing. Alternatively, firms are uncertain of the extent of demand for their new product, but must invest before knowing. Ultimately firms often overshoot, profits decline, and the least efficient firms fail. Was such overshooting likely in banking in the late 19th and early 20th centuries? Evolving telecommunications and transportation technology as well as shifting financial arrangements were influencing both the technology of banking and of the firms to which banks make loans. In this environment, existing banks and potential investors in new banks faced a great deal of uncertainty about the proper scale of the industry, and entry was rapid, relative to GDP growth and population growth. Average profits were driven down in the banking industry, and after 1921, while larger banks remained strong, small bank profits fell significantly. Clearly the demand shocks of the 1920s and the Depression played a major role in the shakeout in banks, but overbuilding appears to have been of significant importance.

SUMMARY

As the U.S. economy grewand evolved in the late 19th and early 20th centuries, the banking industry grew even more rapidly, especially in raw numbers of banks, as well as in assets relative to GDP and numbers relative to population. Contemporary analysts maintained that the growth produced an overbuilt industry. Ultimately, failures shrank the number of banks. Failures first became significant in the early 1920s, continued throughout the 1920s, and became even more numerous during the Depression. They largely ended in 1934, at the time of the formation of the FDIC. A long-held explanation for bank failures during the Depression is contagion, whereby the initial failure of one bank leads to widespread runs on other banks and their failure. According to this explanation, many of the Depression-era failures were inappropriate, meaning that the failed banks were solvent and would have survived without contagion-induced runs. The solution to contagion was deposit insurance provided by the federal government, which put a stop to failures.

Still, given that the cycle of failures began in the early 1920s, long before contagion was evident, one must question contagion as the overriding cause. Instead the banking industry appears to have been experiencing a shakeout, exacerbated by weakened economic conditions during the Depression. While at first blush, the fact that failures stopped virtually simultaneously with the formation of the FDIC implies that contagion must have been at work, other explanations for this simultaneity are just as credible. For example, risky bank profits were certainly boosted by the provision of deposit insurance at premiums that did not reflect bank risk, protecting these banks from failure. Further, the process that drove supervisors to quickly close troubled banks was undercut once deposit insurance was established.

Chapter

3

The Case for Banking Deregulation

INTRODUCTION

If the manufacturing and retailing sectors can be described as the muscle and bone of the U.S. economic body, the financial intermediaries would certainly be the circulatory system. This country's 40,000 banks and savings and loan associations (S Ls play the crucial role of gathering the savings of individuals and businesses and using them to provide loans to other consumers and commercial enterprises. There is no other single industry as necessary to the nation's economic prosperity as the financial institutions. Should the U.S. automobile industry fail, widespread displacement would obviously result the economy would remain undisturbed and could continue to prosper.

Should the financial intermediaries industry collapse, however, the resulting interruption in the flow of funds from net savers to net borrowers would bring the economy to a grinding halt. Almost every business enterprise in the country relies on credit for continued normal operation from financing inventories to expanding plants.

While complete catastrophe is very unlikely, American financial institutions are facing a crisis unprecendented since the early 1930s. Savings and loan associations have been particularly hard hit. Holding almost 700 billion in deposits, these institutions were expected to suffer collective losses of $5 billion in 1981 with 75 percent of the S Ls and savings banks incurring operating losses during the year. Unless economic catastrophe on a lesser scale is sure to overtake the industry But significant sectors of conditions change drastically or some action is taken soon Many solutions have been offered. For some the answer seems to lie in regulating the currently unregulated competitors of banks and S Ls particularly the money market mutual funds.

Others advocate a bail out of the ailing savings and loan industry, 2 leaving basic industry structure unchanged and hoping the economic crisis is soon resolved A growing number of students of the problem are recognizing however, that the regulatory structure surrounding the financial services industry is a part of the problem son testified before the Senate Banking Committee: As banker Lee Gunder What is needed is an approach to legislation and regulation which recognizes the public interest is best served in a competitive marketplace, a marketplace where initiative, innovation, and performance are not restrained by discriminatory laws, complicated rules and unequal regulatory treatment. In other words, rather than regulating the unregulated firms now offering financial services, the banks and S Ls should be freed from at least part of the regulatory network currently binding' them.

There are at least three broad areas where this sort of regulatory reform ought to be seriously considered on the pricing policies of depository institutions both those rates paid by banks and S Ls to depositors and those charged for loans cause severe distortions and should be closely examined. offer are also severely restricted and the liberalization of these powers is an area deserving of attention. Finally, geographic limitations have resulted in hardships, especially for consumers, and ought to be relaxed a step in this direction. The step is one, however, that has met with and will continue to meet with opposition savings and loan associations currently enjoy a protected position. They are, understandably, reluctant to give up that advantage.

Furthermore, the fears created by the 1930s' bank failures are deeply imbedded. But, the world is rapidly changing, and in order to offer the widest range of services to consumers, the regulatory barriers that financial institutions now face must be removed

Restrictions The types of financial services banks and S Ls may Legislation introduced by Senator Jake Garn (R-UT) represents Many banks and ROOTS OF THE PROBLEM Underlying other causes of problems currently facing depository institutions are the volatility of the inflation rate' and its absolute level. Both have increased dramatically in recent years. The 1965 inflation rate was 1.7 percent. In 1970, it had climbed to 5.9 percent. By the end of the decade, it had reached double digits 11.3 percent in 1979 and 12.4 percent in 1980.

This ever-upward trend in the Consumer Price Index has created problems for financial institutions 3 Banks and S Ls historically have relied on the deposits of their customers to provide the raw material with which they make their principal product loans. Over the past few years however, many depository institutions have found it increasingly difficult to attract and hold deposits. Existing legal restrictions on the amount of interest financial institutions may pay on savings accounts repeal the old adage, "A penny saved is a penny earned." Consumers gradually have come to realize the money left in savings accounts earning 5% to 5% percent interest loses buying power in an economy suffering from inflation rates exceed ing 5% percent. They have reacted rationally, seeking investments yielding a larger return but providing the convenience of a passbook savings account demand did not go unfilled for long institutions could not do because of legal restrictions, other firms did market mutual funds. Total investment in these funds has grown from a mere 4 billion in 1978 to $185 billion at the end of 1981.

Growth during the past five years has been particularly rapid as more of the funds were offered to individual investors and start-up costs were lowered In addition, Cash Management Accounts (CMAs introduced by Merrill Lynch, provide checkwriting privileges tied to a brokerage margin account and a Visa credit card. Merrill Lynch has been adding 1,000 CMAs a day at $20,000 minimum. Prudential Insurance Company of America, recently merged with Bache Halsey Stuart Shields, Inc is also preparing to offer a CMA account, as are American Express and several other financial firms.3

As is the case when the market is allowed to work, this What banks and thrift The result was the emergence of the booming money This phenomenal shift of funds away from traditional depository institutions is illustrated in the following graph. Many financial analysts are alarmed by these trends, and the American Bankers' Association points out that these trend lines are conservative estimates. Because of the regulatory framework within which they operate, however, banks and S Ls have not been able to act to retain their deposits as they have been drained further complicate matters, depositors who have left funds in banks and S Ls, for the most part, have placed them in accounts earning rates of interest above 54, to 5% percent allowed on passbook savings.

The six-month certificates of deposit (CDs for example, have become increasingly popular, as have the All Savers certificates and individual retirement accounts. Such a shift of deposits has increased the costs of funds for the depository institutions To Another problem created for banks and S Ls by high inflation rates is related to their role as lenders source of revenue for banks and S Ls is the interest income from the loans they make. Banks generally make commercial loans while S & Ls and savings banks concentrate on mortgage lending The primary Banks obviously also provide consumers loans, but commercial loans represent well over half of the loan portfolios of most banks 0 CD 0 0 5 The interest rates paid by borrowers are simply the prices of the loans. If the interest rate is below the average inflation rate over the life of the loan, the lending institution in effect loses money. This is because its costs salaries, electricity building maintenance, and so forth rise at roughly the rate of inflation. To remain profitable, the prices (interest rates charged by these financial institutions must rise too In some instances, however, banks and thrift institutions have been prevented by state usury laws from raising prices other cases, particularly for S & Ls concentrating in long-term mortgages, the major problem has been a lack of prescience.

S & L executives were no better than anyone else at predicting in 1971, when inflation was 4.3 percent, that rates by the end of the decade would hit double digits. And yet, such exceptional foresight is exactly what would have been required to ensure an S L's profitability today. Table I compares the average yields on mortgages with the inflation rates over recent years.

It is apparent why many savings and loan associations are facing severe financial difficulties. This situation of rising costs of funds and low yielding portfolios was described recently in Harper's magazine by William Quirk as being "like buying apples at twelve cents and selling them for ten cents, a practice with a limited future. If In Year 1975 1976 1977 1978 1979 1980 TABLE I Average Effective Yield on Mortgages Held by S Ls 7.10 7.20 7.35 7.72 8.21 8.79 Inflation Rate2 9.1 5.8 6.5 7.7 11.3 12.4 Sources Edward J. Kane S Ls and Interest Rate Re-Regulation: The FSLIC as an Industry Bailout Program," unpublished paper, September 15 1981, p. 8 2Economic Report of the President, January 1981, p. 293 Exacerbating their problems with inflation are the marketing restrictions imposed on the depository institutions. Not only can American Express, Merrill Lynch, Sears, and other new-style financial institutions offer accounts paying market rates of interest, many of which are also "checkable i.e checks may be written against the account they also face none of the geogra phic restrictions imposed on the depository institutions.

For a population as mobile as that of the U.S., this is important. 6 Systems of electronic funds transfer, moving deposits instantaneously across the country, make possible the dispersion of automatic teller machines (ATMs) throughout the U.S. American Express, Visa International Inc., and Mastercard International Inc. are just a few firms which already take advantage of this new technology or plan to do SO As use of ATMs spreads, individuals will be able to make deposits to or withdrawals from money market or other accounts from almost anywhere in the country.

Similarly, the Sears U.S. Government Money Market Trust, recently introduced, has offices nationwide adding to "one-stop shopping. Banks and, to a lesser extent, S Ls are prevented by law from offering these interstate services directly, however.

Instantaneous transfer of funds through air and telephone lines, moreover, means that an individual anywhere in the country can dial a toll-free number and conduct business with a large number of money market funds without leaving home. Warner Cable a subsidiary of American Express, is currently experimenting in Ohio with home banking, bill-paying, and security-trading for subscribers via their televison sets. Thus, while less-regulated firms are seeking ways to take advantage of new technology, the extensively regulated banks and S Ls are prevented from competing directly.

Traditional financial institutions, in short, are being squeezed between rising costs of funds and increased competition from unregulated firms. To make matters worse, a variety of firms are being allowed to offer services traditionally reserved to banks and S Ls. The result: profit margins are shrinking and, in the case of most S Ls, have disappeared completely. It is this situation which prompts the call for something to be done.

Before discussing what regulations ought to be removed or modified, however, it is instructive to examine why the depository institutions became so heavily regulated in the first place.

HISTORY

In examining the history of banking in the U.S two themes emerge:

(1) a deep-seated opposition to attempts to concentrate financial power, an attitude which has given the states a significant voice in the conduct of financial institutions; and

(2) an attitude of protection toward existing financial institutions which grew from the widespread bank failures of the 1930s.

Decentralization: The history of U.S. banking, more than anything else, reflects the aversion of early Americans toward attempts to concentrate power in a central government. In fact, early efforts to establish a central banking authority, first in 1791 and then in 1816 while successful for a time, were eventually defeated. The power to grant bank charters was considered the sole prerogative of 7 **state**

legislatures. These charters were obtained through special legislative acts, a method which, not surprisingly, was abused.

Reacting to these abuses, Michigan in 1837 initiated a system of free banking could open a bank. New York passed a similar law the following year and soon most other states followed suit. As a result banks were often established in a haphazard manner sometimes borrowing the cash necessary to meet capital requirements just before the bank examiners arrived Anyone meeting specific capital requirements Banks not only provided credit for a growing economy, but also, for better or worse, controlled the supply of currency.

Each bank issued its own bank notes, or currency, based (supposedly) on the quantity of specie, i.e gold or silver coins, held by the bank. During the period of free banking, many banks were opened in remote areas, making it difficult, if not impossible, for note holders to redeem bank notes for specie. This practice led to the term "wildcat banking" because many banks were located where only the wildcats could find them some voice in granting bank charters was during the Civil War. The 1864 National Banking Act, designed to help the federal government finance the war, empowered Congress to charter banks which were allowed to issue currency linked to the number of federal government bonds held as security. These bank notes were printed by the Treasury, thus providing the first national currency. The Office of the Comptroller of the Currency was created to administer federal banking laws.

Few banks sought national charters; state charters were easier to obtain and less restrictive. This prompted Congress in 1865 to impose a 10 percent tax on bank notes issued by state banks a move designed to tax state banks out of existence.

This tactic failed because state bankers discovered they did not have to issue currency to operate profitably. Instead, they encouraged the use of checks drawn on demand deposits. The dual banking system, with both states and the federal government granting bank charters, was born and continues to the present The first successful attempt to give the federal government Tying the supply of currency, as the National Banking Act did, to the number of government bonds held by banks led to problems. During the late 19th century, outstanding government debt was not continually increasing. This led to an unstable and inelastic money supply. Thus, need was perceived for a central bank with the flexibility and authority to deal with currency problems and to manage the banking system. The result was the Federal Reserve Act, passed in 1913. In typical American fashion, it was feared a single central bank would concentrate too much power in too few hands.

Therefore, while overall policy was delegated to the Federal Reserve Board in Washington, the Federal Reserve Act created twelve Federal Reserve Banks distributed throughout the country to ensure consideration of regional problems. Deep-seated resistance to banking monopoly also explains early attitudes toward branching. Most states originally did not allow state-chartered banks to establish branches. In fact, as late as 1910 only twelve states permitted branching. The silence of the 1964 National Banking Act on the subject was interpreted as a branching prohibition for all nationally-chartered banks regardless of state law) until 1922. In that year, the Comptroller of the Currency ruled that any nationally-chartered bank could establish other offices to conduct routine business as long as those offices were not outside the city in which the head office was located. Congress formally endorsed this action with the McFadden Act of 1927 and extended the ruling to state banks which were members of the Federal Reserve System (FRS). Non member state banks remained subject to state laws.

During the 1930s, banks with branches enjoyed a lower failure rate than banks (those with only one office As a result the number of states allowing branching increased. In addition the 1933 Banking Act (Glass-Steagall) removed McFadden requirements that national and state FRS member banks limit their branching to a single city, and made them subject to state branching laws. As the economy recovered from the Depression, bankers again Bank holding companies became a became interested in expansion popular means of growth, triggering attempts to restrict the holding companies.

Company Act of 1956 prohibited bank holding companies from acquiring banks across state lines unless expressly permitted by state law The Douglas Amendment to the Bank Holding The history of U.S. banking, in sum, is a continuing struggle to ensure that financial assets and the power over them remain as dispersed as possible.

Protectionism

The result of free banking was the existence of over 30,000 banks by 1921. Failures were common, averaging 600 per year; yet overall the system worked fairly well as new banks quickly replaced failed ones. for all those in a particular occupation or with some similar bond protected most depositors from heavy losses. The early 1930s, however, saw unprecedented failures as panic and bank runs became all too common. By the end of 1933, only 15,000 banks remained. Many of the customers of the failed banks lost most if not all, their deposits as the existing sources of deposit insurance found themselves unable to handle the massive failures.

The high cost borne by depositors, the disruption of the money supply, and the number of sound banks that failed contributed to tremendous political pressure, clamoring that something be done about the banking industry In response, the Banking Acts of 1933 and 1935 were passed, changing significantly the way in which banks and other financial institutions do business State or regional deposit insurance or insurance 9 The basic goal of the Banking Acts was to prevent widespread bank failures. It was widely assumed, for example, that bankers had contributed to their instability by attracting funds by paying ever higher rates of interest on deposits. To avoid this in the future, Congress prohibited interest on demand deposits and imposed ceilings on the interest paid to time and savings deposits. It was also argued that free banking created too much competition and an overabundance of weak banks. To remedy this, free banking was halted. Applicants for bank charters were now required to demonstrate public need for a new bank and to show that the profitable operation of a new bank would not cause undue harm to existing institutions. Criteria for establishing the soundness of prospective bankers were strengthened. And because bankers were accused of contributing to the over-valuation of shares in corporations in their role as investment financiers the activities of commercial banking and investment banking were divorced.

Congress also sought to safeguard the customers of failed banks through creation in 1933 of the Federal Deposit Insurance Corporation. The FDIC was given authority to insure deposits and to supervise and examine banks to help preserve the health and stability of member institutions. Many observers saw the creation of the FDIC as an implicit commitment by the federal government to bail out the banking system in crisis. Most scholars agree that by increasing depositor confidence in the system, federal deposit insurance represents the most successful of the 1930s' devices to deter bank failures.

By emphasizing the protection of existing financial institutions, however, the banking reforms of the 1930s had the effect of creating a cartel. Branching restrictions allowed banks to define a specific territory for themselves and the 1930s' Banking Acts ensured that existing banks need not fear too much new competition Past dedication to a fragmented financial system may have been justified. J. F. McGillicuddy, President of Manufacturers Hanover Trust Company, writes From a historical point of view, there is much to commend our banking system between various regions of this continent of a country sometimes seems as great as the differences among the countries of Europe, language and long-ago wars aside.

The Economic Diversity

The local orientation of the many banks and S Ls, therefore probably made them more responsive to local needs and encouraged regional growth and development. The protectionist attitude of For a more complete discussion of this point, see pages 12-15. 10 regulators and lawmakers can also be defended from a historical point of view the banking system and there was need to restore faith in it. The new laws substantially strengthened banks' positions, reducing competition and often creating a monopoly in less-populated areas Events of the 1930s severely shook confidence in The wisdom of past legislators in solving problems of their day, however, must not deter today's Congressmen from seeking solutions to fit conditions which have changed dramatically in the past decade. The earlier desirability of protected, fragmented financial institutions should not impede a thorough examination of the regulatory system under which they continue to operate Legislation of 1980 The history of banking regulation is primarily a story of I congressional reaction to financial crisis. Typical is the Depository Institutions Deregulation and Monetary Control Act of 1980 (DIDMCA). The banking industry was being assaulted on many fronts. Interest rates were climbing with no end in sight A rapidly growing number of savings and loans and mutual savings banks were on the verge of failure. Many of the new financial instruments authorized by the regulatory agencies were being challenged in the courts.

Reserve System was accelerating. Disintermediation, the movement of funds from traditional depository institutions into other forms of savings and investments, was becoming a severe problem The exit of banks from the Federal Congress had to act. The DIDMCA included a broad range of reforms through the gradual elimination of ceilings on interest payable on various deposits. Eliminating these ceilings was to occur in phases over six years. To accomplish this orderly phase-out of interest rate ceilings, the Depository Institutions Deregulation Committee (DIDC) was formed. The DIDC consists of five members the chairmen of the Federal Reserve Board of Governors, the Federal Home Loan Bank Board, the Federal Deposit Insurance Corporation, and the National Credit Union Association, as well as the Secretary of the Treasury. (The Comptr6ller of the Currency is a nonvoting member One of the most significant will enhance competition In recent testimony before the Senate Banking Committee, a spokesman for the U.S. League of Savings Associations charged the DIDC with sending the thrifts to their ruin by lifting deposit rate ceilings too quickly. Several examples were cited In September, for instance, the DIDC voted to raise limits on passbook savings accounts at banks and s Ls by percent, a change expected to cost the savings and loan industry 500 million with little prospect of attracting additional deposits or customers.8 Before the rule could go into affect, however, the DIDC reversed itself under a storm of protests. On the other hand, the DIDC has stuck by its approval of ceiling-free 18-month accounts for IRA/Keogh customers beginning December 1, 1981 In addition, the 11 DIDC has refused to restore the housing differential* on money market certificate accounts one of the most popular savings categories. The absence of the differential has, according to the savings and loan industry, led to a shift of funds from S Ls to commercial banks.

Many in the banking industry echo the S Ls' general criticism of the DIDC, but rather than predicting ruin because of the fast pace of DIDC actions, they blame the snail-like rate of changes. These critics point out that in the 1% years since its formation, there has been no change in ceilings on passbook accounts. Leaving the interest rate ceilings in place penalizes smaller savers who lack the resources or sophistication to invest in other financial instruments. In addition, ceilings on the interest that may be paid to depositors precludes banks and S Ls from competing with money market mutual funds and other instruments for the savings of individuals. Thus, the drain of funds from depository institutions continues.

Interest rate ceilings for time deposits of more than one year will not be completely removed until August 1984, and the housing differential is retained on many of these deposits until August 1983. At least a schedule for their removal exists however. Meanwhile, funds continue to flow to less regulated competitors.

The DIDMCA did more than create the Committee. The Act also authorized interest-bearing accounts against which checks may be drawn for all depository institutions. At banks, these take the form of automatic transfer accounts which allow automatic transfers between savings and checking accounts. Negotiable orders of withdrawal (or NOW accounts) were authorized for the depository institutions, and credit unions were granted legislative permission to offer share drafts. These instruments, while somewhat cumber some, increase the range of services available to consumers However, some question why Congress did not achieve these reforms by simply removing the prohibition on interest-bearing demand deposits In addition, the consumer lending powers of S Ls were broadened and they were given permission to issue credit cards and offer trust services. Federally chartered mutual savings banks were granted authority to make business loans.

Addressing another problem, the DIDMCA pre-empted some state usury laws. State interest ceilings were removed for all mortgage loans and for business and agricultural loans of more than 25,000 This was subsequently lowered to $1,000 later in 1980. The Act Commercial banks, by law, must pay 1 percent less than S Ls on many of their accounts. This differential is justified by the belief that its existence ensures a flow of funds to S Ls and, thus, to the housing markets 12 also addressed some complexities of the truth-in-lending laws attempting to simplify the consumer disclosure and notification procedures. To minimize problems, the DIDMCA requires that federal financial regulatory agencies meet certain criteria before issuing new regulations. For example, the need for the new regulation must be clearly established; meaningful alternatives must have been considered, costs minimized, and conflicts and duplications avoided to the extent possible.

The "monetary control" part of the Act dealt with Federal Reserve complaints that the decreasing number of banks under its jurisdiction was frustrating attempts to control the money supply.

Federal Reserve System reserve requirements, therefore, were imposed on the checkable accounts of all depository institutions In return, the Federal Reserve must make certain services available to all depository institutions In the past these services access to the discount window* and check-clearing services, for example) were available only to FRS member banks, many at no additional charge. Under DIDMCA changes the Federal Reserve Banks must determine the cost of providing these services and establish fees accordingly aspects are definitely deregulatory the, proposed interest ceiling phase-out and expanded power of thrifts, for example.

Others increase the regulatory burden universal Federal Reserve requirements, for example. Whatever its ultimate effects the DIDMCA did not resolve the fundamental crisis. If anything today's situation is worse than at the time of the Act All in all, the DIDMCA is a mixed bag of changes. Some Freedom to Fail No solution of the crisis can avoid confronting the issue at the heart of the matter the need for a competitive market, one that provides consumers with the best selection of products and/or services at the lowest possible prices. For this only two conditions are necessary: freedom of entry and freedom of exit.

If new firms may enter at will, even a market with a single firm will approach the competitive ideal, serving consumers in the most efficient manner possible. If the behaves otherwise, the way is opened for another firm to enter, offering a better product and/or a better price. Consumers will be lured from the established firm. The incentives created by freedom of entry thus assure efficient behavior even by a monopolist.

The threat established by free entry loses credibility however, without freedom of exit. A fear of financial losses and potential failure must exist to ensure that managers and owners The "discount window" is the mechanism through which reserves are tempo rarely loaned to banks by the appropriate Federal Reserve Bank 13 of firms adequately attend to consumer wishes ment pledges to protect a particular firm or industry, the conditions evaporate for efficient economic behavior. To ensure that sheltered firms survive, the government almost always turns to restricted entry Yet if the govern This is nowhere more apparent than in the banking and thrift industries. summed up by a former Comptroller of the Currency when he said we believe thoroughly in competition in the field of banking and endeavor to provide it wherever possible without jeopardizinq existing institutions (emphasis added). Similarly, on the state level a banking supervisor remarked Sound and ethical competition is a healthy thing but, of course, not to the extent of hazard to existing banking institutions.

Regrettably, the ideal of a competitive atmosphere and the reality of restricted entry are difficult to achieve simultaneously. If a new bank or S L enters a market and provides better services than existing financial institutions, it may cause the failure of one or more of the existing institutions. Since this is considered unacceptable, the new bank or S & L generally is not allowed to enter even in cases where it is widely acknowledged that existing depository institutions are inefficiently run. As a result, many banks and S & Ls enjoy a monopoly-like if not an actual monopoly) situation especially in less populated areas. because the government has decided financial institutions should be protected from failure regardless of cost. Inferior services thus may be offered at inflated prices to the customers of these institutions because few incentives exist to encourage better behavior The general attitude of federal regulators was They need not fear the entry of new competitors The costs imposed by a poorly run bank or thrift institution They impose other substantial burdens on society do not stop with the inadequately served customers of these institutions.

The primary role of banks and other financial institutions is to distribute the available pool of loanable funds (created by the savings of individuals and businesses Borrowers who are most productive, who best serve the consumer providing desired products or services, and who have the best future earnings prospects ought to receive the available loanable funds In addition, financial intermediaries separate those new ideas and ventures which represent real advances in service to the public from those which do not, providing start-up capital for the former group. When the inefficient management of a financial institution is protected from the discipline of competition This discussion assumes that borrowers are commercial enterprises. As noted earlier, consumer loans, with the exception of mortgages, represent much less than half of total borrowing. However, uneconomic enterprises are encouraged while more productive firms may find themselves unable to obtain funds.

Admittedly, financial institutions differ from other businesses. The liabilities of depository institutions the checking and savings accounts placed there by customers make up over 80 percent of the U.S. money supply. The widespread failure of banks in the 1930s and the resulting instability in the flow of money and credit created real and severe economic problems. But with deposits insured by the federal government, customers need no longer fear for the safety of balances held by an insured depository institution. Widespread panic and resulting bank runs have been largely eliminated as a threat to sound banks It is no longer necessary, therefore, to protect inefficient financial institutions to ensure the safety of sound banks and S & Ls or of deposits in general. This is not to suggest that there is no role of the government in controlling entry into the financial institutions industry.

Because of the extremely important role depository institutions play in providing the U.S. money supply and the flow of credit minimum standards should be established for opening a bank or other depository institution. The adequacy of the new bank's capital structure and the general character of the management should be established as a necessary safeguard of the public funds. Yet there is no need for government chartering agents to continue considering the future earnings prospects of the new bank or S & L. The prospective owners already have done this as a first step in applying for a charter to examine the convenience and needs of the community within which the new depository institution seeks to operate. This too is a fundamental component of the future earnings prospects.

Finally, the continued existence of other banks or S & Ls within the area should be no factor at all in determining whether to approve the charter of a new institution. In short, the protection currently covering financial institutions must be removed inefficient depository institutions must be allowed to fail It also is not necessary. There is one legitimate concern connected with bank failure. Many banks maintain deposits, known as correspondent accounts, with other banks cases, banks which are not members of the Federal Reserve System may keep a portion of their required reserves in this form.

Reserve System members may gain access to some Federal Reserve Bank services in this way. If a bank which holds correspondent accounts should fail, the smaller banks whose deposits are held by the failed bank could be seriously hurt through no fault of their own however, by providing 100 percent deposit insurance for correspondent accounts rather than subjecting them to the $100,000 FDIC ceiling imposed on other accounts In addition, non-Federal. This problem could easily be solved.

WHAT IS TO BE DONE?

Speaking to the Civic Federation in Chicago, Secretary of the Treasury Donald Regan listed four regulatory areas needing attention (1) interest rate restrictions; (2) specialization of financial institutions (3) the regulation of geographic markets and (4) growth of the regulatory agencies. Some bankers have identified roughly the same four categories, calling them pricing powers, place, and prudential restrictions. Other students of depository institutions have slightly different names, but most agree on the broad classifications.

Pricing More than any other regulation, the pricing limitations account for the current crisis of depository institutions. Pricing restrictions are of two basic types: ceilings on interest rates paid on deposits and limits on the interest charged for loans As inflation rates have increased, consumers have found the 544 to 5% percent paid on savings accounts at banks and S Ls unacceptable To understand the impact of these interest rate ceilings on depository institutions, think of savings accounts as the raw materials with which banks and S Ls produce their primary service making loans depositors is analogous to restricting the price a steel manufacturer may pay for iron ore. Obviously, when market price increases as a result of inflation, for example the firm must be able to offer more for the ore. If it cannot, the ore seller will seek customers willing to pay the market price. is happening to banks and savings and loan associations. Deposits are moving to unregulated firms able to pay market rates of interest Depositors have been taking their money elsewhere.

Limiting the rates that may be paid to This is exactly what Of course, some deposits in banks and S Ls pay interest at rates closer to the market return To take advantage of these higher rates, however, the depositor is required by regulations to commit funds for a specified period of time. Those suddenly needing access to savings face a substantial penalty for early withdrawal Needless to say, the unregulated firms offering alternative financial instruments do not face these restrictions.

Very often checks may be written on these accounts Is it any wonder that money market mutual funds, combining near-market returns with accessibility, are attracting customers in droves?

The result has been a draining of traditional, low-cost loanable funds. Savings deposits in commercial banks fell from 191 billion in September 1980 to $158 billion in September 1981 an average decline of $2.75 billion monthly. The savings and loan associations have not fared much better. The deposits in S L accounts paying 535 percent fell by $15 billion during the fifteen months from July 1980 to September 1981.11 Passbook 16 savings accounts that had made up 91 percent of all S L deposits in 1966 and 43 percent as late as 1975, represented only 21 percent of S L deposits by 1980 Recognizing the problems caused by the limits on interest paid to deposits, Congress in 1980 enacted the six-year phase-out under DIDMCA. However, the Depository Institutions Deregulation Committee (DIDC) has yet to allow any increase in the rates paid on savings accounts. Citing objections by the savings and loan industry, the Committee voted 3 to 2 against raising rate ceilings in fall 1981 Representatives in the savings and loan industry claim that any increases in interest rate ceilings at this time will only make their situations worse. Unquestionably, as rates on deposits rise, the costs of banks and S & Ls will also rise in the beginning. As a practical matter, however, most depository institutions are obtaining much of their operating capital at rates above these ceilings, anyway. And, without an increase in the ceilings the outflow of low-cost funds will remain unabated. Even members of the savings and loan industry are willing to admit as much.

Richmond's Security Federal Savings and Loan Association President Edwin Brooks, testifying on behalf of the U.S. League of Savings Association, acknowledged Savers routinely shift their funds from old low rate accounts and passbooks into the new, high-rate market related accounts The balances in older certificate accounts will disappear completely in a short time. The percentage of funds obtained by financial institutions at above ceiling prices is thus constantly rising in any event, and higher rates would at least encourage the retention of consumer deposits. Furthermore, interest rates are not expected to rise to market rates when the ceilings are removed. Savings accounts in banks and S & Ls provide more convenience, familiarity, and safety than most other financial instruments. In addition, an increase in interest paid on savings accounts should lead to funds flowing back to the depository institutions resulting in less dependence on the more expensive funds purchased at market rates. The costs of funds should thus eventually fall. The movement of funds back to banks and S Ls is desirable for other reasons. Most important, the pool of loanable funds available to banks and S & Ls will be enlarged investment in local communities and housing is to be public policy, a necessary first step is increasing the funds local if encouraging. At the last minute, Secretary of the Treasury Donald Regan reversed an earlier vote that would have raised the rates by percent. 17 financial institutions have to loan. If an overriding concern of the government is, as many claim it should be, protection of and service to consumers, the only equitable course of action is a speedy removal of restraints on interest paid to savings accounts.

While ceilings on interest rates paid on deposits are set at the federal level, limits on the prices lending institutions may charge for loans are set by state legislatures. These so-called usury laws generally are justified on the grounds that small borrowers must be protected from the unbridled greed of wealthy bankers. What happens, in fact, is that when interest rates in general rise above the ceiling, smaller borrowers without established credit ratings find themselves unable to obtain loans at all. While these small borrowers are protected from bankers they are forced either to forgo loans or turn to the illicit loan-sharking industry, largely unencumbered by legal considerations. Continued interest rate limits hurt only the small, unsophisticated saver or borrower. Those with more money can always find alternative investments with higher returns or alternative sources for loans. Powers Banks and savings and loan associations face strict legal limitations concerning the kinds of investments they make and the kinds of financial instruments they may offer. In the case of banks, most of these restrictions were established by the Glass Steaga Act (also known as the 1933 Banking Act). They were prompted by arguments that the restraints would help preserve the safety and soundness of banks as well as reducing fraudulent stock practices. In the case of savings and loans, the restrictions were intended to help allocate credit to support the residential market. Congress in 1933 established the Federal Home Loan Bank System to charter federal savings and loan associations.

Though not placed under the interest rate ceilings established for banks initially, the S Ls were subjected to strict requirements mandating that the lion's share of their portfolios be held in the form of real estate mortgages. Citing their current troubles, both the banking and the savings and loan industries are asking for new powers to permit increased portfolio flexibility. The banks blame their present difficulties in retaining deposits on their inability to offer the kinds of financial instruments available from their unregulated competitors. Savings and loan associations, meanwhile, claim that if they had not been forced to hold almost all their assets in long-term mortgages, they would not be suffering their current profit squeeze.

Members of the savings and loan industry further argue that at least until now, S L deregulation efforts have been unbalanced. Regulatory changes affecting the instruments that could be offered 18 consumers and the interest rates that could be paid on some deposits were begun as early as 1978. The first preemptions of state usury laws were not effective until March 1980, however and a mortgage instrument allowing rate flexibility was not authorized until April 1981. Therefore, many individuals within the industry maintain that if interest rate ceilings on deposits are to be lifted, the savings and loan industry should be compensated with increased powers. There is considerable theoretical justification for increasing the powers of banks and S Ls. As Donald Regan remarked in a recent speech The financial markets today change rapidly as one innovation follows another. Institutions have to be able to adjust, and the more specialized an institution the less capable it is of adjusting.13 The financial, needs of consumers and corporations are clearly changing. High inflation rates have made individuals and firms unwilling to hold substantial balances in idle accounts. On the other hand, these customers do not have time to deal with several different firms when taking care of their financial transactions.

The accommodation of "one-stop shopping" represents a significant advantage. Therefore, competitive pressure is building as firms outside the regulatory mesh entangling banks and S Ls cater to customer convenience by offering a wide range of financial services. Increased powers for banks and S Ls should be considered as a means through which they may meet this new competition.

Banks are limited by legislation passed during the 1930s which allows them to underwrite municipal general obligation bonds, but not municipal revenue bonds. At the time the law was written, revenue bonds were virtually unknown. Since 1932 however, revenue bonds have grown from 3 percent of the municipal market to 70 percent.14 Most bankers favor changes in the law that would permit them to participate in the revenue bond market they claim that bank competition in this area would reduce the costs of raising funds for state and local governments. Banks also seek authority to issue a new type of instrument with enough rate flexibility to be competitive with money market mutual funds. Aside from deregulation of deposit rate ceilings the most direct way to accomplish this is to allow banks and S & Ls to offer comingled agency or mutual funds accounts. After all, banks possess unsurpassed experience in managing short-term investments, experience on which many current mutual funds draw by using banks as investment advisors. Should bank customers be denied the direct benefits of this experience Municipal revenue bonds are paid through proceeds generated by the service they were used to build, e.g., sewage treatment, water systems, etc. General obligation bonds, on the other hand, are paid by general tax revenues.

19 While such funds would not immediately increase deposits available for housing, consumer, and commercial credit needs they would offer banks and S Ls an opportunity to retain customers who now are removing funds from traditional savings deposit accounts. Then, as deposit rate ceilings are relaxed and/or short-term interest rates fall, customers of the depository institution could more easily switch their funds back to insured deposits than if they were in money market accounts. Allowing banks and S Ls to offer money market funds also keeps deposits under local management and reduces the flow of funds to the money centers To ensure the widest use of these funds, banks and S Ls could sell shares in any other bank- or S L-sponsored mutual funds. This would permit small banks and S Ls to offer a joint city- or region-wide mutual fund, or to sell shares of a larger institution's fund. The depository institutions would, of course, be subject to the jurisdiction of the SEC where their mutual funds were concerned.

The savings and loan associations are primarily interested in changes allowing them a wider range of assets for their port folios. S & L leaders insist, however, that mortgage money would not disappear if S & Ls gain new powers. In the first place current law requires that 82 percent of an S & L's portfolio be in mortgages if the institution is to qualify for certain tax advantages. More important, however, savings and loan expertise is primarily in providing mortgages. While seeking to reduce their interest rate risk exposure, most industry leaders willingly admit that S & Ls currently lack the requisite knowledge to enter the commercial loan market extensively. The specific list of new powers sought by the thrifts and banks is fairly extensive. In general, the savings and loans want to acquire many of the most important powers now available to bankers. Examples: overdraft loan authority for demand accounts; authority for commercial, corporate, business and agricultural leasing; and opportunities for equipment leasing. Bankers similarly seek to gain major powers available to their nearest competitors the ability to issue mutual funds, under write revenue bonds, and expand real estate lending, among others. Critics of these proposals complain that the changes would eradicate current distinctions between major types of financial institutions. It is very difficult, however, to continue to justify the sharp distinctions between classes of financial institutions particularly when they do not serve the consumer. Why should consumers be inconvenienced by having to deal with several different financial institutions simply as a matter of adherence to a principle established fifty years ago?

Other opponents argue that specialized financial institutions are necessary to ensure the continued provision of mortgage funds. To be sure, S & Ls have considerable expertise in providing mortgage money. Yet other conditions also ensure a supply of housing credit. The demand for mortgage money will continue with 20 or without specialized institutions to provide the funds. The reasons are that (1) housing is a basic necessity; (2) because federal tax codes allow deductions for interest payments, there are tremendous incentives to own a home; and (3) the value of real estate as an appreciating investment can generally be expected. As long as the demand exists, there will be credit supplied. This should be particularly true now that new variable rate mortgage instruments are available, allowing financial institutions to share the risk of future interest rate increases with borrowers.

It has been argued that increased powers for S Ls will not alleviate their current crisis. The problems of the industry, it is said, are the result of tying up their portfolios in long-term low-rate assets not of having too few attractive alternatives for loans No one is suggesting, however, that new powers will be a savings and loan industry cure-all. In fact, the thrifts have made little use of the new powers granted them by the 1980 Act. The trouble is that too much past legislation has dealt with financial institutions on a crisis-by-crisis basis. It is now time to take a long-term view and seek ways to give depository institutions the flexibility to deal with future crises rather than forcing them to bring problems to Congress.

Some managers of many smaller banks and S & Ls express fears that an expansion of powers will force their institutions into areas where their knowledge and expertise is limited. Yet there is no evidence to support this. As suggested with the mutual funds, the smaller banks and S Ls could participate in services offered by the larger institutions, thus providing their customers with a wider range of options financial institutions do not now all offer the same range of services even when that would be possible Furthermore, it is obvious that There is some concern among bankers that providing increased powers to the savings and loans will give them an unfair competitive advantage. S'& Ls have less restrictive branching laws and capital requirements, for example, than banks. If the thrifts are given the wider range of powers which they seek, serious consideration must be given to removing some of these unfair advantages. The liberalization of bank branching restrictions would certainly be a step in this direction. Place Most businessmen recognized the U.S. was a national market rather than a series of local markets, almost 100 years ago. This led to a substantial number of mergers between 1887 and 1904, consolidating many smaller firms that had been operating in limited geographic areas. Yet what has been accepted for every other industry is still not the norm for the depository institutions industry. Ritter and Silber, authors of a text on financial markets, noted. The small unit bank, like the Family Farm, is generally embraced as an integral part of the American Way of Life, regardless of whether or not it is economically viable so that it can stand on its own two feet in terms of costs and revenues. Conversely, bigness is typically equated with monopoly, especially where financial institutions are concerned.

Objective conditions, however, contradict this view of banking transported as does banking. Billions of dollars are transferred daily instantaneously all over the world with the sophisticated electronic systems. Automatic teller machines already provide 2.4-hour service to bank customers. Soon consumers will be able to bank by telephone and television through home computers It is already possible to transfer funds between accounts or between institutions by merely picking up the telephone No other industry deals with a commodity so easily To further complicate matters, consider the mobility of the avcragc American. He works, shops, and plays 6ver wide geographic areas moved would be a perfect complement to the mobility of the average consumer. The obvious conclusion is that funds from local banks should be accessible nationwide It would seem the increasing ease with which money is While the technology exists, the laws do not. Banks are restricted from branching across state lines and sometimes within the states themselves.

Therefore, banks often cannot offer accessibility within a single metropolitan area if state or county lines are crossed. Because the courts have ruled that ATMs are technically branches, even though it is technologically feasible to develop a nationwide system of shared ATMs providing every individual with access to funds in his local bank regardless of where he happens to be, it is not legally permissible at least for banks. These restrictions, on the other hand, do not hamper the individual who qualifies for the gold American Express card with which cash is obtainable anytime, anywhere. Those with money in the Sears money market fund may soon have the same flexibility. Indeed, many other firms are planning to use this ability to transfer funds to provide nationwide maybe even worldwide access to deposits. Banks, however, are prevented by law from offering these services. This means that travelers away from home without the financial resources to invest in a nationwide money market fund better not need cash suddenly restrictions on banks exist because of the 200-year-old fear of undue concentration of financial resources. The U.S. supports almost 15,000 banks; Canada has eleven.

It has been argued that if interstate geographic restrictions are lifted, a few large banks such as Bank of America, Chase Manhattan, Citibank would buy the others, leaving the U.S. with only a handful of large banks with tentacles reaching through- out the country. These banks, goes the argument, would then be able to decide which businesses grow and which fail, which regions thrive and which decline. A move to interstate banking admittedly would result in some consolidation of the banking industry survive in a truly competitive atmosphere. They now exist only because they are protected by restrictions keeping other banks out of their market. The price for this is paid by their customers who are certainly not as well served as those of banks facing more competition as the result of less restrictive branching laws. There is no reason to believe that well-run local and regional banks would not survive, however.

Supporting this contention is strong evidence from the twenty-two states which currently have statewide branching. Without exception, every state allowing statewide branching has some banks that have chosen to open no branches and have survived.

Facing potential competition from at least five of the nation's top ten banks, over 46 percent of New York banks continue to exist while operating one office Many banks would not Some small banks would undoubtedly be absorbed In California more.

Smaller local banks have substantial advantages over potential outside competitors the local market the community's businesses and individuals. Furthermore, many customers prefer to deal with a locally-owned bank provided they are offered similar services as consumers dealing with branches of larger banks. Finally, at least some data suggest that economies of scale are unimportant for banks larger than $50 million. This will be especially true if some sharing of services is allowed for example with mutual funds The most important is their knowledge of 23 Still, there are advantages to interstate banking. In the first place, it would allow consumers access to their deposits over a wider geographic area allowing banks to compete more effectively with firms which offer services nationwide such as Merrill Lynch, Sears, and American Express Most important however, it would increase the degree of competition in the banking market. The mere threat of new competition is often enough to ensure that existing firms give customers the best service possible. Many small New York upstate banks, upon hearing that a New York City bank was about to open a local branch, suddenly have offered free checking, expanded overdraft privileges or other new or expanded services.

Furthermore, the worst banking service often is found in towns too small to support more than a couple of banks. Frequent ly there is a shortage of local business demand for loans, even though there may be adequate deposit volume to support more banks branch of a larger bank. Branches are less costly to establish than a new bank. In addition, depositors would be better served because of the increased competition while the national economy would benefit from an improved flow of loanable funds to areas most in need of them increased economic growth, the branch banker is in an ideal position to facilitate the flow of funds into the community. In fact, evidence suggests that rather than using outlying branches to transfer funds to head offices in urban areas, banks are much more likely to transfer funds among rural offices according to loan demand.

And because Supreme Court decisions of the 1960s clearly subjected bank mergers to the Sherman and Clayton Antitrust Acts, the legal mechanism already exists to guard against "undue concentration of financial power This would be a perfect situation in which to establish a Should this small town suddenly experience Consideration of these arguments led the Department of the Treasury in a January 1981 Report of the President on geographic banking restrictions to conclude that Lliberalization of these restrictions (1) could improve competitive conditions in local markets and subject to the establishment of appropriate controls would not raise significantly the risk of undue concentration of power (2) would increase the range of financial services available to local communities but would have little impact on credit availability (3) does not pose a significant threat to the viability of the small bank as an institution (4) would not have a material impact on the safety and stability of the banking system; and (5) need not threaten the vitality of the dual banking system. Other Problems In addition to the regulations already cited, a number of others are particularly onerous. There is considerable dismay, 24 for example, with the "performance1I regulations imposed on the lending. Institutions of depository institutions, but are directed instead at affecting the way funds are invested and at protecting consumers.

Such regulations began in 1968 with the Truth-in-Lending Act and include the Consumer Credit Protection Act, the Equal Credit Opportunity Act, the Equal Credit Opportunity Act Amendments, the Home Mortgage Disclosure Act, the Debt Collection Practices Act and the Community Reinvestment Act, to name a few. These performance standards levy substantial reporting and regulatory costs that are, as are all costs, eventually passed on to consumers.

To serve the consumer best, only one measure is required increased competition. These have nothing to do with the sound

Another area of concern is the proliferation of regulatory agencies. No fewer than three federal groups exercise examination and supervision powers over some banks troller of the Currency, the Federal Deposit Insurance Corporation and the Federal Reserve System. Savings and loans are in a slightly better position because the FSLIC is part of the Federal Home Loan Bank System. If S Ls begin a more extensive use of their new powers, however, the Federal Home Loan Bank System and the banking regulators will oversee financial institutions with very similar functions. In addition, every state has its own group of examiners. When questions of mergers or new financial instruments or services arise, almost all the regulatory groups get involved. In many cases, decisions take months further reducing the ability of depository institutions to respond to competition from unregulated firms.

The power of the regulators has been expanding in recent years. This fuels fears that rather than accept a more flexible less regulated atmosphere for depository institutions, regulators will insist on controlling the currently unregulated competitors of banks and S & Ls. While this might solve the problem for a time, when the situation changes, some less regulated firm (or firms) will find a way to respond. Then that firm (or firms will be brought under the regulatory umbrella, and find itself unable to respond as conditions change. So another entrepreneur will fill the gap, and in turn be regulated. Reducing regulations thus offers the only course consistent with maximum service to the consumer. the range of possibilities for regulatory change the Office of the Comp The list could continue, but enough has been said to indicate

SUMMARY

Legislative solutions imposed in the past have been outdated by rapidly changing economic conditions.

Chapter

4

Impact of Deregulation on the Australian Financial System

Deregulation of the financial system is generally taken to mean the variety of legislative and economic events that took place in the early to mid 1980s, in large part as a result of the recommendations contained in the Final Report of the Campbell Committee of Inquiry into the Australian Financial System, released in late 1981.

"Deregulation" broadly meant there was a move away from regulating a range of financial activities directly so as to achieve monetary policy, public sector financing and sectoral assistance objectives. Instead an approach was adopted where banks and other financial institutions had much greater freedom to respond to competitive market signals and customer requirements, subject to meeting minimum prudential standards designed to protect depositors and maintain the stability of the financial system.

The success or otherwise of past deregulation should be gauged against this Inquiry's objectives of having an efficient and competitive financial system, providing consumer choice, and maintaining the overall stability and integrity of the system. Also relevant is the Inquiry's concern with fairness, or the equitable treatment of the various users of the financial system. Consequently, the focus of this discussion is restricted to these aspects of the impact of deregulation on the Australian financial system. According to all the above criteria, deregulation has been successful:

- The outcome of deregulating savings and deposit rates, removing lending controls and opening the financial markets up to greater competition has generated billions of dollars of benefits to Australian savers (in more interest earned) and to Australian borrowers (in lower rates paid);
- Deregulation has resulted in significantly greater competition, convenience and diversity of choice for both individual and business users of financial services; and
- The stability and integrity of the financial system has largely been maintained.

Impact on Efficiency

The impact of removing interest rate and lending controls.

Prior to deregulation, Governments sought to use the banking system as a means of achieving monetary policy objectives. Some of the restraints that were imposed on banks included:

- Controls on interest rates which banks could offer on their deposits and charge on certain loans, particularly housing loans;
- Limits on the maturity of deposits on which banks could pay interest; and
- Limits imposed from time to time on the overall growth of their balance sheets.

A direct consequence of these restraints was the rationing by banks of funds available for lending. Lending rate controls made banks a cheaper source of funds than finance companies and building societies, which only increased the potential bank borrower demand, further exacerbating the loan demand/supply imbalance. In this environment:

- Lower income earners were often excluded from borrowing from banks and were forced to borrow, if they could, from more expensive alternative sources;
- Housing loan borrowers able to obtain bank finance were often forced to "top up" their borrowing with more expensive

second mortgages or personal loans from banks, credit unions and finance companies;

- There was widespread depositor cross-subsidisation of lending for housing and other purposes. Interest rate ceilings on bank deposits meant that customers wanting a better yield had to seek out higher rates from more risky institutions outside the banking system. However, customers who wanted greater security (particularly low and middle income earners and groups such as pensioners) or had cheque accounts had no option but to keep their funds in no interest or low interest bank deposits and hence, indirectly, subsidised those fortunate enough to be borrowers; and
- There was little or no price competition between banks.

With deregulation, rationing of funds by banks ended and the dismantling of cross subsidisation between bank customers began. Both led to greater efficiency in the workings of the financial system and more equitable treatment of all bank customers.

User benefits from removal of lending and interest rate controls

With the removal of lending and interest rate controls, bank customers began to receive competitive market-related rates on their deposits and were offered a greater variety of deposit products.

As interest was paid on cheque accounts, and bank depositors became more interest rate sensitive, a shift occurred in balances out of accounts which traditionally had paid a zero or low interest rate to higher yielding accounts, as shown in Figure below.

As a result, the proportion of funds in current accounts not bearing interest has declined significantly, from 20.5% in 1980 to 5.4% in 1995.

Meanwhile the funds in high interest fixed term deposits and CDs have increased from 31.5% to 57.2% of total deposits over the same period.

Figure: BANK DEPOSITS REPAYABLE IN AUSTRALIA (%)

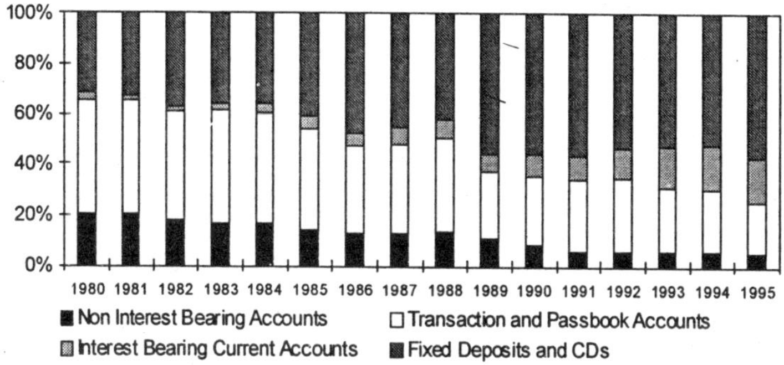

Note: Low interest accounts are non-interest bearing accounts and transaction and passbook accounts.

Source: RBA Occasional paper No. 8.

With the removal of lending controls, banks were in a position to meet a greater share of the borrowing needs of ordinary Australians. Customers in turn benefited from improved access and many also benefited from lower cost borrowing, than had been generally available from non-bank sources pre-deregulation. Not all borrowers, however, paid lower interest. The unwinding of the cross-subsidy to borrowers from those depositors who, prior to deregulation, were receiving no or low interest rates and the removal of interest rate ceilings, saw those borrowers fortunate enough to get controlled rate bank loans prior to deregulation begin to pay market rates. These changes resulted in a significant improvement in the equity of access to bank financing.

Banks' share of lending relative to lending by other financial intermediaries has risen from 58% in 1980 to 77% in 1995. However, it should be noted that the increased share also reflected the conversion of building societies to banks and the absorption of money market corporations and finance companies by some banks. Without these conversions and absorptions, banks' share of lending would have remained unchanged at 58%.

Following deregulation and the lifting of controls on lending, banks turned to borrowing in the professional markets to increase the overall availability of funds for lending purposes. This development, in association with the payment of market-related interest rates on deposit accounts resulted in the overall cost of funds increasing for banks. Banks' shrinking reliance on low interest deposits for lending purposes, from 57% to 14% of liabilities between 1980 and 1995, is clearly illustrated in Figure below.

Figure : LOW INTEREST DEPOSITS AS % OF LIABILITIES

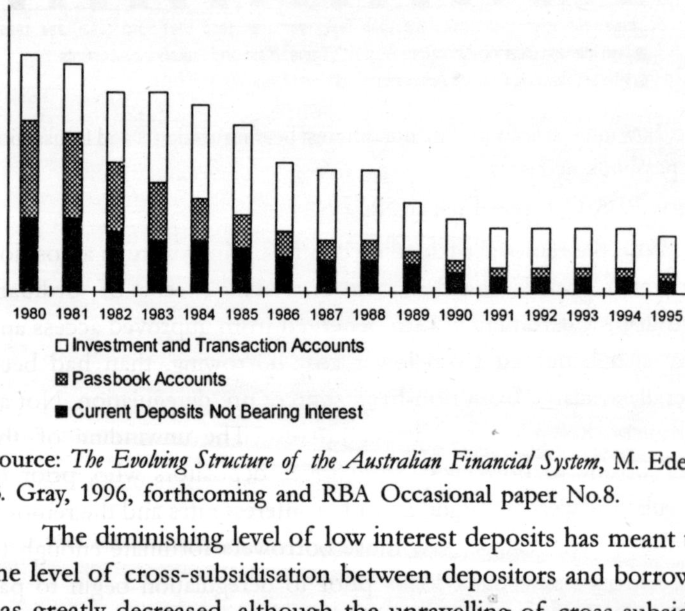

Source: *The Evolving Structure of the Australian Financial System*, M. Edey & B. Gray, 1996, forthcoming and RBA Occasional paper No.8.

The diminishing level of low interest deposits has meant that the level of cross-subsidisation between depositors and borrowers has greatly decreased, although the unravelling of cross-subsidies, particularly as they still apply between transaction account holders and borrowers, still has some way to go.

The deregulatory measures implemented in the early to mid-1980s, the increased competition in both the lending and deposit markets (between banks and other financial institutions), and banks' greater reliance on the more expensive professional money markets for funds, have, in combination, resulted in a reduction in net interest spreads. Between 1980 and 1995, domestic net interest spreads reduced from 5.0% to 3.9%, as can be seen in Figure below.

Figure: DOMESTIC INTEREST SPREAD - MAJOR BANKS

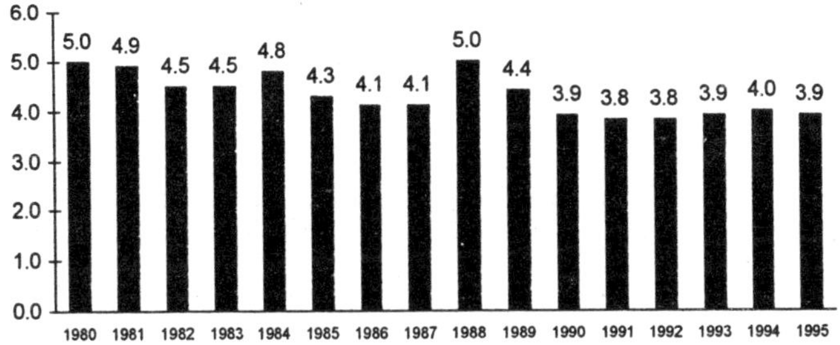

Source: RBA, Annual Report 1996.

This 1.1% reduction cannot easily be quantitatively attributed to its various causal factors. However, it is clear that the Australian economy is more efficient by having the net cost of intermediation, as measured by the interest spread reduced by this amount.

In simple terms, the benefit today to bank savers and borrowers of a 1.1% reduction in interest spread would be equivalent to more than $3 billion. In anyone's language, this is a very large amount.

Improved operational efficiency and reduced costs

The large bank mergers in 1981 between, on the one hand, the Commercial Bank of Australia and the Bank of New South Wales, and, on the other hand, between the National Bank of Australasia and the Commercial Banking Company of Sydney, provided the initial impetus for the resource rationalisation that has taken place since the early 1980s. In addition, the decline in margins, the poor experience with loan losses in the early 1990s and the more recent disaggregation of the banking market that has been taking place, have all acted as inducements to bank management to reduce operating costs and increase efficiency.

In the period since deregulation, the major banks have reduced costs in numerous ways. Between 1983 and 1994, they closed 15% of their branches, particularly in areas where revenues were insufficient to justify their retention. The most significant reductions have occurred between 1990 and 1994, when 12% of branches were closed. Branch closures are still taking place.

Staff numbers in the retail operations of banks have reduced by almost 5% between 1983 and 1994, despite a 25% increase in the volume of retail transactions and a significantly broader product and service base. Between 1983 and 1990, retail banking employment rose by 37%, reflecting the entry of new banks and substantially increased business levels. The main efficiency gains have thus come in the 1990s, with a decline in employment levels of 30% between 1990 and 1994.

These efficiency gains are associated with large-scale reorganisations by banks in the way their personnel provide banking services to personal and business customers. They have outsourced activities that can be provided more cheaply and efficiently by external parties. Finally, they have generally pursued a variety of means to exploit the economies of scale which can operate in many sectors of the financial services market, particularly through the centralisation of certain processing functions and the judicious use of new technology.

These initiatives have resulted in measurable increases in efficiency. The proportion of domestic non-interest expenses make up of the net income earned by banks has declined from approximately 73% to 61% between 1982 and 1995.

***Figure:** NON INTEREST EXPENSES TO NET INTEREST AND OTHER INCOME - MAJOR BANKS (%)*

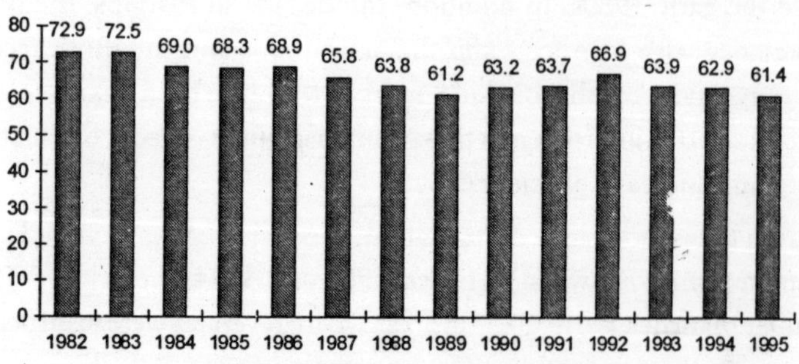

Source: Annual reports of major banks.

Another measure of efficiency improvement is that of operating costs as a percentage of total average assets. Between 1980 and 1995, the banking industry saw an improvement from 4.2% to 2.9% in this ratio as outlined in Figure below.

As total bank Australian assets currently amount to some $456 billion, each 0.1% that can be shaved off this ratio is equal to about $456 million in cost savings a year, relative to that level of assets.

Figure: *NON-INTEREST EXPENSE/TOTAL AVERAGE ASSETS - MAJOR BANKS*

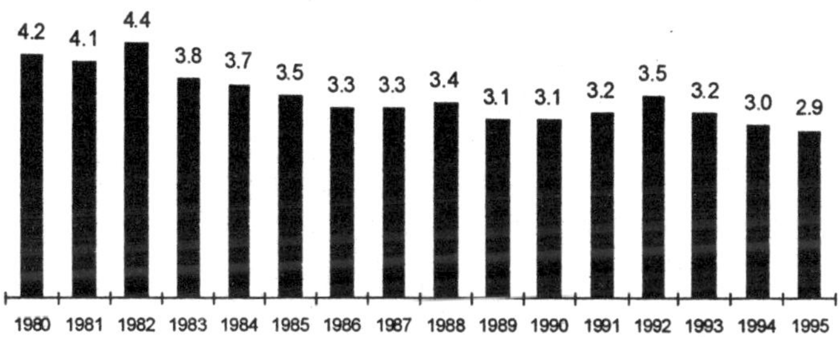

Source: Annual reports of major banks.

Attributing the above significant efficiency improvements across the range of changes that occurred throughout the 1980s is not possible.

For example, rapid asset growth, particularly in overseas markets where corporate lending dominated activities and there was no requirement to build extensive branch networks, also contributed to the improvement in the expense/asset ratio. What is evident, however, is that around 70% of the efficiency improvements occurred between 1981 and 1986.

This period coincided with the two major mergers that created Westpac and the National Australia Bank. The resulting rationalisation benefits contributed to the above efficiency gains. This is evident from the operational efficiency measures for the merged banks. The reductions of 33% in the expense to asset ratio for both Westpac and the NAB between 1982 and 1986, compared to reductions of

14% for the Commonwealth and 9% for the ANZ, suggest that the mergers contributed to the efficiency improvements through this period, to the benefit of users.Although significant efficiency gains have been achieved since deregulation, these gains are not yet enough. Australian banks still need to become more efficient if they are to be globally competitive.

The 1995 study undertaken by the McKinsey Global Institute, showed Australian retail banking productivity as up to 40% behind the levels achieved in the USA.

Figure : RETAIL BANK PRODUCTIVITY - ACTIVITY PER FTE

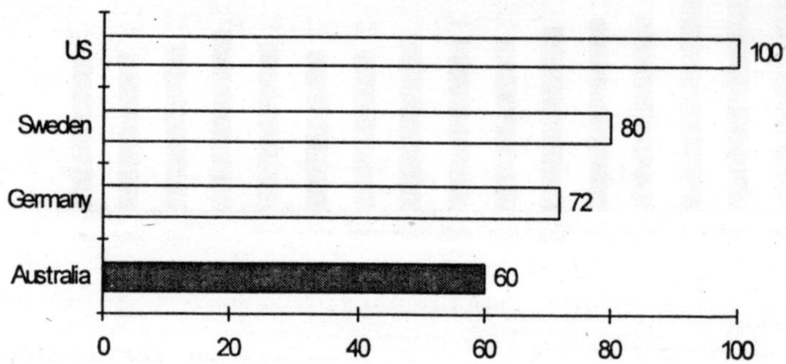

(Index US = 100)*

Note: Composite index of productivity for payments, deposits and credit services, weighted by functional labour input; US, Swedish and German data are for 1992, Australian for 1994.

Source: *Growth Platforms for a Competitive Australia,* McKinsey and Company Australia and the McKinsey Global Institute, page 102.

As the McKinsey report says: "Australian activity levels per capita are well below those in the United States, but are similar to European levels. Transactions per capita are around 47 per cent of the US level, while estimated loan accounts outstanding are around 60 per cent of the US level.

These relatively low per capita activity numbers, when combined with Australia's high number of branches per capita, result in low activity per branch..... Our research suggests that the major cause of lower labour productivity in Australian retail banking is high branch numbers".

The report notes that "Australia has more branches per million population than the United States and many European countries. This is mainly due to the low population densities outside major cities and regional centres, and nature of competition before deregulation, when the convenient location of branches was one of the few competitive levers available to banks. Although industry participants have long recognised the benefits of industry consolidation and the value of alternative distribution channels, they have been deterred from pursuing large scale closures because of historical market and regulatory factors", such as Trade Practices Act and competition policy restrictions on the extent to which consolidation is allowed to take place in the industry.

Figure: BRANCH DENSITY(Branches/million population, 1993)

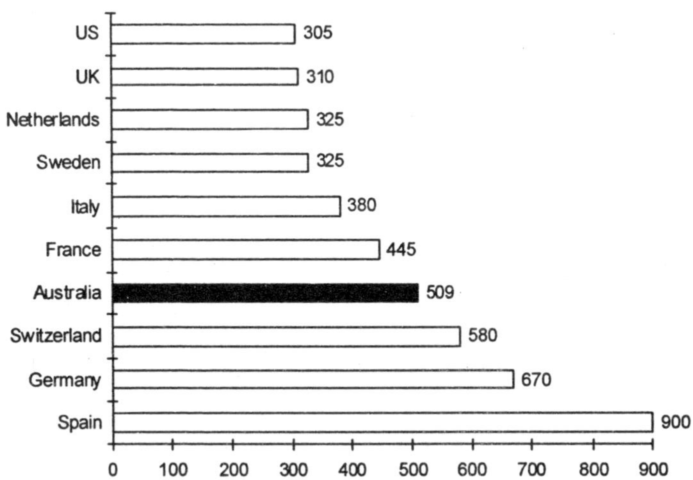

Note: 1994 Business Establishment Survey. All branches of banks, building societies and credit unions included.

Source: Growth Platforms for a Competitive Australia, McKinsey and Company Australia and the McKinsey Global Institute, page 105.

To be able to compete in an increasingly global marketplace and to continue to bring real benefits to customers, both borrowers and savers, domestic banks need to reduce their expenses further, and in particular, the number of branches. Consumers are already benefiting from new ways of transacting business other than by going into branches.

However, they are not prepared to pay the costs of operating both the old and new technologies. For increased efficiency, the number of branches in the Australian banking system needs to be reduced, both through individual bank efforts and through merger rationalisation.

Figure : PRODUCTIVITY IMPROVEMENTS AUSTRALIAN BANKING ($bn)

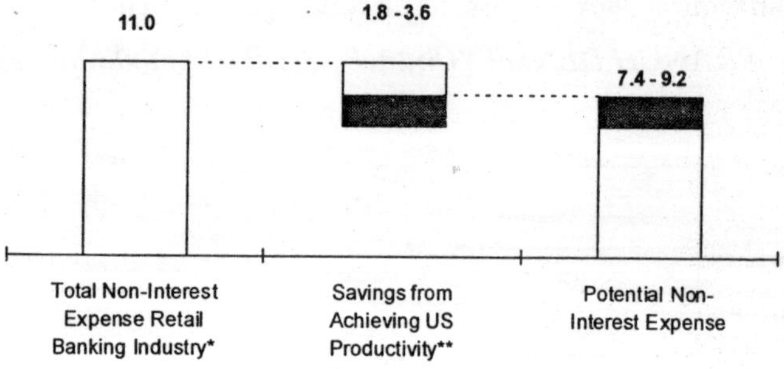

* Assumes that average non-interest expense for a branch is $1.6 million for major banks and $0.8 million for all other institutions.

** Upper bound assumes branch closures spread proportionately across major banks and others. 50% expansion in employees per branch assumed to be required in remaining branches. Lower bound of saving assumes that productivity improvements takes form of employment reduction without savings in premises cost. Employment accounts for around 50% of non-interest expense.

Source: *Growth Platforms for a Competitive Australia*, McKinsey and Company Australia and the McKinsey Global Institute, page 102.

McKinsey have estimated that the benefits to the Australian economy of achieving US retail productivity levels could be between $1.8 and $3.6 billion.

Increased Competition and Diversity of Choice

Increased competition in the financial marketplace has come about as a result of the dismantling of some of the previously described controls, the entry of new competitors as licensed banks and heightened competition among existing players.

This has resulted in significant benefits for consumers and businesses through greater convenience and choice.

Greater Choice of Institution

With the exception of building societies and finance companies that have converted or been absorbed into banks, the choice of institution with which consumers and businesses have been able to conduct their financial services transactions has significantly increased, as demonstrated in Table below.

Table: NUMBER OF FINANCIAL INSTITUTIONS

Type of Institution	1980	1995
Banks	19	43
Building Societies & Credit Unions	765	321
Finance Companies	117	103
Merchant Banks	59	83
Mortgage Originators	0	26
Funds Managers	35	93

Source: Council for Financial Supervisors, Annual Report 1995, CANNEX, Campbell Inquiry, Interim Report, ASSIRT.

The share of assets currently held by each of these different category of institution is shown in Figure below.

This illustrates the importance of the roles played by banks and life offices and superannuation funds in the financial system.

Figure: ASSETS BY INSTITUTION TYPE (as at June 1995)

100% = $956 bn

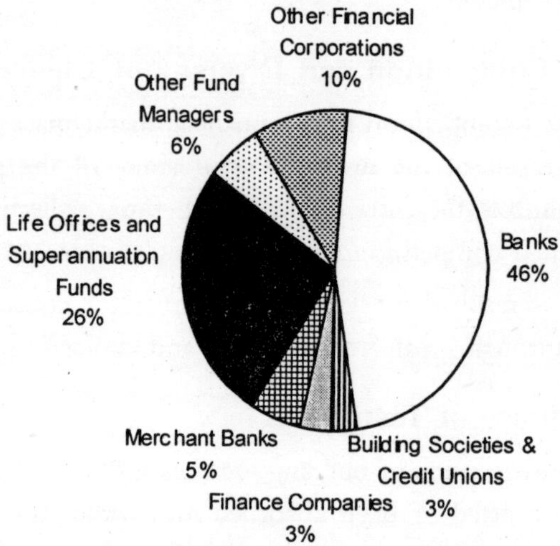

Note: Other funds managers include cash management trusts, common funds, friendly societies and public unit trusts. Other financial corporations include authorised money market dealers, pastoral finance companies, general financiers, general insurance offices, other FCA companies, securitisation vehicles and co-operative housing societies.

Source: RBA Bulletin, April 1996.

Greater Convenience and Choice

Convenience

There has been a dramatic increase over the past two decades in the ease with which banking business can be transacted, brought about both as a result of increased competition in the deregulated market and as a result of the technological innovations that have been introduced.

No longer do bank customers physically need to visit a branch between 10.00 am and 3.00 p.m. (or 5.00 p.m. on Fridays) in order to deposit or withdraw cash, pay off credit cards or transfer amounts between accounts. Not only are the branches open longer hours, but all of these functions can be carried out at the now ubiquitous automatic teller machine, located in shopping malls, in airport terminals and outside most banks. Goods can be paid for and funds often can be withdrawn at more than 100,000 EFTPOS terminals, even more conveniently located at service stations and in supermarkets and other stores. Banks have also begun opening compact banking kiosks at which a broad range of transactions can be carried out in supermarkets or shopping malls during extended hours, seven days a week.

Increased consumer convenience has also come about through innovations that allow customers to pay bills over the phone with a credit card and to carry out a variety of banking transactions any time of the day using the new phone banking services. Home loans can be initiated over the phone or with a mobile banker that visits the customer's residence.

The number of points at which customers can carry out transactions has dramatically increased as have the number of hours per week customers can have banking facilities readily available.

Table: BANK POINTS OF ACCESS

	1980	1995
Bank Branches	5,859	6,655
ATMs	25	7,178
EFTPOS	-	107,702
Telephone	-	11,600,000 *
Internet	-	up to 800,000 **

* This is the number of telephone and mobile phone connections. There are currently 13 banks with extensive phone banking facilities.

** Estimated number of Internet users in mid 1996. Usage growing rapidly, with an estimated 1.9 million households having a PC and 950,000 having a modem in 1995/1996. Most banks have Internet 'home pages' with Advance bank being the only one yet to allow value transactions on the Internet.

Source: RBA Bulletins, Annual Reports, ABA Submission to Campbell Inquiry, Australia Payments System Council Annual Report 1994/95, Telstra, Paul Budde Communications and www.consult.

Table: BANK HOURS OF ACCESS PER WEEK

	1980	1995
Bank Branches	27	33.5-42.5
ATMs	112	168
EFTPOS	-	168
Telephone	-	168
Internet	-	168

Source: Westpac

Businesses are also far better served now than they were 15 years ago, with increasing penetration of desk-banking from the large corporate level to small businesses, allowing customers direct electronic access (via PC and modem) to their bank accounts. Customers review their statements, organise payments to suppliers, receive funds from customers and transfer funds, all via electronic means in their own offices. Banks, particularly the large ones, have also established specialist small business service units. Management information systems are provided to help small business owners run their businesses better and in many cases mobile managers visit small business customers at their workplaces, taking banking services directly to them.

Choice of Product

Product and supplier choice has increased enormously for consumers of bank products. For example, before deregulation, if a customer was eligible for a bank home loan, there were 26 different types of mortgages available. However all were of a credit foncier type with equal monthly payments made up of an interest and principal component. Today there are over 1800 different mortgage products available. Home loan customers can choose between fixed rate and variable rate loans or a combination of both, between loans which afford customers considerable flexibility in their repayments and may even have credit card and savings account options attached to them, to less flexible, lower cost loans. And the loans are available from banks, building societies, superannuation funds, life companies and mortgage originators. Cheque accounts provide another example of the enormous proliferation of choice. Before deregulation, the 10 different cheque accounts offered charged a minimum fee as well as a "per cheque" fee and they paid no interest. Today there are 533 cheque account options available, most of which pay interest on credit balances. Many have no fees except government changes.

Similarly credit and debit card choices are now numerous and include value added benefits and services via the associated loyalty programs that come with many cards. Australians now hold over 7 million credit cards compared to 3 million in 1980 and they can use them at over 350,000 different merchants.

Savings accounts and transaction accounts (all 1,700 different product types compared to almost 700 in 1980) can be chosen by customers on the basis of their specific needs and transaction patterns. All manner of financial products and services now can be tailored very specifically to suit an individual customer's requirements.

The enormous increase in diversity of choice, both of supplier and product, has come about as a result of a more competitive financial services market. The amount of choice will increase further as technology enables providers to match their products and services more closely to individual customer requirements. In addition, the level of the competition in the market cannot be gauged by reference to one particular type of institution and the number of competitors of that type in the market. Different categories of institutions are now marketing the same product types.

Maintenance of the Stability and Integrity of the Financial System

From the mid 1980s, banks were free to set their own interest rates on all lending, and were relatively unrestrained in their ability to grow their balance sheets and increase market share. Like their international counterparts, Australian banks pursued growth strategies, in part reflecting the inflationary and high growth economic environment, driven by (inter alia) overly expansionary monetary policy. The combination of conditions resulted in excessive lending to business (to the property sector and to offshore borrowers in particular) and, subsequently, in large loan losses.

These loan losses did not flow from deregulation itself. They flowed from the combined effect of monetary policy that inadequately adjusted to the impacts of deregulation; an economic environment in which escalating asset values came to be considered the norm; and inadequate credit and operations risk management in the banks. Banks were evolving from the managerially simple world of regulation to the managerially complex world of deregulation. Inadequate risk management was a common institutional failing in a rapidly deregulating environment across the world.

Consequently, in excess of $16 billion of loan losses were written off by the major banks and other financial institutions over the period from 1990 to 1993. Two State banks failed, resulting in additional losses of over $5 billion, as well as a number of non-bank financial intermediaries. Collapses sometimes lead to a loss of confidence in other institutions. For example, the Farrow / Pyramid Building Society situation was a factor in an unjustified depositor run on the Bank of Melbourne. While the Federal Government did not pay directly for any of the collapses, there were tax impacts in connection with the State bank failures. State Government budgets and the taxpayers of those states bore the direct costs.

Despite all of this, the integrity of the financial sector has been maintained and, it could be said, subsequently even strengthened as a result of the adversity. No depositor lost money, and the stability of the payments system was never in question.

Regulators have successfully engineered bank reconstructions or judicious amalgamations of strong and weak banks and, together with action by governments, both in Australia and overseas, have maintained depositor confidence, despite the enormous potential impact on the financial system.

In all instances, the reasons for the banking and payments systems having emerged intact reside in the prudential oversight of banks (including interventionist support when absolutely required), and the ability of banks from a systemic perspective to withstand such shocks because of their strong balance sheet and liquidity management.

The business of banking is about risk management and containment. The ultimate risk is always that the payments system will not operate with complete integrity. In the period since deregulation, the system has withstood some rigorous tests.

A less obvious, but equally positive outcome has been improvement in credit assessment and control and general risk management procedures that have been implemented in all banks in response to the experience.

New Regulation

Explicit controls on banks to assist the Government achieve its policy objectives have, for the most part, disappeared.

In their place, however, a system of prudential supervision and regulation has emerged for each of the main financial participant groupings (banks, building societies, credit unions and insurance companies), and a growing body of consumer protection legislation. Competition policy and prices surveillance have also emerged as important dimensions of the overall financial system regulatory framework.

The regulation listed in Table below, has all been introduced or strengthened in the last decade. Legislation and regulation are increasingly being put in place by Federal and State Government agencies that lack national coherence and deal with problems, or perceived problems, in isolation. These are discussed in later chapters of this Submission.

Over the past decade, the Reserve Bank has regularly released new prudential statements for the banking sector. Often issues are dealt with in a prescriptive manner rather than through a more outcomes-oriented approach.

The risk is that the prescriptive approach can result in "average" regulation, which does not differentiate between the various participants as regards the calibre of their boards and managements, the strength of their balance sheets and their risk management systems.

The challenge is to rely more on the managements and boards of banks to run their businesses within the broader prudential guidelines set by the Reserve Bank and its international counterparts.

The Reserve Bank, however, has recently signalled a modification to its approach and appears to be moving in the direction of placing more reliance on bank management to endorse compliance with pre-approved internal risk management systems, and with external auditors playing a more active audit role.

Table : REGULATION INTRODUCED OR STRENGTHENED SINCE MID 1980s

Protection of Depositors

- Risk based capital adequacy requirements
- Liquidity requirements (6% PAR for banks, 7% PLA and 6% operational liquidity for credit unions and building societies)
- Supervision of large credit exposures
- Restrictions on bank involvement in funds management and securitisation activities
- Guidelines covering bank asset quality
- Primary objects tests for credit unions and building societies
- Prior approval by AFIC or an SSA of service contracts entered into by credit unions
- Intensive hands-on supervision of credit unions and building societies by SSAs.

Protection of consumers

- EFT code of conduct
- Consumer Credit legislation
- Codes of Banking, Credit Union and Building Society Practice

- Expanded role of Australian Payments System Council to monitor and report on the compliance of banks, credit unions and building societies with their respective Codes
- On-going monitoring of credit card pricing in anticipation of a substantial inquiry into the effects on consumers of the deregulation of credit card interest rates
- Restrictions on account keeping fees on retail transaction accounts and pressure on banks to provide "affordable access" to their accounts.

Other social objectives

- Pensioner deeming accounts
- Farm Debt Mediation Act (NSW)
- Occasional and informal pressure on banks to lend more for small business and to lend less for housing
- Localised pressure on banks not to close branches in rural areas
- Deposit taking institutions unable to provide superannuation products on their own account
- Industrial awards often require superannuation to be paid into industry funds
- Extension of Privacy Act to financial institutions

Competition Policy

- Six pillars policy preventing mergers of the four major banks and two major life offices

Banks as Agents of Government

- Administration of the Tax File Number System
- Cash Transactions Reports Act - points system for opening new accounts and reporting requirements for suspect transactions
- Collection of non-uniform State transaction taxes

Source: *How Does Regulation Affect the Future Role and Competitiveness of Banks?* Michael Waterhouse, Australian Banker, page 51, April 1996.

CONCLUSION

Deregulation has largely been very successful, bringing considerable efficiency benefits to the Australian economy, greatly improving the range and pricing of financial services to consumers, and increasing the competitiveness of the financial services markets while maintaining system stability.

However, there is room for still greater efficiency and flexibility. The financial system would be enhanced by a more efficient regulatory framework; that is more nationally consistent in its application across various participant groups; that has the capacity to vary the extent of supervision and regulatory oversight according to the level of risk; and that limits the build-up of increasing layers of regulation.

Chapter

5

Banking Deregulation and its Effects

INTRODUCTION

If the manufacturing and retailing sectors can be described as the muscle and bone of the U.S. economic body, the financial intermediaries would certainly be the circulatory system. This country's 40,000 banks and savings and loan associations (S & Ls) play the crucial role of gathering the savings of individuals and businesses and using them to provide loans to other consumers and commercial enterprises. There is no other single industry as necessary to the nation's economic prosperity as the financial institutions. Should the U.S. automobile industry fail, widespread displacement would obviously result. the economy would remain undisturbed and could continue to prosper. Should the financial intermediaries industry collapse, however, the resulting interruption in the flow of funds from net savers to net borrowers would bring the economy to a grinding halt. Almost every business enterprise in the country relies on credit for continued normal operation — from financing inventories to expanding plants.

While complete catastrophe is very unlikely, American financial institutions are facing a crisis unprecendented since the early 1930s. Savings and loan associations have been particularly hard hit. Holding almost $700 billion in deposits, these institutions were expected to suffer collective losses of $5 billion in 1981 with 75 percent of the

S & Ls and savings banks incurring operating losses during the year. Unless economic catastrophe on a lesser scale is sure to overtake the industry. But significant sectors of -conditions change drastically or some action is taken soon, Many solutions have been offered. For some the answer seems to lie in regulating the currently unregulated competitors of banks and S & Ls — particularly the money market mutual funds. Others advocate a bail out of the ailing savings and loan industry, leaving basic industry structure unchanged and hoping the economic crisis is soon resolved.

A growing number of students of the problem are recognizing, however, that the regulatory structure surrounding the financial services industry is a part of the problem. son testified before the Senate Banking Committee: As banker Lee Gunder- What is needed is an approach to legislation and regulation which recognizes the public interest is best served in a competitive marketplace, a marketplace where initiative, innovation, and performance are not restrained by discriminatory laws, complicated rules, and unequal regulatory treatment.l In other words, rather than regulating the unregulated firms now offering financial services, the banks and S & Ls should be freed from at least part of the regulatory network currently binding' them. There are at least three broad areas where this sort of regulatory reform ought to be seriously considered. on the pricing policies of depository institutions — both those rates paid by banks and S & Ls to depositors and those charged for loans — cause severe distortions and should be closely examined.

ROOTS OF THE PROBLEM

Finally, geographic limitations have resulted in hardships, especially for consumers, and ought to be relaxed offer are also severely restricted and the liberalization of these powers is an area deserving of attention a step in this direction. The step is one, however, that has met with and will continue to meet with opposition savings and loan associations currently enjoy a protected position. They are, understandably, reluctant to give up that advantage. Furthermore, the fears created by the 1930s' bank failures are deeply imbedded. But, the world is rapidly changing, and in order to offer the widest range of services to consumers, the regulatory barriers that financial institutions now face must be removed. Restrictions The types of financial services banks and S & Ls may Legislation introduced by Senator Jake Garn (R-UT) represents Many banks and underlying other causes of problems currently facing depository institutions are the volatility of the inflation rate' and its absolute level. Both have increased dramatically in recent years. The 1965 inflation rate was 1.7 percent. In 1970, it had climbed to 5.9 percent. By the end of the decade, it had reached double digits — 11.3 percent in 1979 and 12.4 percent in 1980. This ever-upward trend in the Consumer Price Index has created problems for financial institutions.

Banks and S & Ls historically have relied on the deposits of their customers to provide the raw material with which they make their principal product — loans. Over the past few years, however, many depository institutions have found it increasingly difficult to attract and hold deposits. Existing legal restrictions on the amount of interest financial institutions may pay on savings accounts repeal the old adage, "A penny saved is a penny earned." Consumers gradually have come to realize the money left in savings accounts earning 5% to 5% percent interest loses buying power in an economy suffering from inflation rates exceeding 5% percent. They have reacted rationally, seeking investments yielding a larger return but providing the convenience of a passbook savings account demand did not go unfilled for long institutions could not do because of legal restrictions, other firms did market mutual funds. Total investment in these funds has grown from a mere $4 billion in 1978 to $185 billion at the end of 1981.2 Growth during the past five years has been particularly rapid as more of the funds were offered to individual investors and start-up costs were lowered.

In addition, Cash Management Accounts (CMAs), introduced by Merrill Lynch, provide checkwriting privileges tied to a brokerage margin account and a Visa credit card. Merrill Lynch has been adding 1,000 CMAs a day at $20,000 minimum. Prudential Insurance

Company of America, recently merged with Bache Halsey Stuart Shields, Inc., is also preparing to offer a CMA account, as are American Express and several other financial firms.3 As is the case when the market is allowed to work, this What banks and thrift The result was the emergence of the booming money This phenomenal shift of funds away from traditional depository institutions is illustrated in the following graph. Many financial analysts are alarmed by these trends, and the American Bankers' Association points out that these trend lines are conservative estimates. Because of the regulatory framework within which they operate, however, banks and S & Ls have not been able to act to retain their deposits as they have been drained. further complicate matters, depositors who have left funds in banks and S & Ls, for the most part, have placed them in accounts earning rates of interest above 54, to 5% percent allowed on passbook savings. The six-month certificates of deposit (CDs), for example, have become increasingly popular, as have the All-Savers certificates and individual retirement accounts. Such a shift of deposits has increased the costs of funds for the depository institutions.

Another problem created for banks and S & Ls by high inflation rates is related to their role as lenders. Source of revenue for banks and S & Ls is the interest income from the loans they make. Banks generally make commercial loans while S & Ls and savings banks concentrate on mortgage lending. The interest rates paid by borrowers are simply the prices of the loans. If the interest rate is below the average inflation rate over the life of the loan, the lending institution in effect loses money. This is because its costs — salaries, electricity, building maintenance, and so forth — rise at roughly the rate of inflation. To remain profitable, the prices (interest rates) charged by these financial institutions must rise too.

In some instances, however, banks and thrift institutions have been prevented by state usury laws from raising prices. Other cases, particularly for S & Ls concentrating in long-term mortgages, the major problem has been a lack of prescience. S & L executives were no better than anyone else at predicting in 1971, when inflation was

4.3 percent, that rates by the end of the decade would hit double digits. And yet, such exceptional foresight is exactly what would have been required to ensure an S & L's profitability today. Table I compares the average yields on mortgages with the inflation rates over recent years. It is apparent why many savings and loan associations are facing severe financial difficulties. This situation of rising costs of funds and low yielding portfolios was described recently in Harper's magazine by William Quirk as being "like buying apples at twelve cents and selling them for ten cents, a practice with a limited future. If

Exacerbating their problems with inflation are the marketing restrictions imposed on the depository institutions. Not only can American Express, Merrill Lynch, Sears, and other new-style financial institutions offer accounts paying market rates of interest, many of which are also "checkable" (i.e., checks may be written against the account), they also face none of the geographic restrictions imposed on the depository institutions. For a population as mobile as that of the U.S., this is important. 6 Systems of electronic funds transfer, moving deposits instantaneously across the country, make possible the dispersion of automatic teller machines (ATMs) throughout the U.S. American Express, Visa International Inc., and Mastercard International Inc. are just a few firms which already take advantage of this new technology or plan to do so. As use of ATMs spreads, individuals will be able to make deposits to or withdrawals from money market or other accounts from almost anywhere in the country. Similarly, the Sears U.S. Government Money Market Trust, recently introduced, has offices nationwide adding to one-stop shopping.

Banks and, to a lesser extent, S & Ls are prevented by law from offering these interstate services directly, however. Instantaneous transfer of funds through air and telephone lines, moreover, means that an individual anywhere in the country can dial a toll-free number and conduct business with a large number of money market funds without leaving home. Warner Cable, a subsidiary of American Express, is currently experimenting in Ohio with home banking, bill-paying, and security-trading for subscribers via their televison sets. Thus, while less-regulated firms are seeking ways to take advantage of new technology, the extensively regulated banks and S & Ls are prevented from competing directly. Traditional financial institutions, in short, are being squeezed between rising costs of funds and increased competition from unregulated firms. To make matters worse, a variety of firms are being allowed to offer services traditionally reserved to banks and S & Ls.

The result: profit margins are shrinking and, in the case of most S & Ls, have disappeared completely. It is this situation which prompts the call for something to be done. Before discussing what regulations ought to be removed or modified, however, it is instructive to examine why the depository institutions became so heavily regulated in the first place. HI STORY In examining the history of banking in the U.S., two themes emerge: (1) a deep-seated opposition to attempts to concentrate financial power, an attitude which has given the states a significant voice in the conduct of financial institutions; and (2) an attitude of protection toward existing financial institutions which grew from the widespread bank failures of the 1930s. Decentralization The history of U.S. banking, more than anything else, reflects the aversion of early Americans toward attempts to concentrate power in a central government. In fact, early efforts to establish a central banking authority, first in 1791 and then in 1816, while successful for a time, were eventually defeated. The power to grant bank charters was considered the sole prerogative of state legislatures. These charters w e r e obtained through special legislative acts , a method which, not surprisingly, was abused. Reacting to these abuses, Michigan in 1837 initiated a system of "free banking."

New York passed a similar law the following year and soon most other states followed suit. As a result, banks were often established in a haphazard manner – sometimes borrowing the cash necessary to meet capital requirements just before the bank examiners arrived. Anyone meeting specific capital requirements Banks not only provided credit for a growing economy, but also, for better or worse, controlled the supply of currency. Each bank issued its own bank notes, or currency, based (supposedly) on the quantity of specie, i.e. , gold or silver coins, held by the bank. During the period of free banking, many banks were opened in remote areas, making it difficult , if not impossible, for note holders to redeem bank notes for specie. This practice led to the term wildcat banking" because many banks were located "where only the wildcats could find them."

Some voice in granting bank charters was during the Civil War. The 1864 National Banking Act , designed to help the federal government finance the war, empowered Congress to charter banks which were allowed to issue currency linked to the number of federal government bonds held as security. These bank notes were printed by the Treasury, thus providing the first national currency. The Office of the Comptroller of the Currency was created to administer federal banking laws.

Few banks sought national charters; state charters were easier to obtain and less restrictive. This prompted Congress in 1865 to impose a 10 percent tax on bank notes issued by state banks — a move designed to tax state banks out of existence. This tactic failed because state bankers discovered they did not have to issue currency to operate profitably. Instead, they encouraged the use of checks drawn on demand deposits. The dual banking system, with both states and the federal government granting bank charters, was born and continues to the present. The first successful attempt to give the federal government Tying the supply of currency, as the National Banking Act did, to the number of government bonds held by banks led to problems. During the late 19th century, outstanding government debt was not continually increasing. This led to an unstable and inelastic money supply.

Thus, need was perceived for a central bank with the flexibility and authority t o deal w i t h currency problems and to manage the banking system. The result was the Federal Reserve Act , passed in 1913. In typical American fashion, it was feared a single central bank would concentrate too much power in too few hands. Therefore, while overall policy was delegated to the Federal Reserve Board in

Washington, the Federal Reserve Act created twelve Federal Reserve Banks distributed throughout the country t o ensure consideration of regional problems.

Deep-seated resistance to banking monopoly also explains early attitudes toward branching. Most states originally did not allow state-chartered banks to establish branches. In fact, as late as 1910 only twelve states permitted branching. The silence of the 1964 National Banking Act on the subject was interpreted as a branching prohibition for all nationally-chartered banks (regardless of state law) until 1922. In that year, the Comptroller of the Currency ruled that any nationally-chartered bank could establish other offices to conduct routine business as long as those offices were not outside the city in which the head office was located. Congress formally endorsed this action with the McFadden Act of 1927 and extended the ruling to state banks which were members of the Federal Reserve System (FRS). Nonmember state banks remained subject to state laws.

During the 1930s, banks with branches enjoyed a lower failure rate than banks (those with only one office). As a result, the number of states allowing branching increased. In addition, the 1933 Banking Act (Glass-Steagall) removed McFadden requirements that national and state FRS member banks limit their branching to a single city, and made them subject to state branching laws. As the economy recovered from the Depression, bankers again became interested in expansion. Bank holding companies became a popular means of growth, triggering attempts to restrict the holding companies. Company Act of 1956 prohibited bank holding companies from acquiring banks across state lines unless expressly permitted by state law.

The Douglas Amendment to the Bank Holding The history of U.S. banking, in sum, is a continuing struggle to ensure that financial assets and the power over them remain as dispersed as possible.

Protectionism

The result of free banking was the existence of over 30,000 banks by 1921. Failures were common, averaging 600 per year; yet overall the system worked fairly well as new banks quickly replaced failed ones. The early 1930s, however, saw unprecedented failures as panic and bank runs became all too common. By the end of 1933, only 15,000 banks remained. Many of the customers of the failed banks lost most, if not all, their deposits as the existing sources of deposit insurance found themselves unable to handle the massive failures. The high cost borne by depositors, the disruption of the money supply, and the number of sound banks that failed contributed to 'tremendous political pressure, clamoring that something be done about the banking industry. In response, the Banking Acts of 1933 and 1935 were passed, changing significantly the way in which banks and other financial institutions do business.

State	Number of Commercial Banks	Percentage Without Branches
Alaska	12	8.33
California	257	33.46
Connecticut	65	16.92
Delaware	20	45
District of Columbia	17	23.53
Maryland	102	18.63
New York	302	46.36
North Carolina	83	18.07
South Dakota	155	67.10
Virginia	234	26.07

The basic goal of the Banking Acts was to prevent widespread bank failures. It was widely assumed, for example, that bankers had contributed to their instability by attracting funds by paying ever higher rates of interest on deposits. To avoid this in the future, Congress prohibited interest on demand deposits and imposed ceilings on the interest paid to time and savings deposits. It was also argued that free banking created too much competition and an overabundance of weak banks. To remedy this, free banking was halted. Applicants for bank charters were now required to demonstrate public need for a new bank and to show that the profitable operation of a new bank would not cause undue harm to existing institutions. Criteria for establishing the soundness of prospective bankers were strengthened. And because bankers were accused of contributing to the over-valuation of shares in corporations in their role as investment financiers, the activities of commercial banking and investment banking were divorced.

Smaller local banks have substantial advantages over potential outside competitors. The most important is their knowledge of the local market — the community's businesses and individuals. Furthermore, many customers prefer to deal with a locally-owned bank — provided they are offered similar services as consumers dealing with branches of larger banks. Finally, at least some data suggest that economies of scale are unimportant for banks larger than $50 million. This will be especially true if some sharing of services is allowed — for example with mutual funds.

Still, there are advantages to interstate banking. In the first place, it would allow consumers access to their deposits over a wider geographic area — allowing banks to compete more effectively with firms which offer services nationwide such as Merrill Lynch, Sears, and American Express. Most important, however, it would increase the degree of competition in the banking market. The mere threat of new competition is often enough to ensure that existing firms give customers the best service possible. Many small New York upstate banks, upon hearing that a New York City bank was about to open a local branch, suddenly have offered free checking, expanded overdraft privileges, or other new or expanded services.

Furthermore, the worst banking service often is found in towns too small to support more than a couple of banks. Frequently there is a shortage of local business demand for loans, even though there may be adequate deposit volume to support more banks, branch of a larger bank. Branches are less costly to establish than a new bank. In addition, depositors would be better served because of the increased competition while the national economy would benefit from an improved flow of loanable funds to areas most in need of them increased economic growth, the branch banker is in an ideal position to facilitate the flow of funds into the community. In fact, evidence suggests that rather than using outlying branches to transfer funds to head offices in urban areas, banks are much more likely to transfer funds among rural offices according to loan demand.17 And because Supreme Court decisions of the 1960s clearly subjected bank mergers to the Sherman and Clayton Antitrust Acts, the legal mechanism already exists to guard against "undue concentration of financial power." This would be a perfect situation in which to establish a should this small town suddenly experience Consideration of these arguments led the Department of the Treasury in a January 1981 Report of the President on geographic banking restrictions to conclude that:

Lliberalization of these restrictions

(1) Could improve competitive conditions in local markets and, subject to the establishment of appropriate controls, would not raise significantly the risk of undue concentration of power;

(2) Would increase the range of financial services available to local communities but would have little impact on credit availability;

(3) Does not pose a significant threat to the viability of the small bank as an institution;

(4) Would not have a material impact on the safety and stability of the banking system; and

(5) Need not threaten the vitality of the dual banking system.

Other Problems

In addition to the regulations already cited, a number of others are particularly onerous. There is considerable dismay, for example, with the "performance" regulations imposed on the lending institutions. These have nothing to do with the soundness of depository institutions, but are directed instead at affecting the way funds are invested and at "protecting consumers". Such regulations began in 1968 with the Truth-in-Lending Act and include the Consumer Credit Protection Act, the Equal Credit Opportunity Act, the Equal Credit Opportunity Act Amendments, the Home Mortgage Disclosure Act, the Debt Collection Practices Act, and the Community Reinvestment Act, to name a few. These performance standards levy substantial reporting and regulatory costs that are, as are all costs, eventually passed on to consumers. To serve the consumer best, only one measure is required — increased competition.

Another area of concern is the proliferation of regulatory agencies. No fewer than three federal groups exercise examination and supervision powers over some banks: the Office of the Comptroller of the Currency, the Federal Deposit Insurance Corporation, and the Federal Reserve System. Savings and loans are in a slightly better position because the FSLIC is part of the Federal Home Loan Bank System. If S & Ls begin a more extensive use of their new powers, however, the Federal Home Loan Bank System and the banking regulators will oversee financial institutions with very similar functions. In addition, every state has its own group of examiners. When questions of mergers or new financial instruments or services arise, almost all the regulatory groups get involved. In many cases, decisions take months – further reducing the ability of depository institutions to respond to competition from unregulated firms.

The power of the regulators has been expanding in recent years. This fuels fears that rather than accept a more flexible, less regulated atmosphere for depository institutions, regulators will insist on controlling the currently unregulated competitors of banks and S & Ls. While this might solve the problem for a time, when the situation changes, some less regulated firm (or firms) will find a way to respond. Then that firm (or firms) will be brought under the regulatory umbrella, and find itself unable to respond as conditions change. So another entrepreneur will fill the gap, and in turn be regulated. Reducing regulations thus offers the only course consistent with maximum service to the consumer.

SUMMARY

First, pricing restrictions should be removed quickly. The ceilings on interest paid to depositors with funds in passbook savings accounts has hurt everyone — the depositors with insufficient balances to move their funds to another instrument and the depository institutions watching accounts of large depositors flow to mutual fund and other financial instruments. In addition, usury laws dry up funds until they are unavailable at any price, at least to consumers without extremely good credit ratings. Second, wider powers should be granted to banks and thrift institutions. Increasingly jealous of their time, most consumers are not going to travel all around town for financial services if they can find them in one location. Furthermore, under the careful eye of the SEC as well as the various banking and thrift regulators, past sins regarding stock market abuses are unlikely to reoccur.

Finally, the mobility of the American consumer must be recognized. If depository institutions are to properly serve their customers, they must be freed from regulations forbidding operations across state lines. Coupling a relaxation of interstate restrictions with a realization that insufficient banks should be allowed to fail in the best interest of society would increase competition in many markets. Financial services would surely follow. Better service for consumers of Current Proposals Several pending proposals typify the current debate on the deregulation of financial institutions. The Garn bill. A major part of the bill drafted by Senator Jake Garn parallels legislation proposed by Richard Pratt, Chairman of the Federal Home Loan Bank Board. savings and loan associations authority to expand their commercial lending activities and to offer checkable accounts to commercial enterprises.

Mutual funds and invest in corporate debt issues. This-legislation would give The thrifts would also receive permission to offer The Garn bill would also reduce restrictions applying to the asset powers of commercial banks. Example: The bill provides the authority for banks to underwrite municipal bonds and banks would be allowed to offer mutual funds. In addition, the bill would expand the power of regulators to promote interstate and interindustry takeovers of failing banks and thrifts. These mergers could only be approved, however, if no other takeovers were feasible. Finally, Senator Garn's bill preempts all remaining state usury laws, with a three-year override provision. The legislation would also uphold due-on-sale clauses in mortgage contracts, thus overriding state preemptions of these clauses.

Senator Garn, who also happens to chair the Senate Banking Committee, seems committed to seeking significant deregulation of the financial services industry. He plans to hold exploratory hearings later this spring on the Glass-Steagall and McFadden restrictions on the banking industry. No legislation has as yet been proposed in these areas.

The Regulators Bill

It was the weakest proposal for regulatory reform comes from the House of Representatives. The Regulators Bill passed there is an attempt to respond to a narrow definition of the current crisis without promoting long-run changes. Bill merely expands the authority of regulatory agencies to approve interstate and interindustry mergers — as does the Garn bill. That is all. Chairman of the House Banking Committee Fernand St. Germain remains opposed to either interstate banking or the blurring of Glass-Steagall divisions.

Administration Proposals

The Reagan Administration supports recommendations that depository institutions be given the right to underwrite revenue bonds and offer money market mutual funds. The Administration favors giving the banks and thrift institutions the power to make direct investments in real estate equity. However, Donald Regan, the Administration's primary spokesman, has suggested that these new activities be carried on through affiliates of bank holding companies, though small banks of less the $100 million would be exempted from the requirement to establish subsidiaries.

While it favors granting wider powers to S & Ls, the Administration has stated that the S & Ls in exchange would have to give up their interest rate differential. (The housing differential, at any rate, is scheduled to be phased out by 1986.) The Administration also supports efforts to allow securities firms to enter the banking business. These banking functions would be carried out by a subsidiary so that reserve and capital requirements would apply. Finally, the Administration endorses a federal preemption of state laws prohibiting due-on-sale mortgage clauses and the federal preemption of state usury laws.

CONCLUSION

Considerable support exists for fundamental changes in the regulatory structure surrounding depository institutions. There is little consensus, however, on the form of the changes. Powerful opposition in the House, moreover, comes from the Banking Committee Chairman. Hearings are being held in both chambers, though, and recognition seems to be growing that some sort of regulatory reform is in the best interest of consumers as well as commercial enterprises. There is a growing cognizance that the depository institutions are being severely hampered in performing this function by 50-year-old laws. The rigidity of the legal structure surrounding the depository institutions has finally made itself felt. The banks and S & Ls, in particular, are experiencing considerable problems because of their inability to respond to changing conditions. The average consumer and the economy in general are suffering. The same regulatory mesh making it difficult for the banks and S & Ls to respond to the changing economic scene has made it difficult for them to serve consumers adequately. an unnecessary burden in the 1980s. Federal deposit insurance protects depositors from substantial loss and significantly reduces the likelihood that public panic will pose a severe threat to sound banks. As a result, the protective attitude surrounding banks and S & Ls is no longer warranted. Not only would the system of financial institutions be strengthened in the long run and the efficiency with which loanable funds are moved be increased, but removing protective entry restrictions in banking would also mean that consumers of financial services would be better served.

The regulatory network, justifiable when established, imposes Furthermore, the fear of concentrated financial power is unfounded. While some consolidation of depository institutions is to be expected if regulations are relaxed, that consolidation will result from the inability of a few inefficient, but sheltered institutions to adjust. Yet most cost savings can be achieved by relatively small institutions. This, plus the antitrust laws, will assure that the scenario of a few huge banks and S & Ls with branches nationwide will remain fantasy. Finally, there is no more fungible good than money; funds flow to those investments with the highest return. There is no reason to believe that would change with the slight concentration that would take place under more liberal branching laws. The fears on which many of the existing regulations were predicated thus are no longer justifiable. And while the regulatory structure is no longer protecting consumers from real dangers, it is imposing substantial costs on bank and S & L customers. Substantial deregulation is the surest means of lowering these costs.

UNPRECEDENTED BANK DEREGULATION HELPED IGNITE CREDIT CRISIS

Author Barry J. Dyke, in the new book, "The Pirates of Manhattan" reveals how unprecedented bank deregulation helped ignite the current credit crisis. For thirty years, bank deregulation was rigorously lobbied for by bankers and Wall Street and it rewarded them with Olympian paydays. Yet bank deregulation has brought imploding hedge funds, blatant conflicts of interest, Enron, WorldCom, a dot.com meltdown, mutual fund scandals, regressive bankruptcy laws, over-leverage, over-speculation, legalized usury, millions of foreclosures, plummeting real estate values, a weakened dollar, an auction-rate securities mess and a world-wide credit crisis.

BNews Imageank deregulation left gaping holes in consumer protection yet no new rules were put in place to insulate consumers from deregulation downsides. Deregulation revealed that banks are not only inept managers of economic risk—but consistently rely on predatory lending for a majority of their profits. Yet banks inevitably get into trouble and continually rely on Congress and the U.S. taxpayer to bail them out. Some bailouts include; the Mexican and Argentine debt crisis, the Savings and Loan collapse, Bear Stearns implosion and the Federal Reserve's opening of the discount window for investment banks to keep them solvent.

A watershed event in bank deregulation occurred in 1978 when the U.S. Supreme Court ruled in Marquette National Bank vs. First Omaha Corporation. That decision ruled that a bank could export the rate of interest from the originating state to other states. In 1979, with the Marquette decision in hand, South Dakota became the first state in the country to repeal its usury (excessive-interest) rate laws. In 1981, Citibank set up its credit card business in South Dakota and began to charge 20 percent interest on credit cards where it had been hitherto limited to charge 12 percent in New York. Since Marquette, high interest rate credit cards have become a vital and main source of profits for Citigroup, Bank of America, JPMorgan Chase, American Express and Capital One—when banks borrowed from the Federal Reserve at forty year lows.

The Depository Institutions Deregulation and Monetary Control Act of 1980 removed restrictions on banks competing for deposits. Recklessly, banks invested billions of deposits into high-priced, risky oil & gas exploration deals. Penn Square, Continental Illinois, Chase Manhattan Bank, Michigan National Bank, Seattle First National Bank and Northern Trust invested enormous amounts in these ventures—as well as billions from hundreds of smaller banks, savings & loans and credit unions. Deregulated but far from enlightened, Penn Square and Continental Illinois collapsed. Another 2900 banks failed or were merged out of existence. A $4 billion 1984 bailout of Continental was the largest bank bailout until the recent June 2008 collapse of California's IndyMacBank.

Continental Illinois, like today's Citigroup, was once a darling of the market, a favorite of analysts and its common stock sold at a premium over other money center banks. Citigroup has not collapsed, yet it has lost 60% of its value since 2005 in its pursuit of a deregulated universal bank model. Yet in the past decade, Citigroup has been at the forefront of virtually every banking and securities scandal in America.

The Pirates of Manhattan reveals another major banking secret—banks invest billions of their reserves—into high-cash value life insurance—not into mutual funds, hedge funds or half-baked stock deals which they are retailing to their customers. With laser accuracy, the author documents that major banks such as Wachovia, Bank of America, Wells Fargo, JPMorgan Chase, Wells Fargo, Citibank, Bank of New York-Mellon and thousands more have invested more than $120 billion of their money into high cash value life insurance for their Tier One Capital—a bank's most important asset. Over twenty-five years, the author, Barry J. Dyke, has acquired extensive knowledge and expertise to write such a book. He has practiced financial planning, founded a pension consulting business, a third party administration company, a health & welfare practice and a registered investment advisory firm, Castle Asset Management. A major point in the book is that due to bank deregulation, life insurance is one of the safest warehouses for people's capital in America. A vast video library www.thepiratesofmanhattan.com/videos.htm supports research in the book.

The book is taking a novel approach selling directly off the internet to wealth advisors and consumers. The book has sold in all 50 states, England, Europe, Canada, Australia and Singapore. As of August 2008, the book is a best-seller.

"A period of financial deregulation resulted in rapid growth in lending, particularly in real estate related lending. Rapidly rising real estate prices encouraged more lending, abetted by lax regulatory systems in many cases. When economic recessions occurred, inflated real estate prices collapsed, leading directly to the failures."

Any business can fail shattering hopes and aspirations of entrepreneurs, employees and other stake holders. Failed businesses also cause loss to national income and put productive assets to waste. Failure of a bank causes all this and much more, because a bank is much more than a mere intermediary in the credit market.

In the process of credit intermediation a bank improves the quality of credit in an economy, because it is a credible, safe borrower for general public and it lends after assessing risks. Further, it transforms maturities by borrowing short from its depositors and lending for longer maturities to businesses. It also affords a reliable payment system for the economy. Failure of a bank disrupts the payment system and may cause perfectly solvent entities to default on their commitments.

On top of these, a bank is a storehouse of private information, which it generates and manages in the process of appraising credit proposals and monitoring its borrowers' operations. Failure of even one bank means loss of that private information which translates into delays in future appraisals and disbursements impacting the growth rate of the economy.

All this makes a bank something very special. At the same time a bank easily tends to degenerate into a very fragile organization unless properly regulated. The essential features of a bank that make it prone to be fragile can be summed up as under:

Banks are highly leveraged, much more than a typical non-financial firm. Leverage, combined with limited liability, encourages banks to hold risky assets offering higher expected returns. This is true for non-financial firms too but their creditors (i.e. banks and institutions) address this problem with loan covenants and close monitoring, some things the banks' creditors (retail investors) cannot do.

As typically banks garner deposits from public for short term and invest in businesses for long terms, they are illiquid. This illiquidity, a by product of their maturity transformation activity, is often camouflaged by stated maturities of assets that may look low. For instance in India, working capital facilities, though sanctioned for short term (one year), are in fact longer-term commitments because both lenders and borrowers count on the facilities being rolled over. Thus, whatever the stated maturity of their assets, banks are illiquid in the sense that rapid liquidation would sharply reduce the value of their assets. This illiquidity makes banks particularly vulnerable to macroeconomic shocks.

Banks need to manage information issues. Over time, they generate private information about their borrowers. For instance they regularly conduct sensitivity analyses on their borrowers' profitability and liquidity. Results of such analyses depend very much upon market conditions. In a booming market it is harder to assess liquidity of borrowers, who can borrow from one source to repay another. This feature is referred to as "good times are bad times for learning". Not surprisingly bank failures are more often witnessed after credit booms.

Like any other organization's, a bank's liquidity problems get mutated into solvency problems, but faster. If forced to downsize its balance sheet (contract its portfolio) the quality of its assets deteriorate, and if defaults take place it may have to take over and sell the assets at fire sale prices. This often causes the assets in bank balance sheets to deteriorate further, thus what starts as a liquidity problem soon becomes a solvency problem.

This sums up the backdrop against which the various causes of bank failure should be considered. Just to set the stage, I describe first an infamous failure of a once well known Indian bank, Global Trust Bank (GTB).

In 1990 India had already taken its slow but firm steps towards economic liberalization. Under the new bank licensing policy Ramesh Gelli, an alumnus of Asian Management Institute, who had been chairman of a bank (Vysya Bank, since taken over by ING in a friendly deal and renamed ING Vysya) earlier received license for starting GTB in 1993. Among other promoters of the banks was IFC, Washington. GTB began operations on the 30th October 1994. It received deposits of Rs 1 billion on its opening day and Rs 10 billion in its first year, making it one of the fastest growing bank in India. It offered a complete bouquet of banking services and positioned itself as "extremely technology savvy, using latest technologies to deliver world-class services to its customers". In 1999 it made forays into electronic commerce.

In January 2001 came the news that GTB was merging into UTI Bank. UTI Bank, with public sector parentage, had a strong brand name, was focused on retail and fee-based income and had a large ATM network. It also had NPA over 4% and rather low spreads. GTB had a strong asset portfolio, lowest NPA among Indian banks, highest spreads and the highest CAR. GTB suffered from low retail presence and poor market perception. The two sides, as seen, were bringing complementary strengths with what seemed scopes for compelling synergy.

The deal however, fell through amid speculations that GTB shares were rammed up a few months before the announcement of merger. It turned out that Ramesh Gelli had lent funds to a disgraced Mumbai broker Ketan Parekh to jack up GTB share prices. Security market watchdog SEBI banned Ramesh Gelli from dealing in the bank's shares and Gelli put his papers and exited from GTB board.

Now began a lingering and painful sojourn of unpalatable discoveries for GTB shareholders / depositors, which ended in the bank being merged with a public sector bank Oriental Bank of Commerce in 2004.

GTB turned out to be overly dependent on capital markets for its income, which explained its high spread during the years of dot com boom. It only had 13% deposits from relatively cheap and stable retail sources. As equities fell, GTB resorted to, in connivance with its statutory auditors Price Waterhouse Coopers, income massaging. (A curious aside- the partner of PWC who had signed the balance sheets of GTB was the gentleman recently put behind bars for his role in misreporting the affairs at Satyam.) Next year it revealed net worth of Rs 4 billion whereas an inspection by the central bank indicated negative net worth. In June 2002 there were panic withdrawals from its branches in Hyderabad and Secundrabad.

The panic was limited to these cities only. Meanwhile bank declared 10% (on face value of its shares) dividend though a net profit of Rs. 0.4 billion was shown after drawing down over Rs. 2 billion from its reserves to write off bad debts. RBI restricted dividend payment and started monitoring the bank on monthly basis. This led to normalization of day to day operations but operating profit remained inadequate to meet the backlog of provisioning requirements. In Feb 2002 an independent accountant appointed earlier by RBI confirmed sticky, hidden and uncovered loans of GTB that indicated the bank to have negative net worth of over Rs. 1.5 billion. GTB was eventually merged with OBC that was eagerly scouting for a bank in the southern states of India.

GTB failed because in its quest for superior spreads it had excessively exposed itself to the capital markets conniving with a broker, who had gone, well, broke after the dot com bubble. The root causes of GTB's failure can be traced to:

a) Information asymmetry between the bank and its depositors and between the bank and its supervisors (RBI)

b) Exogenous shock – bursting of dot com bubble

Why do I do not consider Gelli's almost criminal shenanigans as the cause of failure? Because success driven full blooded managers, bucked by the limited shareholder liability, will always bend rules for that extra 1% of return. Any system aimed at safeguarding banks must first gear itself to safeguard the banks from their managers.

GTB saga sets the stage for considering the more important and most frequent causes of bank failure, which is macroeconomic volatility, both external and domestic. If volatility sharply alters the relationship between the values of a bank's assets and liabilities banks can become particularly vulnerable as was demonstrated in GTB case by equity meltdown of 1999/2000.

This volatility can arise from both external and domestic sources. Change in the terms of trade (also called TOT, denotes relative price of exports to imports) is such an external factor. TOT's are known to gyrate wildly at times. By adverse movement, it can seriously impair a bank's customers' ability to service their loans. Hundreds of diamond polishing units in Surat are closed as Americans have no desire for diamonds at their present prices. If there were a Diamond Polishers' Cooperative Bank at Surat that would have perhaps failed by now. Impact of TOT volatility is more pronounced for countries with high export concentration (that would include all the Asian tigers) and banks with sectoral presence.

Next variable, whose volatility may seriously affect banks, is interest rate. Volatility in international interest rates directly affect private capital flows. It has been seen that the spread between US treasuries and bonds rated Baa is directly correlated with capital flows from developed to emerging economies. Capital inflows boost bank deposits which encourages managers to increase lending even at the expense of somewhat lower credit quality. When the boom collapses and capital flows out the sudden fall in bank deposits force a "fire sale" of bank assets and liquidity problem gets converted into solvency problem.

The third external volatility is the real exchange rates volatility. It can cause difficulties for banks either directly (when there is a currency or maturity mismatch between bank liabilities and assets) or indirectly (when it creates large losses for bank borrowers. It has been observed that sharp real exchange rate appreciation typically precedes a banking crisis. Perhaps because high real domestic interest rates often push local firms towards foreign currency debt exposing them to huge foreign exchange rate risks.

On the domestic side, volatility in growth and in inflation rates makes assessing credit risk more difficult. Empirical evidences suggest that sharp contractions in economic activity increase the probability of bank failures.

There are many empirical evidences suggesting the linkage between volatilities and bank failures. Banking crises are often linked with economic cycles, which can be considered as volatilities in national income. It is also observed that banking crises are often preceded by boom in bank lending and declines in equity prices.

These observations support the suppositions that discriminating between good and bad credit risks is harder when the economy is expanding rapidly because many borrowers are at least temporarily very profitable and liquid. Sharp downturns in real estate and equity prices intensify these crises and fall in asset prices depresses the market value of collaterals.

Another major cause of bank failures is increasing bank liabilities with large maturity or currency mismatches. Bank deposits grow rapidly during boom times and bank assets differ significantly from bank liabilities in liquidity or maturity. Under such conditions a bank becomes very fragile if its risk management policies do not call for enhanced loan loss provisions to capture impact of volatility of bank assets.

In India, banks that were not quite prepared for financial liberalization suffered heavily during the first ten years of the new regime. We do not hear long lasting stories because they were all stolid public sector entities and the government bailed them all out by recapitalization. But the fact remains that banks weaned on controlled interest rates (where short term rates were much higher than long term rates, for instance) would find it difficult to survive in a market driven environment unless they are adequately prepared to embrace the change.

Finally we should recognize the symbiotic relationship between macro economic shocks and bank's fragility. While macroeconomic developments can lead to financial vulnerability, it is equally true that imperfections in financial intermediation can contribute to macroeconomic instability.

Chapter

6

The Bitter Fruits of Deregulation

Remember the good old days when the economic threat was mere recession? The Federal Reserve would encourage the economy with low interest rates until the economy overheated. Prices would rise, and unions would strike for higher benefits. Then the Fed would put on the brakes by raising interest rates. Money supply growth would fall. Inventories would grow, and layoffs would result. When the economy cooled down, the cycle would start over.

The nice thing about 20th century recessions was that the jobs returned when the Federal Reserve lowered interest rates and consumer demand increased. In the 21st century, the jobs that have been moved offshore do not come back. More than three million U.S. manufacturing jobs have been lost while Bush was in the White House. Those jobs represent consumer income and career opportunities that America will never see again.

In the 21st century the US economy has produced net new jobs only in low paid domestic services, such as waitresses, bartenders, hospital orderlies, and retail clerks. The kind of jobs that provided ladders of upward mobility into the middle class are being exported abroad or filled by foreigners brought in on work visas. Today when you purchase an American name brand, you are supporting economic growth and consumer incomes in China and Indonesia, not in Detroit and Cincinnati.

In the 20th century, economic growth resulted from improved technologies, new investment, and increases in labor productivity, which raised consumers' incomes and purchasing power. In contrast, in the 21st century, economic growth has resulted from debt expansion.

Most Americans have experienced little, if any, income growth in the 21st century. Instead, consumers have kept the economy going by maxing out their credit cards and refinancing their mortgages in order to consume the equity in their homes.

The income gains of the 21st century have gone to corporate chief executives, shareholders of offshoring corporations, and financial corporations.

By replacing $20 an hour U.S. labor with $1 an hour Chinese labor, the profits of U.S. offshoring corporations have boomed, thus driving up share prices and "performance" bonuses for corporate CEOs. With Bush/Cheney, the Republicans have resurrected their policy of favoring the rich over the poor. John McCain captured today's high income class with his quip that you are middle class if you have an annual income less than $5 million.

Financial companies have made enormous profits by securitizing income flows from unknown risks and selling asset backed securities to pension funds and investors at home and abroad.

Today recession is only a small part of the threat that we face. Financial deregulation, Alan Greenspan's low interest rates, and the belief that the market was the best regulator of risks, have created a highly leveraged pyramid of risk without adequate capital or collateral to back the risk. Consequently, a wide variety of financial institutions are threatened with insolvency, threatening a collapse comparable to the bank failures that shrank the supply of money and credit and produced the Great Depression.

Washington has been slow to recognize the current problem. A millstone around the neck of every financial institution is the mark-to-market rule, an ill-advised "reform" from a previous crisis that was blamed on fraudulent accounting that over-valued assets on the books. As a result, today institutions have to value their assets at current market value.

In the current crisis the rule has turned out to be a curse. Asset backed securities, such as collateralized mortgage obligations, faced their first market pricing in panicked circumstances. The owner of a bond backed by 1,000 mortgages doesn't know how many of the mortgages are good and how many are bad. The uncertainty erodes the value of the bond.

If significant amounts of such untested securities are on the balance sheet, insolvency rears its ugly head. The bonds get dumped in order to realize some part of their value. Merrill Lynch sold its asset backed securities for twenty cents on the dollar, although it is unlikely that 80 percent of the instruments were worthless.

The mark to market rule, together with the suspect values of the asset backed securities and collateral debt obligations and swaps, allowed short sellers to make fortunes by driving down the share prices of the investment banks, thus worsening the crisis. With their capitalization shrinking, the investment banks could no longer borrow. The authorities took their time in halting short-selling, and short-selling is set to resume on October 3 or thereabout.

If the mark to market rule had been suspended and short-selling prohibited, the crisis would have been mitigated. Instead, the crisis intensified, provoking the US Treasury to propose to take responsibility for $700 billion more in troubled financial instruments in addition to the Fannie Mae, Freddie Mac, and AIG bailouts. Treasury guarantees are also apparently being extended to money market funds.

All of this makes sense at a certain level. But what if the $700 billion doesn't stem the tide and another $700 billion is needed? At what point does the Treasury's assumption of liabilities erode its own credit standing?

This crisis comes at the worst possible time. Gratuitous wars and military spending in pursuit of US world hegemony have inflated the federal budget deficit, which recession is further enlarging. Massive trade deficits, magnified by the offshoring of goods and services, cannot be eliminated by US export capability.

These large deficits are financed by foreigners, and foreign unease has resulted in a decline in the US dollar's value compared to other tradable currencies, precious metals, and oil.

The US Treasury does not have $700 billion on hand with which to buy the troubled assets from the troubled institutions. The Treasury will have to borrow the $700 billion from abroad.

The dependency of Treasury Secretary Paulson's bailout scheme on foreign willingness to absorb more Treasury paper in order that the Treasury has the money to bail out the troubled institutions is heavy proof that the US is in a financially dependent position that is inconsistent with that of America's "superpower" status.

The US is not a superpower. The US is a financially dependent country that foreign lenders can close down at will.

Washington still hasn't learned this. American hubris can lead the administration and Congress into a bailout solution that the rest of the world, which has to finance it, might not accept.

Currently, the fight between the administration and Congress over the bailout is whether the bailout will include the Democrats' poor constituencies as well as the Republicans' rich ones. The Republicans, for the most part, and their media shills are doing their best to exclude the ordinary American from the rescue plan.

A less appreciated feature of Paulson's bailout plan is his demand for freedom from accountability. Congress balked at Paulson's demand that the executive branch's conduct of the bailout be non-reviewable by Congress or the courts: "Decisions by the Secretary pursuant to the authority of this Act are non-reviewable and committed to agency discretion." However, Congress substituted for its own authority a "board" that possibly will consist of the bailed out parties, by which I mean Republican and Democratic constituencies. The control over the financial system that the bailout would give to the executive branch would mean, in effect, state capitalism or fascism.

If we add state capitalism to the Bush administration's success in eroding both the US Constitution and the power of Congress, we may be witnessing the final death of accountable constitutional government.

The US might also be on the verge of a decision by foreign lenders to cease financing a country that claims to be a hegemonic power with the right and the virtue to impose its will on the rest of the world. The US is able to be at war in Iraq and Afghanistan and is able to pick fights with Iran, Pakistan and Russia, because the Chinese, the Japanese and the sovereign wealth funds of the oil kingdoms finance America's wars and military budgets. Aside from nuclear weapons, which are also in the hands of other countries, the US has no assets of its own with which to pursue its control over the world.

The US cannot be a hegemonic power without foreign financing. All indications are that the rest of the world is tiring of US arrogance.

If the US Treasury's assumption of bailout responsibilities becomes excessive, the US dollar will lose its reserve currency role. The minute that occurs, foreign financing of America's twin deficits will cease, as will the bailout. The US government would have to turn to the printing of paper money as did Weimar Germany.

For now this pending problem is hidden from view, because in times of panic, the tradition is to flee into "safety," that is, into US Treasury debt obligations. The safety of Treasuries will be revealed by the extent of the bailout.

Chapter

7

Competitive Dynamics of Deregulation: Evidence from US Banking

Robustness tests: do better banks really gain following deregulation? The previous results show that the link between bank performance and market share became stronger after deregulation, suggesting that relaxed constraints on bank growth improve the average quality of the banking system as better banks gain control of the market over time. An alternative interpretation, however, is that this change reflects nothing more than increased M&A activity after deregulation that is unrelated to bank quality. One possibility, for example, is that banks with more access to resources—large banks, banks with high levels of capital, or banks flush with cash—simply acquire assets without any particular ability to manage those assets better compared with competing banks. Perhaps acquirers are simply luckier than other banks. If true, this idea could explain our results but undermine our interpretation.

To address this issue, we re-estimate our basic regression in Equation (1) for sub-samples of banks that are least likely to be able to acquire other banks. If the performance/market share link strengthens for these banks, then we can conclude that the poor performing banks are indeed facing more competitive pressure after deregulation. To do this, we split our sample in three ways. First, we used size as the criterion and created sub-samples of "small" banks (share of state assets below 1%) and "large" banks (share of state assets above 1%) to test whether the performance/ market share link became stronger for relatively small banks, which are less likely to be acquirers. Second, we split the data based on the availability of cash to a bank by identifying the "low ROE" banks (ROE below the state/year median) and the "high ROE" banks (ROE above the state/year median). Again, the question is whether poor performers became subject to increased pressure after deregulation. Finally, we split the data based on observed growth and created sub-samples of "shrinkers" (banks with a declining market share over the two periods) and "growers" (banks with increased market share over the two periods) to see if performance and market share are linked for those banks losing market share.

These results suggest that the competitive pressures from deregulation led to meaningful reallocations of market share to the better performing institutions. Not only did banks with high ROE gain market share through M&A, but banks with low ROE lost market share. Moreover, within the set of banks that lost market share, those with lowest ROE lost the most. Thus, by increasing pressure on under-performing banks and allowing the reallocation of assets toward stronger performers, this process contributed to the improved performance of the U.S. banking industry.

DEREGULATION AND STATE-LEVEL EXIT TRENDS

The previous analysis examined the disciplinary pressures on surviving banks. We now move our focus to banks that exit the industry. Before continuing, it is worth emphasizing that we define exit quite broadly to incorporate not just failure or liquidation of bank assets but also changes in ownership. Therefore, we are concentrating on the exit of a firm as a separate entity, rather than the exit of assets per se. Bank exit is typically not associated with the elimination of physical assets such as branches or financial assets such as loans, but rather, these assets are simply transferred to the acquiring institution.

For example, branching deregulation allows banks to enter new markets within the state by buying existing banks, or branches of exiting banks, and folding them into their current operation as the target's offices are converted into branches. This strategy avoids the cost of operating a multi-bank holding company within a state and adds services to the customer in the form of convenience. Similarly, interstate banking removes the prohibition on an out-of-state bank holding company's ability to own any assets in a state. Because both forms of deregulation make it much easier for banks to be acquired, we expect exit, which we define broadly as a change in the ownership of bank assets, to rise.

We construct two measures of overall exit: the percentage of banks in a state that exit during the year and the market share of those exiting banks. The second measure is essentially an asset-weighted version of the simple exit rate. We relate these state-level aggregates to deregulation indicators, state effects, and time effects, as in the following basic regression:

(4) [X.sub.j,t] = [[beta].sub.1][BRANCH.sub.j,t] + [[beta].sub.2][INTER.sub.j,t] + [[beta].sub.3][BRANCH.sub.j,t] [UNIT.sub.j] + [[alpha].sub.j] + [[alpha].sub.t] + [[epsilon].sub.j,t],

where [X.sub.j,t] is the exit rate (either simple or asset-weighted), [UNIT.sub.j] is a dummy variable that indicates if the state had unit branching restrictions, [[alpha].sub.j] is a state fixed effect, and the other variables are defined as above. We estimate Equation (4) with and without the unit branching dummy variable. Note that Equation (2) uses state-level data, while Equation (1) uses bank-level data, so there are far fewer observations here.

Primary state-level results. The results, reported in Table 5, suggest that branching deregulation had little impact on the exit rate in states that began with limited branching. For unit banking states, however, we find an increase in the simple exit rate of a little more than 1% per year (1.412-0.325). (38) The increase in the weighted exit rate, however, is never statistically significant following branching deregulation. These results are sensible. Branching deregulation has a bigger effect on the exit behavior of small banks.

Chapter

8

Deregulation of Bank Entry and Branching: Impact on Competition

INTRODUCTION

Competition has been referred to as the fundamental economic regulatory force. In a competitive market, several firms strive to produce goods and services at the cheapest price. Otherwise, more efficient firms, either actual or potential, will eliminate inefficient firms by undercutting their prices. In addition to its favorable impact on prices, competition may also lead to improved product quality and services, and encourage the production of new products and the use of new technologies. It may also lead to the availability of more and better information about products and product quality to consumers. Simply put, ensuring that markets operate in a competitive manner is welfare improving for society. Thus, international support for open markets has grown on account of the benefits of competition (Cabalu *et al* 1999).

In contrast, barriers to entry serve to limit the number of producers or sellers, and thus stifle or restrict competition (Lamberte *et al* 1992). Barriers to entry are factors that allow incumbent firms to raise and maintain prices above costs without fear that new firms would enter the market to contest it (Medalla 2000). In particular, regulations that restrict market entry are among those that have the most direct impact on competition. Such restrictions are typically imposed for public safety or efficiency reasons, including preventing over-investment or overcrowding in certain markets. But primary importance is often placed on the elimination or reduction of government barriers to market entry to enhance the contestability of markets and the competitive process (Grimes 1999). This paper looks at public policy towards bank entry and branching in the Philippines, and its impact on the sector's structure, conduct and performance.

REGULATION OF BANK ENTRY AND BRANCHING IN THE PHILIPPINES

Financial systems in both developed and developing countries have typically been subject to substantial public regulation. The basic rationale for this is that both the payments system, and public confidence in financial institutions and instruments on which the financial system is built, bear the qualities of a public good. Hence, the need for some government intervention to achieve market enhancing outcomes (Grimes 1999). In particular, there are two main reasons for regulating banks. One, regulation of banks provides protection against the risk that failure of one bank might lead to the failure of other banks, even if they are sound. The latter would lead to wider financial instability and overall economic disruption. Two, the asymmetry of information between depositor and bank means that a retail depositor does not have the capacity to assess the soundness of an individual institution. There is, thus, a need to provide some protection for depositors.

In particular, entry into the banking sector is one area that continues to be regulated even in the most liberalized or deregulated financial systems. All OECD countries, for instance, continue to regulate the entry of new domestic banks, although none of them imposes an outright ban on the entry of new banks. That is, new entry requires a license but is otherwise free. Controls on entry in the form of authorization criteria include minimum capital requirements, and more importantly fitness and properness criteria for controllers and managers of banks. On the other hand, the entry of foreign banks is relatively more restricted (OECD 1998). Thus, regulation of entry to the banking industry is primarily a tool of prudential regulation. "Free banking", or the removal of entry and other restrictions without accompanying prudential regulations, is also not deemed as tenable because it could lead to over-competition and excessive risk-taking, and thus compromise the stability and soundness of the banking system.

In the Philippines, government policy on domestic bank entry was initially lax in the 1950s and early 1960s, as the Central Bank of the Philippines (CBP) actively promoted the development of the banking system to finance the reconstruction of the economy after the war (CBP 1974). It became very restrictive beginning in the mid-1960s, as the rapid expansion of the banking system led to increased instability. By that time, the CBP became increasingly concerned over the large number of small banks, and decided to raise minimum capital requirements and essentially prohibited new bank entry (Emery 1976). The CBP also imposed tight restrictions on bank branching, especially in areas identified as heavily or over-branched. On the other hand, the moratorium on the entry of new foreign banks was imposed from the time the CBP began operations in 1949, for nationalistic reasons.

The Philippines' first attempt to reform its financial system occurred in the early 1970s. Among the measures introduced were a formal moratorium on new bank entry, coupled with a more favorable policy towards bank branching. In practice, though, rules on bank branching remained very restrictive and arbitrary (Lamberte and Lim 1987). Minimum capital requirements were again raised because authorities believed that bigger banks would lead to a more stable banking system. To meet the new requirement, mergers and acquisitions were especially encouraged to further reduce the number and increase the average size of commercial banks. Foreign equity participation of up to 30 percent of the voting stock of existing domestic banks was also allowed (Lamberte 1989).

The Philippines formally embarked on a financial liberalization program in the early 1980s, which included the deregulation of interest rates. However, it was noted that interest rate liberalization did not enhance competition because it was not accompanied by the complementary measure of deregulation of entry restrictions (Tan 1989). Again, the latter was due to the monetary authorities' belief that there were already too many banks in the Philippines. But the impact of removing interest rate ceilings depend on the degree of competitive pressure, which would not improve if there is no serious threat of entry into the banking system, or if other regulations such as those concerning branching become binding constraints (Blundell-Wignall and Ishida 1990). Banks' minimum capital requirements were also raised twice in the 1980s, with the intention of building up the sector, especially in the aftermath of the financial crises in the mid-1980s.

Regulations on new domestic bank entry and branching were relaxed in 1989, although in practice the CBP's policy remained restrictive and discretionary. In particular, new branches were allowed only in rural areas (Lamberte and Llanto 1993). It was only beginning in 1992 that restrictions on new domestic bank entry and branching were effectively relaxed, and these were further simplified and made uniform across banks in 1995. New domestic banks, satisfying the laws of incorporation as approved by the Monetary Board, could be established as long as they met minimum capital and other prudential requirements. Geographical restrictions on domestic bank branching were lifted in 1993, and branches could be established anywhere subject to certain prudential requirements, such as those on capital adequacy, liquidity, profitability and soundness of management (Paderanga 1996).

The moratorium on foreign banks, which had been in place since the CBP was first established in 1949, was lifted in May 1994 with the passing of RA 7721. This law partially liberalized the entry and scope of operations of foreign banks in the Philippines. In particular, foreign banks were authorized to operate in the Philippines through (only) one of the following modes of entry: (i) acquire, purchase or own up to 60 percent of an existing domestic bank; (ii) invest in up to 60 percent of the voting stock of a new banking subsidiary incorporated in the Philippines; or (iii) establish a branch with full banking authority. The third mode of entry was operative for only 5 years from the date of effectivity of the Act, and was limited to only 10 foreign banks. Each of the 10 foreign banks was entitled to six branches – 3 in locations of its choice, and 3 in locations to be designated by the Monetary Board. The four foreign banks operating through branches in the Philippines upon the effectivity of the Act were also accorded the same branching privilege. In addition to the ten new foreign bank licenses granted in 1995, there have been seven new locally incorporated foreign bank subsidiaries.

These deregulatory measures were expected to improve access to banking services and enhance efficiency. Tan (1989) had argued that the restricted bank entry policy in the Philippines was responsible for the shallowness of the country's financial sector. In particular, the ultimate effect of the policy of restricted entry into the banking sector had been to shield both the big and small banks from competition, which allowed the big banks to earn abnormal profits and the small banks to operate at high costs. The restrictive bank branching policy also weakened the deposit mobilization process (Lamberte and Lim 1987).

The Asian crisis struck in July 1997, which led to systemic failure of financial institutions in Thailand, Indonesia, and South Korea. In contrast, only one fairly small and newly upgraded commercial bank failed in the Philippines, although the overall performance of the banking sector took a turn for the worse in the aftermath of the Asian crisis. In an effort to strengthen the banking sector, the *Bangko Sentral ng Pilipinas* (BSP) mandated consecutive increases in banks' minimum capital requirements. Furthermore, the BSP again declared an indefinite moratorium on the establishment of new banks and the branch expansion of existing banks, but excluding microfinance-oriented banks, in August 19993. The foreign banks were also exempted from the moratorium on local branch expansion, although the limit of six new branches remained. This policy, together with higher minimum capital requirements, continued to reflect monetary authorities' preference for and strategy of forcing more mergers and acquisitions to reduce the number and increase the average size of banks in the Philippines. Consolidation is in turn expected to result in a stronger and more stable banking system. Thus, prospective investors were encouraged to acquire existing banks instead of applying for new operating licenses, while banks wishing to expand could do so by taking over smaller banks.

RA 8791, or the new General Banking Law of 2000, formalized the moratorium on new bank entry by stipulating that "no new commercial bank shall be established within three years from the effectivity of this Act" (Sec. 8.3). It also tightened the licensing requirement by including an assessment of the bank's ownership structure, directors and senior management in the licensing process (Sec. 8.3). RA 8791 also expanded the coverage of RA 7721 by allowing a foreign bank to acquire up to 100 percent of the voting stock of (only) one bank, but only within seven years from the effectivity of this law. This included foreign banks that had acquired 60 percent of the voting stock of a bank under RA 7721. With the reimposed moratorium on the entry of new banks, the only alternative for foreign banks to enter the domestic industry is to buy into existing domestic banks. Again, this fitted in with the BSP's push for more mergers and acquisitions in the banking system. The BSP had designated a critical role for foreign banks in its effort to consolidate the banking sector, that is, foreign buy-ins were especially encouraged. More consolidation and more openness to foreign banks were seen as positive factors for the Philippine banking system. In particular, a strong foreign banking presence – with credibility and capital – was expected to result in improved efficiency and help to stabilize the banking system during times of stress. However, both RA 8791 and RA 7721 also contained a provision requiring the Monetary Board to ensure that 70 percent of the resources or assets of the entire banking system is controlled by domestic banks that are majority owned by Filipinos at all times.

Overall, government barriers to bank entry, which included direct entry restrictions and higher capitalization requirements, were imposed primarily to limit and reduce the number, as well as increase the average size of banks in the Philippines. The problem was a weak structural base in that the financial system consisted of too many weak small banks, and a few strong, big banks. Bigger and fewer banks, in turn, were seen to promote the safety and soundness of the financial system. However, barriers to entry also had an impact on the banking sector's structure, conduct and performance. The following section briefly discusses these effects.

SOME INDICATORS OF STRUCTURE, CONDUCT AND PERFORMANCE OF THE BANKING SECTOR

Financial structure. The Philippine financial system consists of banks and nonbank financial institutions (NBFIs). RA 8791 classifies banks into commercial banks, universal banks (expanded commercial banks), thrift banks (savings and mortgage banks, stock savings and loan associations and private development banks), rural banks, cooperative banks and Islamic banks. NBFIs include, among others, insurance companies, investment houses, financing companies, securities dealers and brokers, fund managers, lending investors, pension funds, pawnshops and nonstock savings and loan associations. Figure 1 shows the total assets of the Philippine financial system from 1970-99. Total assets of the financial system as a percentage of GDP rose from 63 percent in 1970 to 117 percent in 1983, then fell to 66 percent in 1988 as a result of the financial and economic crises in the mid- 1980s. The ratio rose to around 140 percent in 1997, and again declined to 124 percent in the aftermath of the Asian crisis. The total assets of commercial banks, in particular, grew significantly in the 1990s due to the successive increases in minimum capital requirements, the upgrading of the specialized government banks, and the entry of new domestic and foreign banks.

The Philippine financial system has consistently been dominated by commercial banks. In fact, the importance of commercial banks even increased over time. The banking system accounted for 81 percent of total financial assets in 1999, compared to around 76 percent in 1970. The asset share of commercial banks also increased from around 57 percent in 1970 to 73 percent in 1999. In contrast, the asset share of rural banks fell from around 3 percent in the 1970s to less than 2 percent in the 1999, while the asset share of thrift banks slightly rose to 6 percent in 1999 from 4 percent in 1970. On the other hand, the share of NBFIs in total financial assets fell from a high of 28 percent in 1975 to 19 percent in 1999.

Thus, there has been no significant structural change in the Philippine financial sector in the last 30 years. A bank-dominated financial system is not necessarily bad. The issue is whether such a structure is a market-outcome, or the result of government policy and regulation. In the case of the Philippines, it was clearly the latter. The banking sector has historically been the focus of financial sector policy, development and reform. In contrast, efforts to reform and develop the other sectors of the financial system began only in the mid-1990s.

The easing of restrictions especially on bank branching was very evident in the rapid growth of banking offices in the 1990s. Compared to just 0.5 percent in the 1980s, the number of banking offices in the 1990s grew by 8.7 percent, with all bank categories posting significant growth. In particular, double-digit growth rates were recorded in the number of branches of rural banks beginning in 1990, and beginning in 1992 for commercial and thrift banks. The period after the deregulation of foreign bank entry but before the Asian crisis was also marked by a dramatic increase in the number of commercial and thrift bank branches. The increase in the number of head offices of commercial banks was largely due to the entry of foreign banks beginning in 1995. In terms of number of branches, however, foreign banks were at a serious disadvantage. For instance, private domestic commercial banks had a total of over 4,000 branches in 1999. In contrast, foreign bank branches and subsidiaries had only around 219 branches.

Thus, deregulation of branching in particular had a significant impact on regional access to basic banking services in terms of deposits and loans. Any portfolio shifts from holding savings in the form of physical assets to financial assets would lead to more efficient financial intermediation. In turn, the improvement in financial intermediation would have a positive impact on the economy. In terms of distribution, however, most of the bigger commercial banks in particular were located in Metro Manila. The distribution of financial resources would necessarily be biased in its favor still.

Overall, the Philippine banking system continued to be characterized by the presence of a few large commercial banks and a lot of very small thrift and rural banks. As noted earlier, restricted bank entry policy had fostered such a structure. The following subsections discuss the impact of banking structure on banks' conduct and performance.

Measures of concentration. The continued dominance of a few, large commercial banks raises the issue of market power. Thus, there is a need to monitor the concentration process even in a deregulated environment to detect any further strengthening of the oligopolistic group, and ensure that it does not lead to misuse of market power. In contrast to previous periods, the period after 1995 was characterized by significant movement in the commercial banking sector in terms of new entries and consolidations. In particular, the number of foreign bank branches and subsidiaries increased as a result of deregulation. The number of domestic private banks initially increased in the first half of the 1990s as a result of deregulation of entry, then decreased towards the latter half due to mergers and acquisitions. Although the BSP especially encouraged mergers and acquisitions among the small banks to meet the higher capital requirements, the mergers and acquisitions primarily took place among the biggest banks.

Private domestic banks consistently accounted for over 60 percent of total commercial bank assets. Private domestic banks' share rose to as high as 77 percent in 1994, before subsequently falling to around 67 percent in 1999, with the entry of the ten foreign banks in 1995. If the share of Philippine National Bank (PNB), which passed into majority private ownership in 1995, is included, the share rises to around 76 percent in 1999. On the other hand, the asset share of foreign bank branches and subsidiaries rose from around 9 percent in 1995 to 17.5 percent in 1997, which indicates a decreasing dominance of the domestic commercial banks. Finally, the asset share of government owned commercial banks declined from less than 27 percent in 1980 (accounted for by PNB) to 12.6 percent in 1999. The share of foreign bank branches and subsidiaries in total deposits and loans likewise increased beginning in the mid- 1990s.

Although the actual value of the Herfindahl index (HI) 5 may not be indicative of undue concentration, given its very low values, it would also be useful to look at the trend. The HI was fairly stable from 1990-94. It began to decline beginning in 1995 with the entry of the new foreign banks, indicating that the system was becoming less concentrated. However, this trend was reversed beginning in 1998, which means that the mergers and acquisitions also resulted in increasing concentration. Similar trends are also evident when one looks at the asset share of the three and five largest commercial banks, which are all domestic banks. Before the restriction on new bank entry was eased in 1995, the five largest commercial banks consistently accounted for around half of the sector's total assets. Their share declined to around 37 percent in 1997, but this trend has since been reversed. Also, the wide gap between the five biggest and five smallest commercial banks is stark. As noted earlier, the concern with excessive concentration is that it is a potential source of monopoly power.

Operational efficiency. Operational efficiency is a microeconomic concept, but it is also used to characterize a financial system. In particular, the market structure could be reflected in the spread between the cost of funds and the lending rate: a financial system is considered operationally efficient if the interest spread is low. The latter, in turn, arises from two factors. On a microeconomic level, the more cost efficient banks are, the lower the spread will be under reasonably competitive conditions. On a macroeconomic level, systemic risks also affect the spread. A more stable and confident environment will lead to a lower risk premium over lending, thus leading to a lower spread (Ersel and Kandil 2000). A high intermediation margin would imply a smaller intermediation activity (Tan 1989). One of the structural weaknesses identified in the Philippine banking sector in the past was the large spread between commercial bank deposit and lending rates, which in turn was attributed to high intermediation costs mainly in the form of taxes and reserve requirements, as well as high profit margins (World Bank 1986). Tan (1989) also pointed out that the interest rate differential might not just be due to taxes, but to some monopoly power of the large commercial banks as well. More recently, the World Bank (1998) noted that high intermediation costs continued to be a feature of the Philippine banking system, especially when compared to other Asian economies6. Average net interest margin as a ratio of total assets from 1988-95 was 4.2 percent. Figures for comparable countries like Indonesia and Thailand were 3.5 and 3.1 percent, respectively (Demirguc-Kunt and Huizinga 1997; in Claessens and Glaessner 1998).

In addition to high reserve requirements and the mandated credit requirements, other contributing factors to the Philippines' high intermediation costs were high operating costs and insufficient competition (World Bank 1998). Operating costs of Philippine banks were also found to be significantly higher in the Philippines compared to other Asian economies. In particular, average overhead costs as a ratio of total assets in 1988-95 was around 4.4 percent, compared to 2.9 percent and 2.0 percent for Indonesia and Thailand, respectively. Despite the higher operating costs, Philippine banks were also found to be more profitable. The ratio of net profit to total assets was around 2 percent for Philippine banks during the same period, against 0.9 and 1.1 for Indonesia and Thailand respectively (Demirguc-Kunt and Huizinga 1997; in Claessens and Glaessner 1998). Thus, the World Bank (1998) noted that the "high profits despite high costs indicate lack of competition, which is also evidenced by the fact that there is high concentration in the banking sector…" (p. 23). The partial liberalization of foreign bank entry in 1994 precisely aimed to increase competition and improve efficiency in the domestic banking sector. By increasing competition, it was expected that market forces would reduce bank spreads. Although the entry of more foreign banks led to some changes in the banking structure, particularly the decline in concentration ratios, there has been no significant impact on bank spreads. Table 6 shows domestic commercial banks' average spread and rates of return both prior to and after the restriction on foreign bank entry was eased in 1995. Both only slightly declined during the post-liberalization years prior to the Asian crisis.

Recent studies have examined the impact of the entry of more foreign banks on domestic banks' interest rate spreads and efficiency (e.g., Manzano and Neri 2001, Montinola and Moreno 2001, Unite and Sullivan 2001). Overall, their results indicate that foreign bank entry has had limited impact. Manzano and Neri (2001) noted that the effects on competition might not have been felt immediately because of a period of adjustment for the foreign banks, and/or because liberalization did not go far enough. But ultimately, they attributed the persistence of high bank spreads to the government's macroeconomic policy mix. In particular, the overvalued exchange rate before the crisis encouraged foreign borrowing and dollar intermediation by banks, which dampened the competition for peso deposits and upward movements in the deposit rate. On the other hand, the government's high interest rate policy to defend the exchange rate caused banks' lending rate to remain high. Thus, the impact of macroeconomic factors could have masked the impact of foreign bank entry on domestic banks' interest spread. According to Montinola and Moreno (2001), the scope of liberalization was limited, hence its modest effects on competitiveness and efficiency.

A more in-depth study of the determinants of bank net interest margins would be useful to establish the impact of the structure of bank competition. Apart from the market structure component, regulatory components in the form of reserve requirements and capital to asset ratios, and a risk premium component to account for uncertainty in the macroeconomic environment facing banks would have significant effects on bank net interest margins (Saunders and Schumacher 2000). The persistence of high interest rate spreads despite financial reforms was also observed in Latin America (Brock and Suarez 2000). This was attributed to a combination of microeconomic and macroeconomic factors, including high operating costs, high levels of nonperforming loans, high reserve requirements, and uncertainty in the macroeconomic environment facing banks. In the Philippines, it has also been argued that part of the reason for the high bank spreads is that banks are heavily capitalized and less leveraged. In the years prior to the 1997 Asian crisis, Philippine banks' capital adequacy ratio, defined as the ratio of net worth to risk assets, was between 17-20 percent. Holding equity capital is relatively costly when compared to debt, and so banks that have relatively high capital ratios can be expected to try to cover some of this cost by imposing an extra spread (Saunders and Schumacher 2000).

While the entry of more foreign banks in 1995 has not had a visible impact in terms of reducing domestic banks' interest spread, this does not mean that foreign banks have had no impact whatsoever on domestic banks' operations and the level of competition in the banking sector. Focusing on price or interest competition does not take into account the dynamic aspect of competition and efficiency. The latter refers to the structural response of banks to deregulation as reflected for instance in their balance sheets, that is, the changes in the structure of their assets and liabilities. Audretsch *et al* (2001) noted that competition and anti-trust policies in the developed economies such as the European Union have been based on traditional static models and analyses of industrial organization, wherein technology and consumer demand are given and price (output) is the firm's main, if not its only, choice variable. In contrast to the static models' focus on price competition, more recent dynamic models of industrial organization argue that firms in reality are "engaged in a continuing dynamic competitive process, constantly creating and adopting new products and processes in order to gain advantage over their rivals" (p. 618). And in a dynamic economy, the latter may have a more significant effect on welfare than the former in the long run. The issue is especially relevant to financial markets as they operate in more deregulated and globalized environments, and become increasingly characterized by technological advancements and product innovations. This emphasizes the need to augment traditional analyses of industrial organization, such as Bain's (1956) Structure-Conduct- Performance paradigm, with more dynamic analyses of markets and institutions in order to come up with a fuller depiction of competition (Audretsch *et al* 2001).

In the Philippines, foreign banks traditionally competed with local banks primarily in corporate lending and non-branch based financial services. A survey of selected local banks on their reactions to the entry of more foreign banks in 1995 indicated that the latter has led to a more competitive environment particularly in wholesale banking (Hapitan 2001). The entry of more foreign banks further reduced the already thinning spreads from servicing corporate accounts because of the entry of more local banks in the early 1990s. This induced local banks to tap other segments of the market that would generate higher returns. Thus, local banks shifted their focus towards developing products and services for the middle and retail consumer markets, and to some extent the previously neglected small and medium sized enterprises. Local banks also sought to improve existing product lines and services, especially by introducing technology based enhancements such as phone banking, bills payment, point of sale transactions, and internet banking (AAC 1998). But as Hapitan (2001) also noted, re-engineering was undertaken by the domestic banks as a strategy in itself, and not because of the entry of more foreign banks per se.

Local banks' greater focus on retail operations could also account for the persistence of high banks spreads, both from the cost and profit aspects. Banks whose services are directed more toward retail operations normally have higher operating costs compared to banks that are more oriented toward wholesale markets. This is due to the former's need for more branches, equipment, and personnel to serve retail customers. Higher operating costs then translate into a higher spread (Brock and Suarez 2000). Branches of domestic commercial banks expanded rapidly especially in 1995-97, which accounts for the increasing trend in their operating costs during that period (Figure 5). The shift towards more profitable retail lending could have also allowed banks to maintain their profit margins. The New General Banking Law has allowed foreign banks to fully own an existing local bank, thus relaxing the restriction on branching by foreign banks. In December 2000, Hong Kong Shanghai Banking Corporation (HSBC) acquired a local thrift bank, which could further enhance competition in the middle and retail consumer markets.

SOME POLICY IMPLICATIONS

One area of public policy that has had a significant impact on the structure and performance of the Philippine banking sector is on entry and branching. In particular, restrictions on entry and branching, coupled with other regulatory restrictions on competition, led to an uncompetitive and inefficient banking system. On the other hand, their deregulation enhanced the contestability and competitiveness of the market, and facilitated changes in banking trends. In particular, the results indicate that deregulation of bank entry and branching had a positive impact on financial intermediation and dynamic efficiency of commercial banks.

Government barriers to bank entry are imposed primarily to limit and reduce the number, as well as increase the average size of banks in the Philippines. The problem was a weak structural base in that the financial system consisted of too many weak small banks, and a few strong, big banks. Bigger and fewer banks, in turn, were seen to promote the safety and soundness of the financial system. However, the focus should not just be the size of banks, but whether they are also sound, competitive and efficient. And in the latter aspect, entry barriers have clearly had a negative effect. Clearly a balance needs to be struck between the potential costs and potential benefits of allowing greater competition. In particular, the potential adverse effects of enhancing competition through a lowering of barriers to entry can be addressed by properly applying prudential restrictions already in place, particularly the fitness and properness criteria for bank owners and managers. Although it should also be noted that one merit of having direct entry restrictions in the Philippines is that it frees monetary authorities from political interventions in the licensing process. On the other hand, the policy bias has somewhat shifted in favor of foreign banks. The literature on foreign banking typically asserts that foreign bank entry can render national banking markets more competitive, thereby forcing domestic banks to operate more efficiently (Claessens *et al* 1998) Another potential positive impact of greater foreign participation in the Philippine banking sector is on the ownership structure of domestic banks. Very few domestic banks have remained purely Filipino owned, and foreign stakes could be increased further. This would serve not just to widen the ownership base of domestic banks, but also change the nature of ownership and hence banking in the Philippines. Concentration of ownership of Philippine banks continues to be a concern essentially because of its adverse implications on allocation of credit, the worst case being DOSRI abuses. But any resulting adverse efficiency effects would eventually backfire on the banks themselves, as the cases of Japan and South Korea clearly demonstrated, and with grave consequences for the entire economy. As long as scarce loanable funds are not channeled to borrowers who can use them most productively, the level and quality of investments and, consequently, the rate of economic growth will be severely affected.

Finally, in addition to the policy on entry and branching, there are other key policy issues with respect to competition in the commercial banking sector that need to be examined further. These include other unjustified regulatory restrictions on competition such as the mandatory credit requirements, which are also a contributing factor to the Philippines' high intermediation costs; the effective treatment of the "exit problem", competitive neutrality, mergers and acquisitions, and potential anti-competitive agreements as banks enter into more cooperative arrangements (e.g., the interconnection of networks such as ATMs; operation of international credit card systems or national debit transfer systems).

Chapter

9

Banking Deregulation, Punctuated Equilibrium and Early-mover Advantage

Proponents of the punctuated equilibrium and first-mover frameworks suggest that banks reacting strongly to changes brought about by deregulation will succeed. Alternatively, population ecologists argue that firms are unable to undertake significant change. We support the punctuated equilibrium view - banks that aggressively undertook merger and acquisition (M&A) activity once deregulation was enacted increased their probability of survival. However, we find evidence that "fast-followers" perform better than "first-movers." Banks completing their first acquisition in the second year after deregulation was enacted had better chances of survival than banks completing their first acquisition in the first year, or the third through fifth years.

INTRODUCTION

Deregulation provides the opportunity to observe how firms deal with profound environmental change, since deregulation often results in more opportunity and more competition. Incumbent firms vary in the way in which they respond to the changes brought on by deregulation. The purpose of this paper is to identify which types of bank responses impacted the probability of bank survival as intrastate merger and acquisition (M&A) activity was permitted by deregulation. In this study, we consider previous research that offers contradictory insights on how banks' reaction to deregulation impacts their subsequent performance. Population ecology theory suggests that firms undertaking significant change diminish their chances of long-term survival (Amburgey, Kelly & Barnett, 1993; Barnett & Freeman, 2001; Hannan & Freeman, 1977; Hannan & Freeman, 1984). Punctuated equilibrium theory posits that firms reacting quickly and aggressively to environmental change generate superior performance (Chaney, Devinney & Winer, 1991; Chen & MacMillan, 1992; Eddy & Saunders, 1980; Ferrier & Smith, 1999; Haveman, Russo & Meyer, 2002; Lee, Smith, Grimm & Schomburg, 2000; Lieberman & Montgomery, 1988; Nelson & Winter, 1982; Porter, 1985; Banking Deregulation, Punctuated Equilibrium & Early-Mover Advantage 540 Schumpeter, 1934, 1950; Vanderwerf & Mahon, 1997). Still other research indicates that firms that react slowly, but more comprehensively, outperform first-movers (Grinyer, Mayes & McKiernan, 1988; Hopkins, 2003; Miller & Friesen, 1984; Shamsie, Phelps & Kuperman, 2004; Virany, Tushman & Romanelli, 1992). In order to distinguish between these conflicting perspectives, we test a new set of hypotheses using data from the banking industry as deregulation was enacted throughout the United States. Following is a brief introduction of the research that leads to our new tests.

Intuitively, one could expect that banks responding more quickly and extensively to the environmental change brought on by deregulation will out-perform other banks. Previous research has found that firms that respond quickly to competitive challenges out-perform firms that respond more slowly (Chaney, et al., 1991; Chen & MacMillan, 1992; Eddy & Saunders, 1980; Ferrier & Smith, 1999; Lee, et al., 2000; Lieberman & Montgomery, 1988; Nelson & Winter, 1982; Porter, 1985; Schumpeter, 1934, 1950; Vanderwerf & Mahon, 1997). Within the context of banking deregulation, fast responders have the widest range of choice among the acquisition targets; late responders select a merger or acquisition target from a reduced pool of banks. It follows that fast responders are more likely to select the best acquisition targets. On the other hand, a case could be made that firms that respond more slowly, more deliberately, and in a more limited way may have the advantage. This approach would permit firms to learn from the mistakes of others before deciding if and how to respond. Previous research has provided evidence that firms that exhibit a slower but more effective response to competitive threat out-perform firms that acted quickly but less effectively (Grinyer, et al., 1988; Hopkins, 2003; Miller & Friesen, 1984; Virany, et al., 1992).

Hopkins observed three reasons that slower firm reaction to competitive threat can be more effective: "First, change is delayed until it is clear that change is necessary. Second, change is delayed until there is agreement on what the new strategy should be. Third, the forces encouraging change have gotten stronger because of the delay" (2003: 9). In addition, previous research has identified several contingencies under which late-movers generate superior performance (Shamsie, Phelps & Kuperman, 2004). Early-movers in the banking M&A arena may pave the way for late-movers to perform even better.

To determine whether the timeliness and the extent of a bank's reaction to deregulation is a determinant of the bank's subsequent performance, we explore the relationship between the M&A activity undertaken once intrastate banking M&A activity was permitted by deregulation and changes in bank survival rates. Using 19 years of bank regulatory data (1986 to 2004) across 22 states comprising over 10,000 observations, we find that the chance of bank survival increases over the number, and size, of mergers or acquisitions undertaken in the first five years after deregulation was introduced. We find that banks that undertake M&A activity in the first five years after deregulation was enacted have better rates of survival than banks that conducted M&A in later years, or conducted no M&A at all. As stated above, banks that react in the second year after deregulation was enacted have better survival rates than banks that react in the first year, or in years three through five.

The implication is that banks that react to the environmental changes brought about by deregulation have better rates of survival than firms that do not react, but that no first-mover advantage exists. These results are statistically and economically significant, and are not due to any selection bias that can be attributed to differences in the size and profitability of the acquiring banks.

LITERATURE REVIEW AND RESEARCH HYPOTHESES

Two contrasting theoretical perspectives can be used to predict banks' reaction to deregulation. The punctuated equilibrium paradigm suggests that evolutionary change occurs in periodic bursts, rather than in gradual, incremental steps (Gersick, 1991). Proponents of the punctuated equilibrium framework have shown that firms that adapt to profound environmental shifts by making substantial changes in strategy and tactics outperform firms that do not adapt (Haveman, et al., 2002). Alternatively, Hannan & Freeman (1984) observed that society prefers firms that are accountable, stable and have replicable processes. It is these very characteristics that make firms less capable of change. This limited ability to change is called "structural inertia." The concept of structural inertia has been embraced by population ecologists, who argue that firms that are created in the best form to exist in the market survive; maladapted firms die (Hannan & Freeman, 1977). Firms are poorly equipped to undertake strategic change, and are therefore roughly trapped into a course of action that is largely dictated by their initial form. Proponents of structural inertia suggest that firms are incapable of successful change; thus firms that seek to undertake dramatic change in the face of deregulation should experience decline.

Two Theories from Population Ecology

The punctuated equilibrium framework stems from ecology. In contrast to Darwinism, this model suggests that populations adapt in rapid steps and then exist in equilibrium until another dramatic shift in the environment changes the requirements for survival or success (Gersick, 1991). Deregulation is a classic example of an abrupt change as described by punctuated equilibrium, and calls for rapid adaptation among the affected firms (Fox-Wolfgramm, Boal & Hunt, 1998). Firms that adapt do so in rapid steps interspersed with long periods of equilibrium. Firms able to adapt to dramatically new environmental requirements succeed; ones unable to adapt die. In fact, evidence suggests that firms that make profound, timely change in the face of an abrupt transformation of its environment outperform those that do not change (Haveman, et al., 2002). While the punctuated equilibrium framework stresses the importance of phases of intense change, the population ecology perspective suggests that most types of organizational change are detrimental to firm performance (Hannan & Freeman, 1977). Firms develop processes that routinize most functions; they become adept at repeating tasks in the most efficient manner. Further, riskadverse investors prefer firms that are transparent and stable. By developing effective processes that are readily observable by the public, and that can deliver reliable operating results quarter after quarter, firms possess "structural inertia" (Hannan & Freeman, 1984). As such, population ecologists argue that firms are incapable of change; the environment "selects" firms that took the initial forms that are best suited to deal with current environmental conditions; firms that are poorly suited to meet environmental challenges die. In general, organizational change has been shown to be hazardous; firms that undertake change increase their probability of firm failure (Amburgey, et al., 1993). In particular, Barnett and Freeman (2001) find that firms that undertake excessive organizational change by introducing too many new products simultaneously decrease their chances of survival.

Merger and Acquisition

Research on deregulation finds that it has generally been beneficial at the industry level (Winston, 1998; Winston, et al., 1990; Morrison & Winston, 1989; Werden, et al., 1991). Deregulation has increased competition, reduced prices and costs, increased innovation, and improved service. Deregulation in the banking industry has permitted intrastate M&A activity. This, in turn, has greatly increased M&A within the banking industry. Consistent with general observations about the beneficial aspects of deregulation, research has shown that increased M&A activity within banking has benefited the industry (Stiroh & Strahan, 2003). However, research on M&A generally suggests that acquiring firm shareholders do not benefit from acquisitions (Harford, 1999; Loughran & Vijh, 1997; Lubatkin & Lane, 1996; Porter, 1987; Sirower, 1997). Within the banking industry, Rhoades (1994) finds that of 19 studies on the operating performance of merging vs. non-merging banks, almost all studies find no improvement in bank operating performance after a merger or acquisition. Of the subset of studies that do find some improvement, results are inconsistent.

Taken in isolation, this previous research suggests that increased M&A activity within banking should benefit the industry at large, but should not benefit incumbent banks. However, this view may not be complete in two respects. First, most extant research has not considered firm survival as a measure of performance. This study uses survival analysis in order to determine if the firm's chances of survival was impacted by its level of M&A activity in the wake of deregulation. Second, while M&A activity does not benefit acquiring firms in general, we find that under specific circumstances, M&A can improve firm performance. Using the punctuated equilibrium framework, we suggest that the probability of a successful merger or acquisition increases when deregulation permits M&A activity for the first time. This is because banks can exploit the opportunities that are created during a strategic window such as deregulation. Weak banks that were previously protected by government regulation of banks became available for stronger banks to acquire.

Banking Deregulation and M&A

Historically, the U.S. banking industry was heavily regulated. Among the major restrictions was the prohibition of intrastate branching activity. These regulations were generally perceived as benefiting small or inefficient banks by preventing larger banks from competing with them (Stiroh & Strahan, 2003). From 1970 to 1998, states deregulated, dropping restrictions against intrastate bank branching. First, banks were permitted to expand on an intrastate basis by acquiring other banks. Later, banks were permitted unrestricted branch banking by establishing their own new branches. This form of deregulation created an environment in which M&A activity may be beneficial to acquisitive banks. Where larger more competitive banks were once prohibited from entering certain markets, these banks could now grow through M&A into new potentially lucrative markets where weak competitors had been protected for years.

Thus, since government regulation had constrained banks from growing larger through branching for years, growth through M&A during the first phase of deregulation may have been an excellent path to growth for many banks. Indeed, research at the firm level has found that after deregulation, firms that adapt their strategies perform better than those that do not (Carow, Heron & Saxton, 2004; Smith & Grimm, 1987; Stiroh & Strahan, 2003).

Is a larger, more aggressive response to deregulation better than a smaller response? No studies have examined whether firm performance after deregulation changes over the firm's *rate* of adaptation in response to deregulation. Thus, it is not known whether the rate of adaptation to new deregulation describes the bank's performance after deregulation. Smith & Grimm (1987) found that railroads that made strategic adaptations after deregulation fared better than railroads that did not adapt.

However, Rhoades (1994) finds no evidence of change in financial performance when comparing banks that engaged in M&A activity when compared to banks that did not. This research can be extended in two ways. First, we can use a different measure of performance than the operating performance studies surveyed by Rhoades. Second, we can determine if the relationship between adaptation and performance is continuous. That is, we can determine if there is a relationship between the extent of bank adaptation and bank survival after deregulation. The intensity of a bank's adaptation to deregulation can be measured in two ways - the number of total acquisitions a bank completes in the first five years after deregulation and the size of the acquisitions a bank completes in the first five years after deregulation.

H1: The probability of bank survival is positively related to the total number of acquisitions undertaken in the first five years after the introduction of deregulation.

H2: The probability of bank survival is positively related to the total amount of assets acquired in the first five years after the introduction of deregulation.

Early-Mover Advantage

A broad body of research in competitive dynamics shows that early movers generally out-perform late movers. In product markets, firms that are the first to introduce new products generate superior profit (Lieberman & Montgomery, 1988; Nelson & Winter, 1982; Porter, 1985; Schumpeter, 1934, 1950; Lee, et al., 2000) and superior stock returns (Chaney, et al., 1991; Eddy & Saunders, 1980). Resourcebased theorists predict that first-movers are better able to create proprietary resources that will promote sustainable competitive advantage (Barney, 1986; Conner, 1991; Makadok, 1998; Wernerfelt, 1984). Vanderwerf & Mahon (1997) find that first and early movers generate superior market share across a broad range of situations and industries. Late movers are less likely to be successful because of the existence of well-established competitors and less growth opportunities (Carpenter & Nakamoto, 1989; Lilien & Yoon, 1990; Makadok, 1998; Robinson, Kalyanaram, & Urban, 1994; Shaw & Shaw, 1984; Teplensky, Kimberly, Hillman & Schwartz, 1993). Studies on firm decision-making speed find that fast decision-making is positively associated with firm performance across a number of contexts (Baum & Wally, 2003; Eisenhardt, 1989; Judge & Miller, 1991).

In the same way that advantages accrue to first movers in product markets, similar benefits can be gained by first movers in the M&A arena. While first-movers in the product markets are capturing lucrative customers in new growth areas, first-movers in the M&A market can acquire valuable resources that reside in target firms. Such resources can be combined with the acquiring firm's existing capabilities to build sustainable competitive advantage. Carow, et al. (2004) build a theoretical framework that predicts that the early mover advantage will extend to the M&A process. Acquisition is a powerful mechanism through which firms can acquire critically important assets, and can combine those acquired assets with the existing capabilities within the acquiring firm to create valuable, rare and inimitable resources (Barney, 1986; Barney, 1988; Conner, 1991; Lubatkin, 1983; Makadok, 2001; Penrose, 1959; Sirower, 1997). An early mover may possess superior information that enables it to capture the most valuable assets at the best price (Barney, 1988; Jarrell, Brickley & Netter, 1988). In some industries, large first movers that introduce a new technology can invest heavily to create scale economies, which can be exploited by smaller late entrants (Mitchell, 1991). Unlike the introduction of a new technology, later entrants into the acquisition market do not create scale economies; thus any advantage created by moving first should be more sustainable. Carow et al. (2004) find that first-mover acquirers generate superior performance if they undertake related acquisitions during industry expansion periods. Given this theoretical background, we test the following hypothesis.

H3: The probability of bank survival is negatively related to the time elapsed between the beginning of deregulation and the date of the bank's first acquisition.

Data and Variables

The sample used in this study is taken from the Bank Regulatory database maintained by Wharton Research Data Services (WRDS). The Bank Regulatory database contains five databases for regulated depository institutions, which holds accounting data on savings and loan institutions, bank holding companies, commercial banks, and savings banks. The five databases are the Commercial Bank database, the Bank Holding Companies database, and Merger Description data from the Federal Reserve Bank of Chicago, as well as the FDIC/OTS Deposit and the Research Information System from the Federal Deposit Insurance Corporation (FDIC). The Bank Regulatory database contains data from all five datasets from 1986.

State level deregulation permitting intrastate branching through mergers and acquisitions (M&A) began prior to 1970; the last state to permit such activity was Wyoming in 1998. Since WRDS provides bank data from 1986, we are able to observe the performance of banks within the 22 states that have introduced deregulation after this date (Kroszner & Strahan, 1999: 1441).

Following Shamsie, et al. (2004), we measure bank M&A activity for five years after deregulation. Five years enables us to observe firm responses over a wide timeframe. Firms undertaking M&A later in the study period are considered "late movers." Bank performance and M&A activity is observed for one year before, and five years after intrastate branching through M&A is permitted. For example, since state deregulation began in Illinois in 1988, "pre-deregulation" performance is taken from 1987. "Post-deregulation" performance is observed from 1988 to 1992. In Colorado, pre-deregulation performance is taken from 1990, and post-deregulation performance is taken from 1991 to 1995. For all banks in our sample, survival rates are recorded through 2004.

Study Variables

The following variables are used in the empirical analysis.

Firm Performance. Following Zuniga-Vicente & Vicente-Lorente (2006), firm performance is measured as survival time. We measure survival time as the number of quarter-years the firm existed after deregulation was enacted until 2004.

Bank-level M&A activity. The level of M&A activity for each bank is measured in three ways. First, we consider the amount of time that elapsed from the beginning of deregulation to an acquiring bank's first merger or acquisition. Five dummy variables were created – one for each year of observed postderegulation activity (YR1-YR5). If a bank completed a merger or acquisition in the first year after deregulation, YR1 is coded one, and the other dummy variables coded zero, and so on. Second, we take total bank assets acquired through M&A over the first five years of deregulation. This is equal to the cumulative book value of all assets acquired through M&A

by banks in the first five years after deregulation. Third, the total numbers of mergers or acquisitions completed per bank are used as another measure of M&A activity.

Control variables. Since it is possible that the largest or most profitable banks are best-suited to undertake successful acquisition, we control for this selection bias by including the initial profitability and size of banks as regressors. Additionally, we include the change in U.S. real GDP from the beginning of deregulation to the end of the study period (Bureau of Economic Analysis, 2006) to capture the effect of the macroeconomic environment on bank M&A activity and survival rates. Since states deregulated banking in different years, the five year study period for each bank is unique.

Therefore, the rates of real GDP growth during each time period are unique.

EMPIRICAL ANALYSIS

Descriptive Statistics

The initial size of the acquiring bank, and the total assets acquired by acquisitive banks are logtransformed in order to correct for the skewness of the distribution of bank size. As expected, the total number of bank acquisitions is positively correlated to the level of bank assets acquired, and the bank survival time is positively correlated to the rate of real economic growth in the country during the same time period. Despite an intuitive expectation that larger or more profitable banks are more likely to survive, note that bank survival time is weakly correlated with initial bank profitability and with initial bank size.

Discussion

In this analysis, we find that banks that respond to deregulation out-perform banks that do not. Firstresponder banks did not perform as well as banks that reacted later in the time period. Banks that acquire more banks, and acquire more bank assets, increase their chances of subsequent survival. There are many reasons this relationship should exist. The business press recognizes that firms that frequently use acquisitions to grow become adept at completing and implementing acquisitions (Computerworld, 2005; Economist, 2006). Cisco and General Electric have built their market-leading positions through acquisition, and are routinely among America's most admired companies (Demos, 2006). It is likely that firms conducting more mergers or acquisitions within the first years after deregulation are benefiting from a learning curve effect. Intuitively, we see that firms that conducted more acquisitions in the first five years after deregulation are more likely to have acquired key implementation skills over that time, and that those competencies translate into superior firm durability.

While the learning curve may be an important explanatory effect, the superior survival rates that we observe among banks that completed more M&A transactions may be explained by other factors. Across a broad range of contexts, research shows that firms that react to environmental change out-perform firms that fail to react, or react inappropriately (Vanderwerf & Mahon, 1997). The resource-based view (RBV) of the firm suggests that firms that are among the first to acquire other firms can appropriate the acquired firm's competitive resources, and combine those newly acquired resources with their own, thus developing new resource combinations that provide the firm sustainable competitive advantage (Barney, 1986; Barney, 1988; Conner, 1991; Lubatkin, 1983; Makadok, 2001; Penrose, 1959; Sirower, 1997). Our third hypothesis builds upon a broad literature in competitive dynamics, the resource-based view of the firm, and mergers and acquisition. Firms that respond *first* to the environmental change introduced by deregulation did not perform as well as fast-followers. This suggests that a curvilinear relationship exists between bank response time and bank performance. Several factors can influence the relationship between bank response time and subsequent survival. First mover firms make pioneering mistakes due to a lack of experience and precedents to guide their actions. Late movers have both the disadvantage of a weaker set of acquisition firms as well as the lack of acquisition experience. Second mover firms have a better selection of available target banks than late movers, as well as the ability to learn from the early mistakes of the first mover companies. First-movers may invest in creating public awareness of the benefits of bank M&A through marketing expenditures, while second movers can be free-riders, benefiting from the goodwill created by the firstmovers.

After an initial wave of acquisitions are observed by target banks, some target banks that were relatively vulnerable to acquisition may drop defensive tactics and agree to be acquired. This may make a second wave of acquisitions less acrimonious and costly to acquiring banks. Fast-follower banks may generate superior performance by taking the extra time to develop a comprehensive acquisition plan. It may be somewhat surprising that the level of bank M&A activity in the wake of deregulation is not related to acquiring bank financial performance, particularly in light of Smith & Grimm's (1987) finding that changes in M&A activity explained changes in railroad financial performance. In analysis not shown here, we find no relationship between bank financial performance and M&A activity in the wake of deregulation.

This is consistent with the findings of many studies surveyed by Rhoades (1994). The difference between our results and Smith & Grimm's results can be explained by the difference in the sample sizes used in the two studies, and the extremely homogenous financial performance of all of the banks in our sample when compared to the railroads in Smith & Grimm's sample. Whereas Smith & Grimm's sample contained only 20 railroads, our sample contains 10,217 banks. Further, the financial performance of the railroads in Smith & Grimm's sample is substantially more volatile than the financial performance of the banks in our sample. For example, Smith & Grimm find that railroads that did not react to deregulation experienced a mean decline of 6.32% in ROI, with a standard deviation of 9.06 over four years. The mean change in ROI of the banks in our study sample is only 0.3% with a standard deviation of 0.03. This study uses a different performance measure than earlier research on early-movers in M&A. While Carow et al. (2004)

find that firms generate superior abnormal stock returns when they are among the early-movers in an acquisition wave, we use survival rate as our dependent variable. Their research finds that investors react favorably to first-mover acquiring firms; we find that there is no change in first-mover acquiring bank profitability. This means that Carow et al. (2004) find that the investment community "liked" a fast move in the wake of deregulation, and bid the stock prices of such banks higher. We find that a first-mover has a lower probability of survival than a fast-follower. This suggests that the market initially over-valued the importance of being a first-mover after banking deregulation was enacted.

Other research that detects an advantage accruing to first-movers relative to other early-movers is set in product markets. This is not surprising, since customer-facing organizations that are first to market with a new product can capture early marketshare (Lieberman & Montgomery, 1988; Nelson & Winter, 1982; Porter, 1985; Lee, et al., 2000). In the punctuated equilibrium context of banking deregulation, it is not necessary to be a first-mover. Rather, being a "fast-follower" seems to be superior. As discussed earlier, fast-followers react quickly enough to exploit market opportunities before they disappear, but a short response delay enables them to learn from first-mover mistakes.

Note that this analysis does not capture the full period of banking deregulation within the United States. U.S. banking deregulation began prior to 1970; the FDIC data is not available until 1986. As a result, our analysis estimates the relationship between bank's reaction to deregulation and firm survival after 1986. We can not conclude that this relationship holds before 1986. The findings presented here are important. First, not only do we extend existing research on deregulation and environmental change, but also we provide the first evidence that there is a continuous improvement to bank performance as the bank's reaction to deregulation increases. Stronger reactions to deregulation are superior to weaker reactions to deregulation. Second, we utilize the research on first-mover advantages and merger and acquisition to provide new insights into the environmental changes brought about by deregulation. We show that the broad set of findings on first-mover advantage in product markets does not extend to the punctuated equilibrium context of deregulation and banking M&A studied here.

Our study raises important new questions. First, were the banks that were acquired soon after deregulation different from banks that were acquired later? This study finds that banks that acquired other banks in the second year after deregulation was enacted out-performed other acquiring banks. Is part of this phenomenon due to the fact that the earlier banks that were acquired the most valuable? Perhaps the banks acquired in the second after deregulation were a form of "low-hanging fruit" that provided the most valuable competitive resources to the banks that acquired them. Later acquired banks may have been less valuable. Second, this analysis examines changes to bank survival rates during a short time frame as deregulation was introduced. Do the relationships found here hold during times when deregulation is not being implemented? Perhaps acquisition *always* benefits acquiring banks, not only during periods of deregulation. We hope this study sparks continued interest and study of banking deregulation as an opportunity to understand the punctuated equilibrium framework.

Chapter

10

The Real Effects of US Banking Deregulation

INTRODUCTION

In the 1970s, commercial bank faced restrictions on interest rates, both on the deposit and lending sides of their business. They were restricted for the most part to classic financial intermediation – deposit taking and lending – to the exclusion, for example, of underwriting many corporate securities and insurance products. And, banks were limited in the geographical scope of their operations. No state permitted banks headquartered in other states either to open branches or to buy their banks, and many states prohibited or restricted intrastate branching. Today, almost all of these restrictions have been lifted. Interest rate ceilings on deposits were phased out in the early 1980s, state usury laws have been weakened because banks may now lend anywhere, limits to banks' ability to engage in other financial activities have been almost completely eliminated, as have restrictions on the geographical scope of banking. As a result, our banking system is now more competitive and more consolidated than ever – both vertically and horizontally.

This chapter focuses on how one dimension of this broad-based deregulation – the removal of limits on bank entry and expansion – affected economic performance. In a nutshell, the results suggest that this regulatory change was followed by better performance of the real economy. State economies grew *faster* and had *higher* rates of new business formation after this deregulation. At the same time, macroeconomic *stability* improved. By opening up markets and allowing the banking system to integrate across the nation, deregulation made local economies less sensitive to the fortunes of their local banks.

Below I explain first how relaxation of geographical restrictions on bank expansion proceeded historically, and why our somewhat unusual history of state-level regulation and deregulation presents an attractive setting to study how the financial system affects the real economy. I then present the evidence that banking deregulation led to substantial and beneficial real effects on our economy. The findings are important for at least two reasons. First, they demonstrate the tight link between "Wall Street" and "Main Street." Finance is not only affected by the fortunes of the industrial sector, but the reverse holds true as well. This mutual dependence highlights the importance of financial regulation not only here in the United States but, perhaps even more critically, in emerging economies without a well developed set of financial markets and institutions. Second, the results support the idea that competition and financial market openness are beneficial. This finding would be accepted as non-controversial when applied to industrial firms – for most economist, free trade and competition are akin to motherhood – but is much less accepted when applied to the financial sector.

Bank Deregulation as an Empirical Laboratory

The evolutionary history of banking regulations in the United States offers researchers a unique opportunity to study the effects deregulation, particularly those related to restrictions on banks' ability to expand within and across state lines, because they were imposed at the state level and because states changed their regulatory restrictions on expansion at *different* times. Although there was some deregulation of branching restrictions in the 1930s, most states either prohibited branching altogether (the "unit banking" states) or limited branching into the 1970s. At that point, only twelve states allowed unrestricted statewide branching. Between 1970 and 1994, however, 38 states deregulated their restrictions on branching.1 In addition to facing branching limitations within the state, until the 1980s cross-state ownership of banks was effectively prohibited by states' application of the Douglas Amendment to the 1956 Bank Holding Company (BHC) Act. This amendment prohibited a BHC from acquiring banks outside the state where it was headquartered unless the target bank's state permitted such acquisitions. Since states chose to bar such transactions, the amendment effectively prevented interstate banking. Change began in 1978, when Maine passed a law allowing entry by out-of-state BHCs if, in return, banks from Maine were allowed to enter those states (entry meaning the ability to buy incumbent banks). No state reciprocated, however, so the deregulation process remained stalled until 1982, when Alaska and New York passed laws similar to Maine. State deregulation was nearly complete by 1992, by which time all states but Hawaii had passed similar laws.

The first two columns pertain to within-state branching deregulation. The first column presents the year in which each state permitted branching by means of merger and acquisition (M&A) only. With this form of deregulation, an expansion-minded bank could enter a new market either by buying an existing bank in that market and folding its operations into the acquirer's existing operations, or by buying individual branches of existing banks. The second column reports the year in which each state first permitted unrestricted branching, thereby allowing banks to enter new markets by opening new branches. In most cases, branching by M&A occurred first, then unrestricted branching deregulation occurred soon thereafter. This time clustering makes it hard to isolate the impact of M&A branching from the impact of permitting new branches; moreover, it turns out that most banks enter new markets by buying existing banks or branches rather than by building new ones. So, in the empirical analysis I will construct a single branching indicator based on the date at which a state first permitted branching by M&A.

Column three reports the year in which states first entered into an interstate banking agreement with other states. With interstate deregulation, a state opened up the possibility that an outside banking organization could acquire its incumbent banks. This form of deregulation, however, did not permit these newly acquired banking assets to be folded into the acquirer's banking operations outside the state. State- level moves toward interstate banking therefore did not lead to interstate *branching*. In 1994 though the deregulatory process was completed with passage of the Interstate Banking and Branching Efficiency Act of 1994 (IBBEA), federal legislation that mandated complete interstate banking as of 1997 and encouraged states to permit interstate branching. IBBEA permitted states to opt out of interstate branching, but only Texas and Montana chose to do so. Most other states did protect their banks by forcing out-of-state entrants to buy existing branches rather than open new ones.

The staggered timing of state-level moves to deregulate both branching and interstate banking restrictions provides an ideal laboratory to explore empirically how these regulatory changes affected banking and the real economy. Because of the cross-state and over-time variation in the regulatory status of different states, both unobserved state differences and aggregate shocks (and any secular trends) can be fully absorbed with the inclusion of fixed effects, while leaving sufficient variation in the regulatory variables to estimate their effects on state- level financial and real variables. Moreover, by using the *state* as the relevant unit, the resulting panel data set is balanced because states do not enter or exit the sample. Thus, there is no need to worry about (or attempt to correct for) survivorship biases that can plague attempts to draw inferences from bank- level or firm- level data. To be concrete, the research method boils down to estimating a regression using stateyear observations with the following structure:

(1) *Y*st = “t + $s + (1*Branch*st + (2*Bank*st + *OtherControls*st + ,st

where *s* indexes states, *t* indexes time, *Yst* is the dependent variable of interest, “t is a yearspecific fixed effect (estimated by including a set of year indicator variables), $s is a statespecific fixed effect (estimated by including a set of state indicator variables), ***Branchst*** is an indicator set to one after a state permits branching (by means of merger and acquisition), and *Bankst* is an indicator set to one after a state permits interstate banking. Thus, the deregulation indicators equal one in all state-years following deregulation, and they equal zero in all stateyears prior to deregulation.

Endogenous Deregulation?

Before describing the results, it is worth considering briefly *why* banking regulations remained static from the 1930s to the middle of the 1970s, and why they began to change across all states from the 1970s to the early 1990s. Several developments probably contributed. In the mid-1980s, for instance, the Office of the Comptroller of the Currency took advantage of a clause in the 1864 National Bank Act to allow nationally chartered banks to branch freely in those states where savings institutions (S&Ls and savings banks) did not face branching restrictions. The Comptroller's action was instrumental in introducing statewide branching in several southern states. Another impetus behind deregulation may have been the rash of bank and thrift failures in the 1980s, which increased public awareness of the advantages of large, well-diversified banks. As part of the 1982 Garn-St Germain Act, for example, federal legislators amended the Bank Holding Company Act to allow failed banks and thrifts to be acquired by any bank holding company, regardless of state laws (Kane, 1996).

More broadly, Economides, Hubbard and Palia (1996) show that small banks lobbied successfully in the 1930s for both generous deposit insurance and tight limits on branching, despite the objections of large banks. White (1998) shows that the small bank lobby continued its success over the subsequent 40 years by gaining increased levels of deposit insurance coverage all the way up until 1980 when this limit was last raised (to $100,000). Thus, the influence of small banks may explain the relative stability of these regulatory institutions from the 1930s through the 1970s. Kroszner and Strahan (1999) suggest that the emergence of new technologies in both deposit-taking and lending beginning in the 1970s tipped the balance in the political arena from the traditional beneficiaries of geographical restrictions – small banks – toward more expansion- minded, large banks. As evidence, we show that deregulation occurred earlier in states with fewer small banks, in states where small banks were financially weak, and in states with more small and bank-dependent firms. We also find that a larger insurance industry delayed deregulation when banks could compete in the sale of insurance products. Interest group factors related to the relative strength of potential winners (large banks and small firms) and losers (small banks and the rival insurance firms) therefore can explain the timing of branching deregulation across states.

Given these political economy explanations for banking reform, can we interpret the results from equation (1)? The results in Kroszner and Strahan (1999) suggest that aggregate forces such as technological change affected all financial services firms and created increasingly strong pressures for regulatory regime change; however, interest group factors determined the exact *timing* of when a particular state changed its laws. Thus, a cross-state comparison of state growth or business cycle volatility might be misleading, or at least difficult to interpret. For example, consider comparing states in a single year, say 1987. If states permitting interstate banking had more large banks than states that did not yet permit interstate banking, it could be that regulation led to structural changes favoring large banks (i.e. regulation caused the structural change), or it could be that states with more large banks deregulated before states with fewer large banks (i.e. regulation was caused by the cross-state differences in structure).

The estimators reported here, however, are not likely to be affected by the political economy factors. By including the state fixed effects in the model ($*s*), all of the cross-sectional variation (such as when a state deregulates) gets removed; coefficients are driven by *changes* in variables after a state alters its regulations. Persistent differences across states (e.g. large-bank dominated states vs. sma ll-bank dominated states) do not affect the results. Instead, we look at how a state's banking structure *changes* after it deregulates, on how its growth performance *changes* relative to its level before deregulation, and on how the volatility of its busine ss cycle *changes*, again relative to its volatility prior to regulatory change.

How Banking Changed after Deregulation

We can only expect deregulation to have had large effects on the real economy if there were important changes in the structure and efficiency of the banking industry resulting from the reforms. To summarize briefly the key changes, relaxing restrictions on bank expansion led to larger banks operating across a wider geographical area. Increases in *local* market concentration, however, did not occur. This makes sense because the restrictions on branching and interstate banking generally did not apply to local markets, with the exception of a few "unit banking" states that did not permit branching in any form. Thus, deregulation led banks to enter new markets, but it did not spur banks to consolidate within a local market.

Here, I report the estimated coefficients on the within-state branching indicator (*Branchst*) and the interstate banking indicator (*Bankst*) from the fixed effects model described in equation (1) above. In column (1), the dependent variable equals the acquisition rate in a state- year, defined as the total dollar value of assets in banks acquired during the state- year, divided by total banking assets in the state at the beginning of the year. The results suggest, as expected, that acquisitions increased sharply following interstate banking deregulation. The coefficient implies that the annual acquisition rate rose by 1.64 percentage points after interstate reform — quite a large jump relative to the unconditional mean of 2.77 percent. In contrast, there was no significant increase in bank acquisitions following branching deregulation. Banks tended to expand by purchasing branches of existing banks after branching reform rather than by acquiring all of the branches and other assets of whole banks, so the acquisition rate of whole banks did not rise (for details, see Stiroh and Strahan, forthcoming).

Local market concentration equals the deposit Herfindahl-Hirschmann Index (HHI), calculated as the deposit-weighted average of the HHI indexes of the Metropolitan Statistical Areas (MSAs) in a state/year. The HHI for each local market is defined as the sum of squared market shares, where market shares are based on branchlevel deposit data from the FDIC's *Summary of Deposits* dataset. To illustrate how this variable is computed, consider a bank (or banking company) that owned 10 branches within an MSA. This bank's market share (measured in percentage terms) would equal the sum of all of its deposits in those 10 branches, divided by the total deposits held in by all bank branches within that MSA, times 100. For a market with a single bank owning all of the branches, the HHI would equal 10,000, whereas in a perfectly atomistic market the HHI would approach zero.

The declines were most pronounced following branching deregulation. For example, the share of assets held by banks with less than $50 million in assets (in 1994 dollars) fell by 1.6 percentage points (relative to a mean of 8.9 percent), the share of assets held by banks with assets between $50 and $100 million fell by 2.0 percentage points (relative to a mean of 10.3 percent), and the share held by banks with assets between $100 and $500 million fell by 2.2 percentage points (relative to a mean of 23.2 percent). After interstate banking the share of the smallest banks declined, while the share of other banks did not change significantly.

Did these structural changes cause meaningful changes in the efficiency of a state's banking industry? In earlier research, Jayaratne and Strahan (1998) report that the banking industry became significantly more efficient following reform. They find that non-interest costs fell, that wages fell, and that loan losses fell after states deregulated branching. These cost reductions led, in turn, to lo wer prices on loans (although not on deposits).

The mechanism for this better performance seems to be changes in the market shares of banks following deregulation. Prior to regulatory reform, well-run banks faced binding constraints on the markets in which they could operate. When these constraints were lifted, however, assets moved toward the better run banks as they gained the opportunity to acquire market share.

The beneficial dynamic effects of competition following deregulation can be seen graphically in three figures reported below. We simply plot the correlation between a bank's profit rate (return on equity) and its subsequent asset growth. We find that this correlation is low during the late 1970s, when the better banks were constrained by regulations, then rose sharply during the period of regulatory change – the period when better banks were gobbling up market share – then fell back during the beginning of the 1990s. The figure illustrates, somewhat crudely, the dynamic effects of deregulation. Here, we plot the average market share of banks with above- median profits, averaged across states, after first separating states into three groups: states that have permitted branc hing since the 1930s or before (12 states); states that limited branching (23 states), and the "unit banking" states that did not permit any form of branching (16 states). The figures illustrate the detrimental effects of these constraining regulations. For example, in unit banking states, the higher-profit banks typically held 50 percent or less of the assets in a state; after those states relaxed their regulations, however, these better banks' share rose to 65 to 75 percent of the state's assets. States that limited but did not prohibit branching experienced qualitatively similar effects following deregulation, although these effects were somewhat smaller.

The Real Effects of Deregulation

Did the beneficial changes in banking have quantitatively important effects on the real economy? The answer to this question is important not only for helping us gain an understanding of what has happened in the United States, but also for considering how banking systems across the world ought to be structured and regulated. In recent years, a growing number of researchers have studied how different financial regulatory regimes across countries affected financial stability and economic performance. For example, Rajan and Zingales (1998) and Cetorelli and Gambera (2001) test how differences in financial development and banking structure affected growth across different industries. Demirguc-Kunt, Levine and Min

(1999) find that countries open to foreign entry have had better performing banks.

More recently, Barth, Caprio and Levine (2002) document how various dimensions of banking laws and regulations – e.g. restrictions on bank activities, restrictions on entry, capital adequacy regulations, deposit insurance, supervision and regulation of banks, and government ownership of banks – vary across the world and relate these differences to measures of economic performance and stability. While the cross-country approach has much to teach us, one of the difficulties inherent in such studies is the fact that many kinds of policy regimes tend to go together.

For example, Laporta, Lopez-de-Silanes and Shleifer (2001) find that government ownership of banks tends to occur in countries with substantial corruption and poor long-run growth performance. Similarly, Djankov, La Porta, Lopez-de-Silanes and Shleifer (2002) find that entry regulations also tend to be most prevalent in countries with corrupt political institutions. Thus, it becomes difficult in cross-country studies to determine what specific factor matters; for example, is entry regulation bad or does it simply proxy for other sorts of government constraints that can only be overcome through bribery?

As noted above, our focus is on the U.S. experience; the relative homogeneity in the economic and legal infrastructure across states presents a strong advantage from an empirical standpoint because the many "invisible" barriers to effective contracting and economic performance are either not present or do not vary substantially across states.

Having said that, the hope of this researcher is that the conclusions drawn for the U.S. states will carry over to other environments such as emerging economies. I will focus specifically on three questions. First, what were the effects of banking reform on states' growth perfo rmance? Second, what were the effects of reform on entrepreneurial activity? Third, how did reform affect state-level business cycle stability?

Growth Effects

In the early Twentieth Century, Joseph Schumpeter (1969) argued that efficient financial systems promote innovations; hence, better finance leads to faster growth. On the other hand, Joan Robinson (1952) believed that the causality was reversed; economies with good growth prospects develop institutions to provide the funds necessary to support those good prospects. In other words, the economy leads and finance follows. Recent theoretical developments have fleshed out two potential causal links from financial systems to growth. Financial markets can matter either by affecting the volume of savings available to finance investment or by increasing the productivity (or quality) of that investment. These theories show that an improvement in financial market efficiency can act as a lubricant to the engine of economic growth, allowing that engine to run faster.

Empirical research in recent years has increasingly provided support for the Schumpterian view that financial market development can play an important causal role in driving long-run growth. For example, King and Levine (1993) demonstrated that the size and depth of an economy's financial system is positively correlated with its future growth in percapita, real income. While this evidence is suggestive, it can not rule out the possibility that financial development and growth are simultaneously driven by a common factor not controlled in the empirical analysis. Rajan and Zingales (1998) and Cetorelli and Gambera (2001) attempt to answer this criticism by exploiting cross- industry differences in financial dependence.

They show that in countries with well-developed financial markets, industries that require more external finance grow faster than "cash cow" industries that can finance investment with internally generated funds. Levine, Loayza and Beck (2000) attempt to establish a causal link from finance to growth by using pre-existing legal differences across countries as instruments for the development of the banking system; they show that the exogenous component of banking development is positively related to growth performance. Another way to establish that better finance (or, specifically, better banking) can lead to faster growth is to find policy changes that lead to more efficient finance (banking) and see how the economy responds. In earlier work, Jith Jayaratne and I did just this. We showed that improvements in the financial markets can spur faster economic growth by studying state-level branch banking deregulation. Using data from 1972 to 1992, we estimated the change in economic performance before and after deregulation and found that annual growth rates accelerated by one-half to one percentage point. In that study, we worked hard to rule out other interpretations of the finding. For example, we showed that states did *not* deregulate their economies in *anticipation* of future good growth prospects. We also found no other concomitant policy changes that could account for the result, and no consistent political changes, such as a change in the party controlling the state government, around the time of deregulation. Below, I re-estimate this growth model using a slightly different sample period (1976 to 1996) and including some additional control variables.

The personal income data are reported by the Bureau of Economic Analysis and converted to constant dollars using the Consumer Price Index. Over the sample period, real personal income grew at an annual rate of slightly less than 1.5 percent. The standard deviation of the growth rates equals 2.79 percent, with a minimum of about -15 percent in North Dakota in 1980, and a maximum of about +17 percent, again in North Dakota in 1978. Overall there is clearly more variability in year-to-year growth rates for small states like North Dakota, but in Jayaratne and Strahan (1996) we were careful to rule out the possibility that the growth increases were driven by a few of these small states. In the interest of brevity, I will not report these tests here.

Effects on Entrepreneurs

The results so far suggest that growth accelerated after deregulation. But following the logic of Rajan and Zingales, just as cash-constrained firms benefited most from financial development, bank-dependent firms ought to have benefited the most from the banking deregulation and associated improvements in finance.

Entrepreneurs or potential entrepreneurs are likely to be highly dependent on banks and other financial markets because they have not had the opportunity (yet) to generate cash flow that can support investment. Indeed, Schumpeter himself emphasized the role of financial markets in getting funds to young firms as a key channel through which finance can affect long-run growth. To test this idea, I now explore how the level and growth in new business formation changes following banking reform.

To measure business formation, I use new business incorporations in each state and year from 1976 to 1996. This series comes from the individual states, as reported and compiled by Dun & Bradstreet. Business incorporations is not a perfect measure of the rate of business formation in a state, but it offers the best proxy available that is compiled on a consistent basis over a relatively lo ng period. Dun & Bradstreet also report a series on business "starts" that is an offshoot of their credit database. Since this series only goes back to 1985, it is not helpful in exploring how the changes in banking that began in the middle of the 1970s affected entrepreneurship and business formation. 17 Nevertheless, the starts data can help verify that business incorporations track closely the rate of business formation in a state. It turns out that new incorporations per capita and business starts per capita are consistently positively correlated with each other; the cross-state correlation ranged from a low of 0.58 in 1994 to a high of 0.72 in 1988. There is one important exception, however. The number of incorporations in Delaware is about *20* times the average number of incorporations in the other states (per capita), while the number of starts in Delaware is very close to the average. This difference reflects favorable legal treatment of incorporations in that state. In addition, measures of banking structure in both Delaware and South Dakota are skewed by the presence of credit card banks in those states. We therefore drop both of these states from all of our regressions.

As a further check on the data, incorporations per capita and starts per capita can be compared with the number of new establishments per capita, which is available from the Small Business Administration starting in 1989. An establishment is not a firm;

rather, it is an economic unit that employs people, such as a plant, a factory, or a restaurant. Nevertheless, we think that the number of new establishments ought to be highly correlated with the economic quantity that we are trying to observe – the rate of creation of new businesses. Again, it is highly correlated with both incorporations and starts. From 1989 to 1994, the cross-state correlation between incorporations and new establishments ranges from 0.52 to 0.57, and cross-state correlation between starts and new establishments ranges from 0.41 to 0.65. Thus, new incorporations in a state seem to capture new business formation.

In a typical state and year, there are about 2.5 new incorporations formed for every 1000 people living in a state. The mean growth rate is 2.06 percent per year, slightly higher than the growth in real per-capita income. Notice that the variation in the growth of new incorporations is about four times higher than the variation of overall income. Consistent with the Schumpterian logic, both the level and growth of entrepreneurial activity increased following banking deregulation. The regression coefficients suggest, for example, that the annual level of new incorporations per-capita increased by 9.8 percent after branching deregulation, and by 5.7 percent after interstate banking reform. In the specifications using the growth rate, the increase only occurred following deregulation of branching. Thus, the effects on entrepreneurial activity of branching deregulation appear to be larger and more persistent than the effects of interstate banking, consistent with the effects of the two reforms on personal income growth. It is also worth noting that the *magnitude* of the increase in the growth of new incorporations is substantially larger than the increase in personal income growth following reform, although the standard errors are also substantially larger due to the greater variation in this series.

Business Cycle Effects

The evidence so far points to substantial benefits of opening up banking markets to potential entry and greater competition, for entrepreneurs looking to start businesses and, perhaps through their efforts, to faster overall economic growth. Cross country evidence is beginning to emerge suggesting that opening up financial markets to foreign entry can also create benefits associated with macroeconomic stability (Barth, Caprio and Levine, 2002). There is some evidence from studies at the bank level, however, that risk-taking may increase with the reductions in franchise value that come following banking deregulation (Keeley, 1990, Demsetz, Saidenberg and Strahan, 1996, Hellman, Murdock and Stiglitz, 2000, Bergstresser, 2001). How did banking reform in the U.S. affect macroeconomic stability? In a recent paper, Morgan, Rime and Strahan (2002) analyze this question from both a theoretical and an empirical standpoint. We show first that following interstate banking deregulation in the United States, the banking system became substantially better integrated nationally. Prior to deregulation, the U.S. had a balkanized system composed effectively of 50 little banking systems, one for each state.

After interstate deregulation, however, an average of about 60 percent of a state's banking assets were owned by a multi-state (or, sometimes multinational) banking company. The theoretical effect of this banking integration on business cycles, however, is ambiguous. In Morgan et al, we start with a banking model in which bankers can prevent moral hazard—by monitoring firms—and they can commit moral hazard—by neglecting to monitor. These hazards make the equilibrium rate of investment in the economy depend on the level of firm collateral and bank capital; these state variables give firms and bankers a stake in future investment outcomes, but shocks to either variable cause equilibrium investment to fall, i.e., collateral crunches and bank capital crunches are both contractionary.

We then show how integration of banking – that is, linking up the banking systems of two formerly separate economies – changes the effects of these two kinds of shocks. It turns out that both collateral and capital shocks remain contractionary after integration, but their magnitudes change: bank capital shocks become less important after integration, but the effects of collateral shocks gets bigger. The intuition for this result is straightforward and general. A banking company that is diversified across two economies can import capital if lending opportunities in one economy are strong relative to the availability of local bank capital. In contrast, a collateral shock in one economy will lead the integrated bank to *export* their capital and lending, thus worsening the resulting downturn.

The dependent variable in these regressions equals the absolute value of the residuals from the personal income growth regressions, and the growth in new incorporations regressions. Thus, the dependent variables in can be thought of as the *magnitude* of the deviation from expected growth in state personal income and new businesses, conditional on the employment shares in a state, the state's average growth rate (the state fixed effect), and shocks to the U.S. economy as a whole (the year fixed effects). The results suggest that overall state- level business cycle volatility fell after interstate banking and the associated financial integration.

The coefficients suggest a decline of 0.31 to 0.47 percentage points, which is large relative to the unconditional mean of 1.26 percent. The effects of branching deregulation are not significant, although this should perhaps not be too surprising because branching deregulation allowed integration *within* a state rather than *across* state lines.19 The results for the volatility of the growth of new incorporations also point in the same direction – toward less volatility following deregulation – although the coefficients on both deregulation indicators are not significant at conventional levels.

The theoretical analysis suggests that the explanation for better macroeconomic stability following deregulation is better insulation of a state's economy against shocks to its own banking system. In a disintegrated banking system, like the one we had in the 1970s and early 1980s, shocks to bank capital lead to reductions in lending, thereby worsening the downturn. In contrast, with integration a state can import bank capital from abroad (i.e. from other states) when its banks are down. If this explanation really holds, then the correlation between economic performance and banking performance ought to weaken with deregulation and integration. The results provide strong support for the idea that interstate banking deregulation severed the link between local economic performance and the performance of local banks.20 According to the estimated coefficients, a 10 percentage point reduction in the growth of bank capital held by local banks would be associated with a decline in personal income growth of 1.2 to 1.4 percent prior to interstate banking reform. After reform, however, this correlation becomes indistinguishable (statistically) from zero.

The regression coefficients, for instance, suggest that a 10 percentage point reduction in the growth of local bank capital would be associated with a decline in the growth rate of new incorporations of 4.5 to 5.4 percent, again prior to interstate banking reform. After reform, however, this correlation also becomes indistinguishable (statistically) from zero. So, integration has salutary effects on business cycles by insulating the local economy from the ups and downs of the local banking system. Of course, the kind of cross state integration that we experienced following interstate deregulation would not be expected to insulate states to shocks to *all* banks in the United States.

Banking deregulation of restrictions on branching and interstate banking lifted a set of constraints that had prevented better-run banks from gaining ground over their less efficient rivals. Big changes in the banking industry followed deregulation: many acquisitions and consolidation, integration across state lines, and a decline in the market share of small banks. These changes allowed banks to offer better services to their customers at lower prices. As a result, the real economy – "Main Street" as it were – seems to have benefited. Overall economic growth accelerated following deregulation, and this faster growth seems to have been concentrated among new businesses. Sometimes we think that higher returns necessarily bring higher risk. But in the case of banking deregulation, volatility of the economy *declined* as growth went up.

FINANCIAL DEREGULATION AND THE EAST ASIAN FINANCIAL CRISIS

East Asia's attraction to foreign savers was a direct result of genuine growth in that region. This required productive investment in the construction of physical and human capital to increase the future productivity of workers. In turn, workers engaged in capital construction required food, clothing and shelter etc. (consumption), which was generally provided by the savings of other people. Because human capital are qualities such as education and knowledge, only physical capital contributes to the genuine growth of GDP per capita also seen as living standards.

To understand why there is so much attraction to foreign savers, we need to see what the region in question can offer investors. Investors have a choice of how to finance their investment: using their own saving from wages/salaries, from business profit, or by borrowing or 'drawing' on the saving of other persons. Although using personal saving or business profit for investment may be simpler, it is not always the most cost-effective since the priority of nearly all firms is to profit maximize. In order to do so, drawing on the savings of others allows access to a greater pool of saving and rate of investment, despite the downside regulations to protect the interests of savers and dependence on a continued flow of other persons' savings. In the case of East Asian economies, decades of uninterrupted growth in living standards were partly based on high domestic saving (what is left after consumption spending on living expenses). In comparison, foreign investors' living standards were higher and so an investing economy (such as the US) would likely choose to supplement its domestic saving with foreign saving. Foreign saving is made through the current account of the balance of international payments; when this account is in deficit, the country is drawing on foreign saving each year by the extent of the deficit. This therefore provides a surplus for the East Asian economies.

Allocation of savings is rationally decided by a person's expectations of return and risk and hence a greater risk of loss requires a greater expected future return. However since the future is unknown and therefore inherently risky, the assessment of return and risk are mostly affected by the emotional state of the decision maker. When prices accelerate or plunge to unsustainable heights or depths respectively, it could be said that greed and fear are dominating rational calculation. In a boom, expected returns are exaggerated beyond what is physically possible, while risk is either totally ignored or foolishly imputed at zero (as explained above) when this can never be the case, since the future always holds some kind of risk.

From the saver's point of view, equity is riskier than debt, but because of the attraction of higher expected returns from equity in the event the venture is successful, greed will allow this risk to be accepted. From the investor's point of view who fully intends to honour the commitment to repay debt, the issue of debt is more risky than equity because the funds must be repaid even in the event of project failure which could lead to business and personal bankruptcy.

From the point of view of both savers and investors, international transactions in saving also involve exchange rate risk. When foreign savings are transmitted to the host's country, foreign currencies are bought for domestic currency at one exchange rate, but when these foreign savings are repatriated, a less favourable exchange rate may apply. *For example, if the exchange rate between the Australian Dollar and the Yen is one to one, I will spend AUD 1 million to receive YEN 1 million. However, when I have to repay, if the Yen is worth two Australian Dollars, I will have to pay the equivalent of AUD 2 million in return.

Provided that I invest in an Asian business however, I will hedge against all exchange rate risk, because the profit made will be in the currency that I have to return the debt in. This will always be the case in a booming economy with high savings and high and productive investment.

The ensuing inflow of foreign funds would raise the growth rate of the money supply because there is greater investment and hence greater saving (from GDP=C+I+G+X-M). When investment increases, the money supply increases. Greater saving also leads way to greater spending because a certain amount of the saving is used on extra consumption (which also increases GDP). As mentioned before, physical capital increases due to investment and so the demand for labour increases also.

Rural-urban migration occurs due to the higher investment as well. Because there is a high level of investment, there are both more jobs available in urban factories developing new technologies. Because of the higher demand for labour, the opportunity cost of urban living has increased. Because of this increased rural-urban migration there is more demand for land due to a greater population density. When demand rises for urban living, urban land prices increase. Both urban land price increases and population density are an indication that more real estate should be built.

Because of the increased growth in money supply, the economy appears to be stronger from a foreigner's perspective. The exchange rate between an East Asian country and another country will be much higher than before - see example (*) above. This effectively increases profits immediately. Other factors of extra profit include the extra demand for labour. Since there is more demand for labour, employers can offer lower wages because the job market is more competitive. Higher demand for urban living and increased consumption also means that the large amount of real estate being built will attract a large number of buyers. Another source of buyers are investors in real estate. Auctions especially will allow the people to bid the price up much higher than usual due to the large number of buyers.

Because of the large number of buyers of real estate, there will be many more loans from banks and a large number of loans requested. Banking at this time is risky because the principal amount loaned out by banks involves the debt being repaid with interest earned from on-lending to investors. The ability for borrowers to repay the principal with interest cannot be guaranteed; especially when depositors are not prepared to lend as long as it takes for the principal amount and interest to be paid back. This risk is only reduced in 'normal' banking because the deposits are 'rolled over' from one depositor to another which is reliant on customer confidence.

A loss of confidence due to rumours or facts, can trigger a large number of people to withdraw their deposits making it impossible for banks to store funds from depositors and therefore also impossible to issue funds to borrowers. This can lead to banking collapse in which banks are forced to call in loans from credit worthy businesses, its employees, suppliers and customers to help meet the banks' commitments to depositors. Bankruptcy of competent entrepreneurs and their employees takes years to recover because they are such scarce resources. Generally some kind of banking regulation is necessary to withdraw funds in the event that loans do not perform (such as having adequate reserves of capital).

An excessive propoition of savings was funneled into real estate where overinvestment occurred and losses were made. Building in anticipation of rising prices lead to an over supply of buildings, excessive vacancies and hence falling prices and the inability to service loans. Banks accepted real estate mortgages as security for loans, but the security was an illusion because the market value of the asset fell below the value of the loan.

When there has previously been a high inflow in anticipation of a high level of business activity and profit, a large rise in interest rates to combat inflation will have the dramatic effect of increasing lending which attracts more funds and tends to raise the value of the currency for which interest rates are being raised. However, the rise in interest rates will decrease business activity in the local economy and reduce profit on equity, so a large outflow will occur and the currency value will fall. A panic effect thus sets in with people withdrawing money from banks due to exchange rates falling (because the interest rates do not cover the devaluation of the currency). If interest rates did cover the devaluation of the currency, business and bank failure would set in because of the inability to repay debt - further driving the devaluation of the currency. Other triggers for the crisis included the flotation of several currencies after fixed exchange rate regimes, beginning with the Thai Baht with others following, resulting in a similar result of currency devaluation.

Professor Stiglitz's solution to the Asian Financial Crisis is to increase government spending and deficits and print more money. He claims that 'such a "Keynesian" response would have prevented recessions in the wake of the crisis, in contrast to what he calls the IMF's "alternative theory", which supposedly aggravated or even caused the contractions in output. The IMF's reaction to the crisis was to allow public finances to exert a stimulating impact on their economies, which deepened the reversal of capital outflow pushing the recession further than what it would have originally reached.

Since the main cause of the initial crisis was due to investment - by financing investment, the IMF did more harm than good. The increase in investment spending is shown in the following table excerpt from Japan Economic Institute - Report No. 33 - August 28, 1998.

Table 1: Japan's Balance of Payments, 1993-1998 (in billions of yen)

Current	Account Balance
1993	14,669
1994	13,343
1995	10,386
1996	7,158
1997	11,436

The rise shown here in 1997 Current Account Balance would have been even greater had not the Bank of Japan intervened in the market in April and again with the Federal Reserve Board in mid-June to address the imbalance between the supply and demand for foreign and domestic currencies.

In conclusion, when dealing with international finance, we must always consider why particular events occur rather than taking them for granted, and even then there are always different opinions of what will happen. All of these opinions must be taken seriously to prevent future crises from occurring and will help to keep the economy stable in general. Investment should be to promote a better lifestyle for all rather than for profit-maximisation. Risk-taking should be based on the risks themselves rather than the emotional state of the investor at the time. Ordinary people should take the time to understand the financial world that we are living in today. The day that people lay aside their greed and have nothing to fear is the day where the world economy will be truly global.

Chapter

11

Technology, Firm Strategies, Jobs, and Earnings in Retail Banking

Using data from extensive on-site interviews conducted in 1997, 1998, and 1999, the authors examine trends in job content and earnings in selected jobs in two American banks. Firm restructuring and technological changes resulted in higher earnings for college-educated workers. The banks followed different strategies in implementing these changes for lower-skill jobs, with different effects on bank tellers in particular.

The authors conclude that technological change can provide opportunities for workplace reform but does not determine its effects on jobs and earnings; these effects are contingent on managerial strategies. This focus on organizational processes and managerial strategy provides a complement to accounts of growing inequality that center solely on the role of individual skills and technological change.

Explanations for growing wage inequality over the past three decades have made much of the role of technology. College graduates have seen their wages rise, while workers with less education have seen their wages stagnate and even decline. This pattern is consistent with an account in which technological innovation has increased the demand for skilled workers in the American labor market, but direct evidence on this relationship remains rare. Most often, the effect of new technology has been inferred from the growing wage differentials themselves, a strategy that is ultimately "too crude to give us much insight into the actual nature of the changes that are occurring" (Bound 1996:155).

In this paper, we discuss changes in a subset of key jobs, and their associated earnings, in the retail banking industry. During the 1980s and 1990s, banking saw a dramatic influx of new information technology, as well as pronounced changes in the organization of work. Drawing on case studies of the branch jobs in two large American banks, our goal is two-fold: to examine the extent to which the stylized account of skill-biased technological change actually holds with respect to these jobs, and to identify additional organizational factors that may help to explain why some branch workers' earnings have risen while others' have dropped.

Specifically, we ask the following questions: To what extent did technology drive the workplace restructuring in our case study banks? Did the implementation of new technology result in similar changes in job titles, job content, and earnings in the two banks? Or were there important differences in how technology was implemented, and therefore in the effects on worker outcomes? Finally, did managerial strategies also have an independent effect on the redistribution of skill requirements, responsibilities, and earnings within the organization?

Our study begins with the premise that decisions governing the distribution of new technologies in the workplace are not determined solely by the skill requirements of the technology itself. Managers also consider the larger dictates of business strategy, and their decisions about technology must be considered in the context of strategically driven work restructuring.

These strategic considerations may also result in a differential distribution of rewards, even among workers who participate in technological upgrading. Our industry-focused case studies examine these managerial decisions, with the goal of providing a deeper and more nuanced understanding of some of the mechanisms that have contributed to rising inequality.

TECHNOLOGY, STRATEGY, AND EARNINGS

The structure of jobs and earnings in the American labor market has changed greatly in the past two decades. Starting in the 1970s, average earnings stagnated or even declined. Though college graduates largely escaped these trends, those with less education did not, and earnings inequality increased dramatically. Technological change has emerged as the leading explanation for this increase. From this perspective, substantial numbers of American workers are not meeting the demand for technological acumen and thus find their wages declining, while at the same time, skilled workers are reaping the benefits of their qualifications.

The empirical evidence supporting this intuitively appealing explanation remains sketchy and mixed. Industry-level (Autor, Katz, and Krueger 1998; Berman, Bound, and Griliches 1994) and establishment-level (Doms, Dunne, and Troske 1997) research suggests that computers and skilled labor are complementary. Analyses of individual earnings data are less definitive: some evidence suggests that jobs in higher-technology workplaces require higher levels of skill and thus command higher wages (Krueger 1993), but there are alternative explanations for these relationships (DiNardo and Pischke 1997). Further, research focused more directly on jobs tends to show that technological change has indeterminate effects. Technology may upskill jobs, deskill them, or render them obsolete, even within the same firm (Adler 1992; Adler and Borys 1995; Gappelli 1996; Hirschhorn 1984; Moss 2001; Rule and Attewell 1989; Zuboff 1988). Levy and Murnane (1996), for example, showed that one bank's changes in formal skill requirements for back-office accountants were not easily explained by changes in computerization.

The picture is further complicated because technological change as defined in the inequality literature typically refers to a broad but vague assortment of unobserved changes in the production process. The term "technological change" can refer not only to changes in machines, computer hardware, and computer software, but also to changes in the way that work is organized (Bresnahan, Brynjolffson, and Hitt 2000; Hunter and Lafkas 2000). Thus organizational restructuring—including the introduction of new work practices—may also have implications for skills and earnings (Cappelli et al. 1997; Fernandez 2000; Smith 1997).

Finally, changes in technology and work practices may themselves be driven by managerial business strategies. For example, research in the service sector has shown growing use of market segmentation strategies. Segmentation strategies, in guiding the deployment of technology and the reorganization of work, can lead to job stratification. Higher-value customer segments have been found to be associated with higher wages and better opportunities for workers in a diverse range of industries, including fast-foods and retail sales (Bailey and Bernhardt 1997; MacDonald and Sirianni 1996), computers and high-tech (Colclough and Tolbert 1992), telecommunications (Batt and Keefe 1998; Batt 2000), nursing homes (Eaton 2000; Hunter 2000), and financial services (Keitner and Finegold 1996).

Given this complexity, evidence from the ground—the firms and the specific workplaces in which restructuring occurs and technology is actually implemented —may advance our understanding of the underlying processes that have led to increased inequality. This evidence is critical, for it has become clear that firms are responding to increased competition and restructuring work in ways that are not easily captured by deterministic views of technology. The business press abounds with examples of innovative companies that have created high-quality and well-paid jobs, yet just as prevalent are accounts of low-wage strategies, deskilled jobs, and substitution of contingent workers for full-time workers.

Firms may also use technology to differentially reorganize jobs: upskilling in some parts of the organization, automating and routinizing in others. Thus restructuring and technology can interact to produce different outcomes for workers, within the same industry and even the same firm. Firm-level research is required to shed light on some of the mechanisms that have produced the aggregate trends in wages, showing in more detail the ways in which technology is introdu ced into the workplace and how it transforms job content and skill requirements, and adding explanatory power to our accounts of change in the labor market based on surveys of individuals or industries.

In this paper, we therefore examine the strategic and technological trends that have led to changes in front-line banking jobs, drawing on both industry-level analysis and case studies of two large American banks. We note that changes within organizations can affect earnings outcomes through two routes: they may change the distribution of workers across jobs with different wages, or they may alter the content of particular jobs and thus the wages that those jobs command (Gappelli 1996; Attewell 1987). Our study concentrates more directly on the second route and less directly on the first; to fully capture changes in the distributions of workers would require an equilibrium-style account of net effects on the wage structure both within and across firms (as well as beyond the banking industry). Instead, our case studies examine how technology is actually implemented in the workplace (with an eye toward variation), and the extent to which managerial strategy plays an independent role in that process. Our goal is to deepen current understanding of the forces underlying the polarization of wages and jobs.

AMERICAN BANKING IN THE 1980S AND 1990S

Competition and Technology

From the 1940s until the early 1980s, competition in the American banking industry was restricted. The Bank Act of 1933 (usually called the Glass-Steagall Act) established commercial banking as a distinct entity by separating both the ownership and the activities of commercial banks from those of other financial service providers. The Federal Deposit Insurance Corporation insured individuals' deposits against bank failure, banks with FDIC charters were prohibited from offering investment and insurance products, and many states had strict regulations prohibiting or limiting interstate banking. The resulting stability in the industry especially characterized its retail side, which provided financial products and services to individuals and small businesses through local branches.

The 1980s and early 1990s, in contrast, have been characterized as "the most turbulent period in banking since the Great Depression" (Berger, Kashyap, and Scalise 1995). Banks introduced a vast array of new information technology-hardware, software, and telecommunications equipment-spending about $60,000 per employee on information technology over the 1980s (Keltner 1995). The introduction of Automatic Teller Machines (ATMs) and new back-office processing technologies dramatically decreased the costs associated with handling and processing individual transactions. New software dramatically improved the ability of banks to manage their huge stores of customer data. Telephone banking, and more recently PC-based banking, also appeared as alternative channels for delivery of retail financial services.

These new technologies interacted with gradual deregulation [3] to reshape the industry. Deregulation had three major effects. First, it prompted consolidation of the industry. The loosening of interstate banking laws allowed banks to expand their operations across state lines and encouraged a wave of banking mergers. Improvements in technology made consolidation more desirable, allowing economies of scale and reducing the costs associated with back-office processing. Thus the banking industry shrank from over 12,000 banks in 1987 to only 8,000 banks by 1995 (Berger, Kashyap, and Scalise 1995), and consolidation continues to this day.

Second, deregulation heightened price competition among banks. New technologies intensified the competition, improving banks' ability to adjust prices and terms of financial products. Basic financial services began to resemble commodity products. As margins on these standard products diminished, reducing payroll costs through tighter and more flexible staffing arrangements became integral to survival in the industry.

Third, as deregulation broke down barriers between banks and other financial services providers, banks began to offer investment products through their branch networks, often in partnership with mutual fund companies. They also explored partnerships with insurance companies (witness the 1998 merger of Citicorp and Travelers). Increasingly, banks had to compete for their traditional deposit customers with brokerage houses and money market funds, each of which began to offer standard products such as checking accounts. With this opening of markets, banks began to develop and introduce technologies designed to make the cross-selling of multiple financial products efforts more effective. Integrated databases provided more complete information on customer relationships and transaction patterns, and more sophisticated software helped banks to identify sales opportunities and to act on those opportunities (by prompting employees to make sales inquiries, for example).

These new systems also enabled banks to sharpen their customer segmentation strategies. Banks directed "transaction-based approaches" (Keltner and Finegold 1996) toward customers with low profit potential, seeking to lower costs by replacing teller service with ATMs and telephone banking. By contrast, "relationship banking" strategies.

FOREIGN BANKS

In their twenty years since their entry into Australia, foreign bank performance has been considered a failure. This paper will canvass this and related issues and argue that some of these perceptions may have been based upon inappropriate expectations. It will be argued that the foreign banks have been an important component in the ongoing process of Australian financial system efficiency improvement and globalisation.

September 2005 was the twentieth anniversary of post-deregulation foreign bank entry into Australia. Today of the sixteen initial licensees, only two, Citigroup and HSBC, retain their subsidiary licences. The sixteen new entrants were representatives of the world's largest (and at that time) most successful banks, and also represented Australia's major partners for trading and investment. Thus, they appeared to possess the attributes necessary to make a success of their new Australian operations, yet this has not necessarily been the case.

This paper will canvass the entry of foreign banks into Australia to provide a survey of what we do and do not know about foreign banks operating in Australia.

Despite the initial promise, foreign bank entry into Australia has been considered a failure from the perspective of size, profits and market activity. But too much may have been expected, based upon inappropriate assumptions which created expectations that were never likely to be fulfilled.

The paper is structured as follows. First, the process of foreign bank entry into Australia will be considered. Second, the impact of the foreign banks upon the Australian banking system and the activities of the foreign banks will be discussed. The paper will conclude by offering some directions where further research and discussion would be valuable.

FOREIGN BANKS IN AUSTRALIA

Australia has an established history of restriction upon foreign bank entry post-World War Two. The last foreign bank licensed in Australia prior to deregulation was the Bank of China, which was granted a branch licence in 1942, but which closed in 1972. Several other foreign banks were established in the mid-to-late nineteenth century.

Between World War Two and the Campbell Inquiry, foreign banks entered Australia as representative offices or as merchant banks and finance companies, or often, if conducting intermediation, via joint ventures with a locally incorporated partner (AFSI, 1980). The mining boom in the late 1960s saw the merchant bank and finance company community expand to meet the demand for finance which the regulated banking sector was unable to meet (Pauly, 1987).

In the early 1970s the Bank (Shareholdings) Act was passed, restricting ownership of an existing bank to 10% of shares issued, and reflecting a view that domestic ownership of this key sector was important. Regulations were introduced, effectively prohibiting foreign ownership of more than 50% of a non-bank (Pauly, 1987), subject to a few exceptions, for either institution specific or historical reasons (AFSI, 1980).

This situation came to an end with deregulation of the Australian financial system. In September 1984, applications were accepted from foreign banks for banking licences and restrictions upon non-bank status for foreign banks were lifted. Sixteen foreign banks were invited to take up banking status in February 1985, and fifteen eventually established subsidiaries.

It was originally envisaged that these sixteen licences would be the complete ration of such licences (AFSI, 1981, pp. 444-445). Subsequently foreign banks have been permitted to apply for a full bank licence as a subsidiary, or as a foreign bank branch, provided that their activities are restricted to wholesale banking operations.

DEREGULATION AND THE PROCESS OF FOREIGN BANK ENTRY

A study commissioned for the Campbell Committee by Davis and Lewis (1982) recommended the entry of foreign banks on several grounds. These included increased competition in banking and particularly the transfer of special skills that would lead to lower costs in Australian banking. The initial lack of branch networks for foreign banks was expected to stimulate interbank markets. The foreign bank submissions to the Campbell Committee emphasised their preference for bank rather than non-bank status and, with the exception of Citibank, they emphasised that their main area of operations would be in the wholesale market.

Davis and Lewis (1982) identified foreign bank advantages to be: (i) a significant knowledge capital from its international dealings; (ii) the ownership of new technology; and (iii) superior skills in funds allocation. Offsetting this were the domestic banks' possession of local knowledge and the diseconomies often referred to as the 'liability of foreignness' (Berger, et al., 2004, Miller and Parkhe, 2002). These diseconomies include monitoring, staff turnover, diseconomies of scale for retail operations, and factors such as culture, language, and market structure acting as barriers to entry.

The inquiry process also highlighted the preference of multinational banks to operate in the host country as a branch compared to the general preference of multinational firms to operate as a separately incorporated subsidiary. The branch is the preferred organisational form for banks as it places the resources of the entire bank behind the branch, and thus engenders confidence (Davis and Lewis, 1982).

The main reason given by the Campbell Committee for admitting foreign banks was the spur to competition, seen as a more effective threat to the entrenched position of the incumbent banks than potential domestic entrants (AFSI, 1981). Foreign banks already had resources and knowledge capital. Many were already established in Australia as non-banks, had international standing and the public confidence which that brings, and were considered to be less likely to be inhibited by the possible risks and costs of entry into a new market.

The election of the Hawke Labor Government in March 1983 prevented the full implementation of the Campbell Committee's recommendations regarding foreign bank entry. (2) Major domestic bank mergers in June 1981 pre-positioned the domestic banks to withstand the impact of foreign bank entry (Hall, 1987) and made the issue of foreign bank entry urgent (Pauly, 1987, p. 44). The Hawke Government established the Martin Review which considered (in part) the foreign bank issue. This Review recommended allowing foreign bank entry under more restrictive conditions than those recommended by the Campbell Committee. They included a one-off tender for bank licences with the number of licences being limited to between four and six (AFS, 1984, p. 71).

The Federal Government announced in September 1984 that it would accept applications from foreign banks for banking licences, and declared a twelve-month moratorium on foreign investment restrictions for non bank financial institutions. The guidelines adopted were essentially those of the Martin Review, including the expectation that a full range of banking services was to be offered. However, a local equity participation requirement was relaxed. Forty-two applications were received, while at the same time more than a hundred new or restructured foreign-owned merchant banks were established (Pauly, 1987).

Reciprocity, together with an expectation of a geographical spread in the location of the new banks, were suggested as possible criteria for selection of successful applicants. The reciprocity issue was considered by Pauly (1987) to be particularly important from the perspective of Australian bank's ability to enter the Japanese market. (3) In February 1985, sixteen licences were awarded, over twice the number originally expected. The large number of licences issued was justified on the basis of the quality of the applications. Pauly (1987) argued that political considerations such as reciprocity led to the expansion of the number of licences issued. Nine out of the sixteen applications were approved with complete foreign ownership (Batten, 1993, pp. 44-45) and in the case of the Japanese banks the Japanese Ministry of Finance was assigned three Australian licences, which were then allocated to the successful Japanese banks (Pauly, 1987, p. 85). With the exception of J. P. Morgan, which elected not to take up its licence, all of the foreign banks were operating in Australia by May 1986.

The subsequent Martin Report led to the removal of the previous ration of foreign bank licences and permission for foreign banks to operate in Australia as branches, rather than as wholly owned subsidiaries, provided their activities did not imperil Australian retail depositors.

FOREIGN BANKS: IMPACT AND ACTIVITIES

The entrance of foreign banks into Australia has been regarded as a failure, particularly when measured against their target of a 20% market share within five years of entry (SCOFPA, 1991). (4) Other contributing factors were their lack of impact upon the retail market, due to the expectations of the Martin Review (Ackland and Harper,

1992, FSI, 1997; p 595, Kavanagh, 1991), and the poor profits of some entrants (Ferguson, 1990). This poor performance has been attributed to the high entry barriers faced (SCOFPA, 1991, p 151), with the foreign banks being considered the 'cannon fodder' of deregulation. It has been argued that the foreign banks were never likely to succeed, given the creation of four dominant banks by the mergers of 1981 and the increased spending of these four banks to increase these barriers to entry (Ferguson, 1990).

Size and Market Share

The foreign banks did not anticipate the corporate collapses of the late 1980s when, in 1985, they forecast their 1990 market-share. The impact of loan losses from the corporate collapses of the late 1980s upon the foreign banks' capital bases considerably reduced their ability to make the loans necessary to meet the initial target of 20% market share. Given their relatively small size, the corporate collapses affected the foreign banks in a disproportionate manner (Sykes, 1994, pg 2). Within three years of entry, the foreign banks had revised their projected market share to 15% (Reinecke, 1988) and the grant of more licences than expected had resulted in downward revisions of expected profits.

Interestingly, recent data illustrates that the foreign bank market share is 18%, close to the pre-deregulation target. Williams (1998a, and b) found that foreign banks in Australia were generally larger than foreign merchant banks and those banks with larger parents generally had larger Australian operations. However, in terms of competitive implications, it is worth noting that a global study by Claessens, et al. (2001) found that it is the number, not the size, of foreign banks that acts as a competitive stimulus to the incumbent banks.

Profits

The foreign banks had stated that their main areas of operations would be corporate lending, followed by money-market operations, and trade finance and they expected to earn 40% of their profits from corporate lending. The resulting exposure in a competitive, newly deregulated, market generated considerable problems when the corporate collapses of the late 1980s occurred. Losses resulted, including in some cases, the loss of their start-up capital and some subsequent capital injections (Ferguson, 1991).

These losses led to the perception that foreign banks were not profitable, although their profit experience is more accurately described as mixed (Linklater, 1989). Table 1 details the profit outcomes for the period 1986 to 1993 and provides a more balanced view. Losses were concentrated in the period 1989 to 1991 and several made profits over the majority of the period. Some banks, such as Bankers Trust and Citibank, have generated returns higher than the incumbent Australian banks (Valentine, 1990).

The Japanese-owned banks have reported the most consistent results. They eschewed retail banking activity in Australia, and were disproportionately active in off-balance sheet activity (Reserve Bank of Australia, 1987). Batten (1994) considered that their lower losses reflected their avoidance of a growth-oriented strategy. The other foreign banks were more willing to accept lower profits in order to gain market share (Batten, 1994, p 9, Metcalfe, 1989,). By avoiding the retail sector the Japanese banks have not borne the costs and losses associated with overcoming entry barriers.

Foreign banks are generally less profitable (on average) than their domestic counterparts, and profits are more variable. They are less reliant upon intermediation, as measured by net interest margins, and are more reliant upon fee income (non-interest) income. However, there is considerable variation, reflecting two factors: (i) the different strategies pursued; and (ii) the different levels of risk. Claessens, et al. (2001) found that foreign banks operating in developed nations generally have lower interest margins, profits, and overhead expenses than the incumbent banks, with the reverse holding for developing nations. It was also found that foreign bank entry resulted in lower profits, non-interest income, and overall expenses for the incumbent banks in the host nation.

Williams (2003) found that increases in competitor market-share acted to reduce foreign bank profits. It was argued that the concentration of the Australian banking system acted as a barrier to entry to the foreign banks. Further, it was found that those banks operating in Australia as licensed banks, as opposed to merchant banks, earned an average of 1.5% lower return on assets. Banks from nations with higher levels of home GDP growth experienced higher Australian profits, possibly reflecting a substitution between international and multinational banking. Those foreign banks with a larger Australian presence were generally more profitable in Australia.

Risk

As can be seen the lower average profits of foreign banks have been accompanied by higher average levels of capital and bad loans. The higher levels of capital most likely reflect the need to hold a buffer of extra capital against realised loan losses, possibly at the request of the prudential regulators. The higher levels of provisions for loan losses and doubtful debt expense reflect higher risk loan portfolios and possibly, due to their smaller size, less diversified portfolios. These results are unsurprising, given the wholesale market focus of the foreign banks, combined with the bad debt experiences of the late 1980s and early 1990s. Again these measures display the highest variation for the foreign banks, demonstrating the diversity of strategies and experiences of this group. Naughton and Harvie (1996) argue that the post-deregulation volatility experienced by the Australian banking system reflected Minsky's 'financial instability hypothesis' and that entry of the foreign banks was a significant factor in this volatility. However, these post-deregulation losses were not isolated to the foreign bank sector, with the State Bank of Victoria and the State Bank of South Australia showing the largest losses (Gizycki and Lowe, 2000).

Retail Banking

The Campbell Committee clearly stated that foreign banks should not be required to offer a full range of banking services. But the Martin Review reversed this position and it is likely that this retail requirement was motivated by political rather than economic considerations. As noted by Pauly (1987, p. 87), it was the retail banking issue that later drew public attention away from the fundamental restructuring of the wholesale finance markets which had resulted from foreign bank entry.

It was expected that much of the competition in retail banking to be generated by the foreign banks would come from the joint venture banks (Chase AMP and National Mutual Royal Bank), and also Citibank and Bank of America. However, of the four foreign banks initially expected to provide a retail banking presence in Australia, only Citibank continues to provide retail services.

Edey and Gray (1996) considered that the foreign banks retained a focus away from the retail markets. Few examples of completely new foreign entrants to banking markets can be found in the retail sector (Bourke, 1990). As indicated by Guillen and Tschoegl (2000), international retail banking is a relatively rare phenomenon. Ferguson (1990) argued that National Mutual Royal Bank was the most successful of the foreign banks in the retail sector. The joint venture was sold to ANZ Bank for $400 million, a 68% return over the period, or a 12.6% annualised return. Pope (1993) concluded that the foreign banks that have realised the best returns in Australia have done so by avoiding the retail sector. But Edey and Gray (1996) have considered that some innovations in retail banking were the result of foreign bank entry, particularly in the area of credit cards. The lack of impact of the foreign banks in the retail sector was due to large established customer franchises.

Other foreign banks that have attempted a retail banking strategy are Barclays Bank and NatWest, and more recently ING and BankWest. Barclays and NatWest both withdrew from retail operations in the early 1990s. As a result of these withdrawals, foreign retail banking has been described as a disappointment (Ackland and Harper, 1992, p. 64; FSI, 1997; Martin, 1992). This experience provides some support for the argument that forcing the foreign banks to participate in particular sectors of the economy would result in inefficiencies (AFSI, 1981, p. 442).

The more recent foreign entrants to retail banking, ING and BankWest, have pursued quite different strategies. ING has positioned itself quite successfully as an internet bank, offering convenience and high yield for depositors and using mortgage brokers and securitisation to deliver housing loans. By contrast, BankWest is the 'rebadged' R & I Bank of Western Australia, now owned by HBOS. The strategies of ING and BankWest are tending to converge, with both emphasising internet delivery, where the barriers to entry are considered to be lower. The foothold needed in retail banking by BankWest was acquired rather than developed on a green-fields basis, suggesting that allowing takeovers of existing banks and non-banks could have been the main route to generate competition in this market. Given the political climate of the time, large-scale foreign takeovers of Australian financial institutions was unlikely. The Reserve Bank of Australia considered that the experience of the first fifteen foreign banks has demonstrated that obtaining sufficient size in retail banking to overcome the existing barriers to entry is "extraordinarily difficult—if not impossible" (Reserve Bank of Australia, 1994, p. 17).

Wholesale Banking

Foreign banks and merchant banks increased the level of competition in wholesale banking (Milbourne and Cumberworth, 1991). Foreign bank profits in the wholesale market have been mixed with some adversely affected by the corporate collapses of the late 1980s, while others reported consistent profits. The Reserve Bank of Australia (1994) considered that the over-use of credit which preceded the corporate collapse of the late 1980s could be attributed in part to the entry of the foreign banks and their desire to have an immediate market share.

The foreign banks were disproportionately active in off-balance sheet financing (Linklater, 1989). Their balance-sheet composition also reflected their wholesale focus, with a greater emphasis upon bill financing and foreign currency liabilities and a larger proportion of foreign currency assets than domestic banks. This continued, with the foreign banks in 1994 having high relative market shares in the areas of foreign exchange, derivative securities, and funds management (Reserve Bank of Australia, 1994). They had worse bad-debt experiences but maintained an average capital ratio of 15% (BIS risk weighted guidelines) as compared with an average of 12% for all banks operating in Australia (Reserve Bank of Australia, 1994).

The foreign banks have generally been the most active in providing off-balance sheet, loan-like credit substitutes (see Table 4 above). The foreign banks also bear the proportionately highest level of foreign exchange risk, measured as foreign exchange liabilities minus assets. The situation for off-balance sheet, market-related activity is less clear-cut due to the lower level of voluntary disclosure by the foreign banks in this area. Accordingly, the earlier statement by the Reserve Bank of Australia (1994) that the foreign banks are disproportionately active in this area must be accepted for guidance.

Efficiency

Studies of efficiency and economies of scale in Australian banking are relatively rare, and those considering foreign banks are rarer still. Hogan (1991) and Williams (1997) looked at ratios such as operating profit to average assets (or operating expenses) and reached mixed results. These simple ratios have been criticised as inadequate measures of bank efficiency because they fail to account for the multiple inputs and outputs produced by banks. More recent studies by Avkiran (2000 and 1999), Neal (2004), Sathye (2001), and Sturm and Williams (2004) have estimated Australian bank efficiency from the perspective of a firm using multiple inputs to produce multiple outputs by applying a number of different techniques. (15) Of these, only Sathye (2001) and Sturm and Williams (2004 and 2005) have directly addressed the issue of foreign bank efficiency in Australia. Sathye (2001) used a single year's data (1996) and found domestic banks to be more efficient on average, but that this difference was not statistically significant, due in part to sample size limitations. Sturm and Williams (2004) used a larger sample and longer time-period than previous studies, and concluded that bank efficiency improved over the post-deregulation period and that foreign banks were more efficient than domestic banks, due mainly to the foreign banks demonstrating superior scale efficiency. It was also found that the Big-Four banks exhibited decreasing returns to scale, probably because of over-expenditure on banking infrastructure (particularly in retail banking) in order to construct barriers to entry. This finding was consistent with that of Stearn and Tress (1983). Similarly to Claessens, et al. (2001) Sturm and Williams (2004)also found that foreign bank entry acts as a spur to innovation and efficiency.

Some of these results stand in contrast to Berger, et al. (2000), who found that foreign-owned financial institutions are generally less efficient in developed nations. Sturm and Williams (2004) argue that the rationing of foreign bank licences resulted in the selection of foreign banks with attributes enabling them to overcome the 'liabilities of foreignness' (Miller and Parkhe, 2002).

The issue of economies of scale and foreign bank entry has received considerable discussion during the deregulation process. (16) Foreign banks were considered to possess inherent economies of scale, as a direct extension of their other international operations, and so were capable of competing immediately with the incumbent banks (Reserve Bank of Australia, 1994).

Sturm and Williams (2005) estimated a model of foreign bank efficiency in Australia aimed at identifying causal factors that represent a limited form of the global advantage hypothesis. It was found that the limited global advantage hypothesis was supported particularly for banks from the United Kingdom. The policy of following clients was found to reduce efficiency, as measured using a revenue-based model. Thus it can be concluded that the policy of following clients increases size, but not profits or efficiency. The market share of competitor banks, particularly the Big-Four banks, was found to act as a barrier to entry, especially in the retail market. Acquisition, as represented by the case of BankWest, reduced the efficiency impact of this barrier to entry. It was also concluded that internet banking, as represented by ING Bank, did not improve the efficiency of revenue creation, at least in the start-up phases. No evidence was found of any parent-size effects upon efficiency.

Conclusion: What Do We Know and What Don't We Know?

On first inspection, it would seem that the foreign banks possessed attributes that would guarantee their success in Australia. They were hand-picked and represented a cross-section of the largest and most successful banks in the world. Their home nations were (and are) Australia's major trading and investment partners, with well-established financial systems. In many cases the parent banks had extensive experience in multinational operations. Further, the Australian financial system was newly deregulated, providing new opportunities in a previously highly structured and restricted market. With hindsight, however, the foreign banks might be seen as the shock troops of deregulation (Ferguson, 1990) and would not necessarily survive their experience.

The lag between the formation of the Big-Four Australian banks and the entry of the foreign banks allowed the incumbent banks time to position themselves for the foreign bank's entry and so lessen their impact. The barriers to entry were particularly apparent in retail banking, but it was unreasonable to expect active involvement in retail banking.

While the foreign banks suffered large losses in the early 1990s, their losses were far less than those of the State-owned banks, which had the advantages of incumbency and established networks. The foreign banks, with smaller, more concentrated and more wholesale portfolios experienced some large losses associated with high-profile corporate collapses accentuating public perceptions of loss.

The entry of the foreign banks can be seen as important in the on-going process of efficiency improvement and innovation, as well as increasing the globalisation of the Australian financial system.

Overall, our understanding of the drivers of performance of foreign banks is still relatively meagre; and our knowledge of the organisational and strategic choices made by the foreign banks is still relatively poor. However, some of the unique features of the Australian experience offer potential for useful contributions to the study of multinational banking; and the issue of offshore banking in Australia is an area that offers potential for fruitful and relevant research. The application of case-study type approaches to foreign banking is also another worthwhile possibility, particularly in the areas of mergers and internet banking.

Chapter

12

Business Cycles in a Financially Deregulated America

A very long time ago, in 1980, Brookings published my paper entitled "The Central Role of Credit Crunches in Recent Financial History" (Wojnilower 1980). Presumably the emphasis of this and subsequent articles on the transcendent role of financial institutions and credit in business fluctuations is what led the chairman to invite the present paper, although I am an economist practicing in the financial rather than the scholarly or government community.

The 1980 article concluded that cyclically significant retardation or reduction in credit and aggregate demand occur only when there is an interruption in the supply of credit – a 'credit crunch.' Such interruptions may be prompted, intentionally or accidentally, by the destruction of lenders' incentives through regulatory rigidities … or the emergence of serious default problems in major institutions or markets. Following such episodes … the authorities … and the private markets … have deliberately reshaped the financial structure so as to prevent the recurrence of that particular form of credit supply interruption. It went on to argue that removal of the regulatory constraints would lead to more frequent and inherently much more dangerous default crises. In fact this has happened, as will be recounted here, necessitating a series of breathtaking lender-of-last-resort rescues by central banks and governments. The potential for such crises continues to multiply, while the means for dealing with them are diminshing.

Although the Brookings paper included the business cycles of the essentially noninflationary period 1953-1965, while it was being written and published US inflation was racing toward double digits. American political and economic hegemony was eroding, and the chronically depreciating dollar spread the inflationary bias worldwide. Commodity prices in general and oil prices in particular were multiplying. Labor unions in the US and elsewhere applied relentless upward pressure on money wage rates.

Crucial to furthering the inflationary outcome, financial deregulation was inhibiting the tightening of Federal Reserve monetary policy. Removal of official interest rate ceilings kept credit flowing despite successive upsurges in nominal interest rates to unheard of levels — levels so high that most experts took for granted they must be severely restrictive, when in actuality they were not. Meanwhile the new competition among deregulated financial institutions led to bankruptcies with potential for systemic disruption, deterring the authorities from pressing tight policies home.

How changed are today's circumstances! The Cold War is over. The hegemony of the dollar is unchallenged; left to its own devices, it tends to appreciate. American business and technology are viewed as leading a world economy globalized to an extent that would have been incomprehensible in 1980. In the industrial countries, inflation is subdued. Oil and other commodities are abundant: their relative and absolute prices have fallen. In the US, labor union power has collapsed, part of a pervasive rightward shift in political tastes.

With such a sea-change in political and economic climate, it is not surprising that the US business cycle has been gentler and kinder. From 1953 through 1982, as registered by the National Bureau of Economic Research, there were seven business downturns (plus at least one "close call"), each associated with a credit crunch due to governmental regulations or actions. Since then, notwithstanding ample turbulence and failures in financial markets, only a single mild recession of eight months has been recognized, and the timing of its onset was unrelated to any serious credit disruption. With the dollar free of pressure or challenge, and inflation markedly decelerated, it is an easy path of least resistance for the Federal Reserve to forestall recessions by responding openhandedly to threatened or actual financial crises. And so it has.

Thus, for the US, the narrow business-cycle aspect of my Brookings paper has been inapplicable. To this distant American observer, however, the model appears to have remained useful in explaining cyclical setbacks in many other nations that suffered severe banking shocks after 1980. The list, not necessarily accurate or complete, might include: Australia, New Zealand, and Japan; Scandinavia and the U.K.; as well as Canada, Brazil, Argentina, and Mexico. Obviously I am unqualified to pronounce detailed judgment on these instances.

But even for the US, the approach remains a useful way of examining the macroeconomic consequences of financial change. Although recessions have been largely avoided, the financial system continues to play a prominent role in shaping business fluctuations. Depending on its particular organization and response, real shocks will result in different economic outcomes. Reciprocally, shocks that originate in the financial sector can and do affect the path of the real economy. The process of mutual adaptation between finance and the economy never comes to rest. Nor, consequently, do asset prices or business conditions.

The present paper undertakes a highly selective review of the last fifteen years or so from this standpoint, focusing on the changes in financial institutions, instruments, and practice most influential on the ebb and flow of credit expansion and general business.

DEMOLISHING THE FINANCIAL ZOO

From the 1930s on into the 1980s, the American financial system resembled a well-run and orderly zoo. The various species — banks, securities dealers, insurance companies, etc. — were neatly caged within functional and geographical specialties, prevented and protected from competition with one another. Although competition remained active within each cage, specialized and benign keepers made sure it did not assume lethal proportions. And as in a real zoo, it was just as safe for the public to view a lion as a rabbit: deposit insurance and other safeguards were firmly in place.

This arrangement, which reflected the country's traditional agrarian localism and hostility toward bankers and monopoly, intensified by the disaster of the 1930s, worked well for the thirty years or more during which it was free from serious internal or foreign challenge. Inflation and interest rates remained low, and the rate of saving higher than it has been subsequently. But the tranquil zoo was doomed by technological innovations that rendered the geographical and functional separations grossly inefficient and impossible to preserve. The zoo was technologically and ideologically obsolete in a world increasingly dedicated to freedom and hostile to authority (Wojnilower 1992b).

Deregulation smashed the constraints on deposit and lending rates, geographical scope, portfolio behavior, and other practices that had segregated and sheltered the various financial intermediaries. Each previously secure and tame animal suddenly became both prey and predator. The population within the cages, already excessive by competitive standards, was hardly suited to life in the wild. And now each species had to compete with every other. Some fell extinct, others adapted, and new ones emerged. Although institutions named banks, insurance companies, securities dealers, and so forth, survive to this day, their appearance and behavior would be largely unrecognizable to a 1960s observer.

For firms suddenly facing vanishing profit margins, finding new revenue sources became a desperate matter of survival. The predictable consequence was a rush of lending in unfamiliar fields, unfamiliar instruments, and to unfamiliar clientele. The risks were unavoidably enormous, but preferable to the certain death most deregulated financial businesses faced were they to stand still.

THE EXPLOSION OF CREDIT

Just when the inflationary experience of the 1970s and early 1980s was generating virtually insatiable credit demand, financial deregulation made it easy for would-be borrowers to obtain command over "other people's money" cheaply and with few strings attached. Inordinate credit demand was matched by extraordinary eagerness to lend.

During the first half of 1980, the US experienced a sharp but brief recession triggered by 20 per cent loan interest rates and the imposition of direct credit controls on an already shaky economy. As soon as the recession became visible, however, interest rates were lowered and the controls lifted soon after. The resurgence in credit growth and economic activity — and inflation — was immediate and substantial.

Notably failing to participate in the recovery, however, were the thrift institutions and homebuilding industry which depended on these intermediaries for mortgages. Savings banks and savings and loan associations were hampered in attracting deposits because the rates they were allowed to pay remained partly regulated. Meanwhile their income from fixed-rate mortgages, mostly acquired in the low-interest rate past, was barely adequate to meet interest rate expense. The "crunch" in the mortgage industry became crippling as short-term interest rates rebounded to near 20 per cent by mid-1981, touching off yet another, more severe, and longer-lasting recession (Wojnilower 1985).

Renewed easing of monetary policy in 1982 launched a strong and durable business expansion that lasted almost eight years until the oil price eruption caused by the Iraqi seizure of Kuwait in 1990. The 1982 business revival featured a virtual explosion in credit. At the trough of the recession and onset of the recovery, consumer price inflation collapsed down to 2 per cent, while virtually all except money-market interest rates remained in double digits. But even in this economy just emerging from recession, double-digit real rates did not perceptibly deter credit expansion. It happened to be the time when the regulatory authorities, frightened by the consequences of their own measures explicitly intended to exterminate specialized home-mortgage lending institutions, undertook to liberalize the prudential rules and to ignore if not encourage violations. From a severely depressed 1.06 million housing starts in 1982, homebuilding vaulted to 1.70 million starts a year later. Consumer credit also surged, fueled in part by new legislation that forbade (previously pervasive) discrimination against female borrowers, a liberalization propitiously timed to suit lenders frantically seeking new clients. Similar credit eruptions took place later during the 1980s in the financing of mergers and acquisitions, so-called "leveraged buy-outs", junk (low quality) bond issuance, real estate investment trusts (REITs), and even "emerging markets", notwithstanding the recency of the Mexican crisis of 1982 and other country credit disasters that effectively decapitalized several of the largest banks.

With so much lending to novel borrowers in novel instruments, pushed by inexperienced lenders spurred by high liquidity and desperate need for income, major defaults were to be expected — and materialized. The authorities, rightfully concerned about systemic collapse, were kept busy putting out fires. Each time they succeeded, market participants became more complacent with respect to risk-taking. With widespread economic slack prompting relatively easy monetary policies in much of the industrial world, and the dollar appreciating strongly until late 1985, the US authorities had little difficulty in cauterizing the problems (the most serious of which was the failure of the Continental Illinois Bank, the 17th largest in the country). By the same token, however, market participants had little difficulty in accumulating fresh tinder to ignite.

THE PLAZA INFLATION

In the fall of 1985, at the notorious "Plaza" meetings in New York, the major powers agreed on policies to bring down the dollar in the context of world-wide monetary easing. Thus was the stage set for a classic credit-inflation business cycle, including a boom in stock prices.

But as we know by hindsight, the game did not play out quite so simply. In the early stages, the inflationary implications were overwhelmed by a collapse in oil prices. Also the US and Japanese monetary authorities were initially reluctant and laggard participants (Volcker and Gyohten 1992). But after mid-1986, US inflation began to creep up. The falling dollar (eventually down 40 per cent from its peak) became a matter of serious international concern and dispute, and the Federal Reserve raised short-term interest rates several times. Nevertheless, stock prices continued to advance until August 1987, when US Treasury bond yields began one of the most intense rises in history, shooting up nearly 3 percentage points to almost 10 1/2 per cent in October.

It appeared that some sort of credit panic, to be followed by recession, was in the offing, just as had happened at previous business cycle peaks. What gave way first, however, was neither the credit structure nor the economy, but the stock market. From the August peak to the low plumbed early afternoon Tuesday, 20 October, New York stock prices plummeted 37 per cent, of which 23 percentage points took place on notorious Black Monday, 19 October, 1987 (Brady 1988). Virtually instantly, the crash spread worldwide.

The plunge threatened to bring down both the credit and the payments system. The natural reaction for banks and others who normally finance securities dealers and clearing houses would have been to reduce credit lines, an action that would have precipitated still more forced sales of stock and, very likely, some spectacular bankruptcies. The danger was, if anything, most pronounced late Tuesday morning, when it appeared as though the previous day's catastrophic losses might be repeated. It was conceivable that checks due from some brokers and clearing houses might not be forthcoming or honored, and that the banks failing to pay such checks might themselves come under suspicion.

Had this disaster been allowed to happen, subsequent economic history might have been very different. The episode would have fit neatly into the "credit-crunch-to-business-downturn" schema. But there was no crunch and there was no downturn.

Federal Reserve Chairman Greenspan publicly guaranteed the liquidity of the market. The White House persuaded major companies to buy back their own stock. Near 2 PM Tuesday the tide was turned by major buying in the stock option and futures markets from sources that have not been identified. What rules may have been bent or broken to prevent disaster, and who made these resolute decisions (perhaps against the advice of legal counsel) is not known.

Soon market functioning was back to normal. But central banks understandably feared the drop in asset values might lead to a recession and a stock market relapse. The Federal Reserve relaxed its posture of restraint and lowered interest rates. The economy continued onward and upward. In such odd fashion, the stock market crash actually forestalled the cyclical downturn the authorities earlier had been prepared to accept.

DERIVATIVES – A WARNING

Because there was so little economic impact, some important lessons of the experience are in danger of being overlooked. The key propellant of the headlong plunge was selling by some fifteen "portfolio insurers", institutional investors who were following a program of automatically selling futures in response to declines in the market value of their portfolios. Three such institutions and one mutual fund reportedly accounted for a major proportion of total market sales (Brady, op.cit.). Every successive drop in value triggered an exponentially increasing quantity of such sales.

Actual (as opposed to textbook) markets consist of human dealers willing to risk capital on bids and offers, and of lenders willing to finance them. Facing a literal selling avalanche, these mortals figuratively and often literally refused to answer the telephone. Trading breakdowns and halts occurred in all stock-related markets. Some of these interruptions are believed to have accentuated the decline, others may have helped to cushion it. Be that as it may, markets are a human institution and as such have limited ability to withstand unbounded waves of one-way orders.

The experience exemplifies the systemic risk inherent in the practice of multiplying "derivative" securities — futures, options, and mixes thereof — which embolden market participants to take larger and more leveraged positions (partly by using derivatives to circumvent rules designed to limit risky exposures). By now the "notional" value of derivatives contracts is in the trillions (millions of millions) of dollars. To be sure, today's leading derivative-market participants have developed more sophisticated computer models to guide their operations, which extend far beyond the stock markets. Although these models are for the most part proprietary and not subject to outside examination, they are constructed by leading experts and probably are as good as the state of the art permits. Whether that is good enough may be questioned, but is not the critical issue. The lesson of 1987 is that such programs are apt to be quite similar to one another. In time of stress they give identical instructions to all users, to sell the same or similar instruments on a grand scale. But when market makers are overwhelmed, the instantaneous liquidity assumed by the models vanishes, and with it the allegedly hedged character of the portfolios.

Insofar as financial futures, options, and derivatives have a function beyond offering enticing betting opportunities, it is to enable the public to buy insurance, however illusory, against macroeconomic risks such as tight money or recessions. To the extent market participants thereby feel relieved of the need to worry about such eventualities, the authorities' difficulties in economic stabilization are escalated. That a derivatives crisis will occur sooner or later, I regard as virtually certain. Whether the economic consequences turn out to be small or large will depend, as in 1987, not on the monetary regime but rather on (among other random factors) the willingness, competence, and freedom of the relevant officials to provide immediate and effective lender-of-last-resort relief.

THE RECESSION OF 1990

With monetary policy eased worldwide after the crash and stock markets regaining their footing, the US economy barely paused in its climb. In Spring 1988 the Federal Reserve had to resume pushing rates up, as growth and inflation reaccelerated. The consumer price index reached a year-over-year increase of 5 1/2 per cent in summer. (This may seem low relative to the double-digit increases of 1980-1982, but recall that in 1971 the Nixon Administration had felt impelled to impose wage and price controls at a time when inflation was 4 per cent and abating.)

The rise in short rates brought to a head the savings-and-loan-association crisis, as it became evident that vast numbers of depositors stood to lose their money. But so serene was the public's confidence in deposit insurance, that no runs developed. This gave time to marshal a political consensus for a huge governmental bail-out that successfully protected depositors. Many commercial banks also came under pressure, the smaller ones because they too were essentially thrift institutions oriented toward real estate, and the larger ones mainly because of involvement in real estate and other financing undertaken on unrealistic assumptions, including permanently low short-term interest rates. Through merger and failure, thousands of depository institutions were eventually liquidated. Yet despite some sensational bankruptcies, nothing resembling a credit crunch transpired.

Neither, until August 1990, was there a recession. Until then business fluctuated narrowly, while aggregate labor and industrial capacity utilization held at high pitch. For most of 1988 and 1989, the dollar tended higher, particularly against the yen. World stock markets soared, with New York surpassing its 1987 high in August 1989 on the way up to a crest reached a year later.

The US economy is judged by the National Bureau of Economic Research to have started to contract in August 1990, immediately before the Iraqi invasion of Kuwait and upspike in world oil prices. Was the minimal August decline just noise, or was it the onset of a genuine cyclical recession that would have unfolded even had there been no oil shock? I share the opinion expressed by Chairman Greenspan that, absent the oil crisis, no recession would have begun then. Whether, when, and in what circumstances a recession might have developed had there been no oil shock (or for that matter, 1987 stock market crash) will forever remain a mystery.

THE "HEADWINDS"

The analysis is muddied by the contemporary emergence of a new regulatory phenomenon. It was expedient for politicians and the public to blame the supervisors for the financial turbulence and its costs. Although these charges were partly warranted, it was at least equally true that the supervisors' warnings often went unheeded, and that their preventive efforts sometimes were thwarted by political pressure. To forestall repetition of yesterday's disasters and deflect future criticism, the authorities reacted by developing more formal regulatory criteria. The most notable instance was the 1988 Basle accord among the major financial powers. This set an eight-per-cent-of-risk-assets capital requirement for commercial banks. The accord pleased the major Western commercial banks because it was seen as restraining competition from Japanese banks, and it also suited the Japanese authorities trying to rein in their financial bubble.

American bank examiners applied a harsher standard. The Basle accord defined Government securities holdings as free of default risk, therefore requiring no capital. The US authorities imposed an additional "leverage ratio" standard that stipulated capital against all assets, and in rising proportion as a bank's soundness was deemed to be threatened (Syron and Randall 1991). Subsequent legislation added an interest-rate risk factor (penalizing holdings of longer-dated maturities) to the capital requirement.

How much, if at all, this "revenge of the supervisors" might have slowed credit expansion and the economy in the run-up to the 1990-91 recession is unclear. But statistical and anecdotal evidence is ample that it materially impeded the economy during the recession and the unusually sluggish early years of the subsequent recovery. Bank stock prices gave little warning that particular banks were in trouble. But once the lightning began to hit, almost all banks found it difficult to raise additional capital, whether from the public or through increased earnings. With higher capital ratios being aggressively enforced, the only available response was to reduce risk assets, notably loans. The best loans were terminated first — because they were the ones that borrowers could repay. New business and mortgage lending, especially to smaller customers, was severely curtailed. The sale of securitized packages of consumer and other loans, which improved capital ratios by removing these assets from balance sheet totals, accelerated greatly. Since they were trying to reduce rather than expand assets, banks also bid much less aggressively for deposits and other funds, opening wider the door for mutual funds (of which more below) (Wojnilower 1992a).

The insistence on higher capital ratios when capital was inaccessible forced banks to shrink their balance sheets, with adverse consequences to the flow of credit. The impact paralleled that of a central bank open-market sale of securities that absorbs bank reserves and compels banks to reduce assets and liabilities. Although the economic effects were particularly severe (and well documented) in the northeastern part of the US known as New England, where banks had been deeply involved in financing a defunct real estate boom, they were national in scope (Brown and Case 1992). It was to these problems that Chairman Greenspan was referring when, on several occasions, he described the economy as battling "a fifty mile an hour headwind." The bank capital squeeze was an important reason why the Federal Reserve kept short-term rates unusually low for a long time, enabling banks to refurbish capital from earnings generated by the large differential between money market and other interest rates.

The state of affairs became known as the "credit crunch". Any resemblance to the crunches of earlier years, however, was in name only. Coming during a time of easy money, the early 1990s *capital* crunch was fundamentally different from the earlier *liquidity* crunches triggered by monetary tightening. In the early 1990s the Federal Reserve would have preferred faster expansion of credit. The previous crunches were credit contractions desired by the authorities, but which got out of hand.

In the course of administering all these rules, the official supervisors became involved in detailed private managerial decisions to a degree that, in the days of the financial zoo, would have been regarded as intolerable government meddling. Not surprisingly, the private-sector managers became determined to rebuild capital to levels that would rule out vulnerability to such official interference in the future. This prolonged the crunch, but in the event they largely succeeded. Thus a classic pattern was repeated: supervisors were determined to avoid recurrence of a loss of control — and supervisees to avoid loss of self-determination.

Today many banks view themselves as overcapitalized and again have become aggressive lenders at exceptionally low returns for added risk.

THE RISE OF MUTUAL AND HEDGE FUNDS

The prolonged weakness of the depository institutions — thrifts and commercial banks — opened the door to new competitors. Of these, so-called money market funds are probably the most important, not only because of their success in attracting household balances, but also for their significant role in drawing consumers into other mutual funds, especially equity investment funds.

In the US, retail money-market fund balances, which comprised over $600 billion in September 1997, typically are subject to check-writing for transactions over $500. As such, they are included in, and account for some 15 per cent of M2. Money market funds are useful also to many wholesale investors: so-called "institutional" money market funds held another $335 billion. Money market funds were created in the early stages of deposit-rate deregulation, when banks were allowed to pay market rates only on deposits of at least $100,000, for the purpose of pooling smaller amounts into sums exceeding that threshold. The decision of the authorities not to prohibit such pooling, as they could have, reflected their desire for the eventual abolition of all deposit rate regulation, which now has been substantially accomplished. In this as other instances (Eurodollars come easily to mind), a device designed to circumvent regulation turned out to have strong staying power long after the regulatory obstacle had lapsed. But unlike at the beginning, only a small fraction of money market funds currently is invested in domestic bank deposits. The bulk is in commercial paper and other short-term credit instruments, replacing funds that used to be provided by commercial banks.

Although the market value of money market fund investments necessarily fluctuates, individual subscribers always buy and redeem shares, on demand, at exactly $1. In the few instances in which market values of the underlying assets have dropped materially below $1, the fund sponsors have contributed additional capital to make up the difference. Unlike the other components of M2 or M3, the funds are backed by neither an official lender of last resort nor deposit insurance. Nor are there legally required reserves, only some prudential investment rules.

By introducing millions of people to mutual funds, money market funds spearheaded an enormous expansion of mutual fund investment. Bond-type mutual funds now are about as large as money-market funds, and equity mutual funds somewhat larger than money and bond funds put together, for a combined aggregate over $4,200 billion — exceeding 10 per cent of the country's total financial assets. Twenty years ago mutual fund assets were a mere $50 billion. Over 40 percent of American households now own equities through mutual funds or directly (indirect holders through defined contribution pension plans or variable annuities issued by insurance companies not included). Fewer than 3 per cent of the population, a US Treasury official estimated at the time, may have owned stock in 1927 (Sobel 1968).

Within most of the large mutual fund groups, shareholders may make overnight transfers by telephone at minimal or no cost between stock and other funds, including money market funds subject to check. Much of the stock acquisition by mutual funds necessarily has come from the household sector, and is an intra-sector transfer in the flow-of-funds accounting sense. But from the public's point of view, there is a large gain in liquidity. It is much simpler and cheaper to rearrange or liquidate mutual fund than stock portfolios. How volatile might be the public's management of fund shares during a time of persistent inflation, recession, or stock price decline has not been tested, because we have not experienced such times since mutual funds became so important. In the aftermath of the 1987 crash, withdrawals were small and did not continue for long. But after the Japanese stock market crash two years later, Japanese mutual funds suffered prolonged major outflows.

The risk of selling panics probably is more pronounced on the part of the funds' youthful professional managers, whose median age is said to be under thirty. Their compensation depends on outperforming one another and they have prompted many large securities price fluctuations by their herd-like response to "news". But whether the panic originates with mutual fund shareholders or managers, this is yet another sector in which the Federal Reserve's lender-of-last-resort responsibilities are liable to be tested.

An interesting question is whether the novel political configuration in which a powerful segment of voters owns shares may eventually constrain monetary policy. The criticism hurled at Chairman Greenspan from all political sides (and his lack of defenders) for mild cautions as to the elevated stock price level, and for a 1/4 percent federal funds rate increase in March 1997 at a time of full employment, is ominous.

Another financial intermediary that, like mutual funds, is not new but has grown to global importance is the hedge fund. A hedge fund is, in effect, a private unadvertised mutual fund limited to wealthy investors willing to incur high risk for high return. Unlike US mutual funds, hedge funds may engage in unlimited short-term trading, take short positions, and borrow. Because hedge funds are essentially unregulated and many are legally domiciled in Caribbean and other tax havens, reliable data are few. Their aggregate capi the market. (Of course the funds do not always operate in moblike fashion; anecdotes relate how, near quarterly statement dates, managers have engaged in uneconomic transactions for the purpose of damaging the market valuation of competitors' holdings.)

In most hedge funds, investors must put up sizable minimum investments, but in an interesting analogy to the birth of money market mutual funds, there are instances of investors in non-US funds fractionating their holdings and reselling them in smaller participations. US-domiciled hedge funds hitherto were limited to a maximum of 100 investors to avoid having to register and be regulated as a mutual fund, but this limit has just been raised to 500 for individuals with financial assets of at least $5 million and fiduciaries with $25 million. Significantly, institutional investment in hedge funds is increasing rapidly, and the formation of new funds is being facilitated by sophisticated servicing provided by some securities dealers who are assuming the transactional burdens. There is thus the potential for this intermediary to become significant for its mass as well as its velocity.

THE SLOPE OF THE YIELD CURVE

Hedge funds provide perhaps the purest illustration how the spread between short and long-term interest rates acts as a pivotal incentive for the financial sector to expand or contract the quantity of credit. A market participant able to borrow at or only slightly over the money market rate is virtually always able to reinvest at a higher rate, but the wider the "spread", the more likely it is to exceed transactions, information, and other costs of business. This is the case not only for hedge funds but for all market "insiders". The money market for wholesale participants is, of course, worldwide. The lowest cost of funds is that which happens to prevail anywhere, although for borrowings in one currency destined for investment in another, the foreign exchange risk (or its cost of hedging) must be taken into account.

From late 1992 to early 1994, a prodigious incentive for such "transformation" of short-term funds into longer credits was provided by the low 3 per cent federal funds rate maintained by the Federal Reserve to bolster a sluggish economy and, as described earlier, the banking system. When to the surprise (one wonders why?) of money market participants this rate was raised in early 1994 under circumstances auguring further increase, the market shock was profound. Distress selling of government bonds was widespread, sharply lifting long-term rates around the world with little respect for the substantially differing fundamentals from country to country (Massaro 1997). In the US the drop in bond prices precipitated a number of financial failures, principally through a panic in the market for mortgage-related securities. Treasury bond prices suffered severely because markets for morgage-backed and some other interest-bearing securities dried up under the selling pressures. Not being able to raise required cash by selling the securities they would have liked to sell, many managers had to liquidate what could be sold, namely US government obligations. This is exactly what we should expect whenever a broad sell signal is given by the derivatives models.

After the shock of the 1994 rate increase had worn off, the situation became in some respects even more attractive for hedge funds. US longer-term rates had gone up but, despite the higher money rates, the cost of wholesale financing fell. This was because of the problems of Japan, which produced an extraordinary and destructive rise in the yen/dollar exchange rate. In September 1995 the Bank of Japan responded by lowering its discount rate to a mere 1/2 of one percent. (Although this was labeled an "emergency measure", the rate remained there as of October 1997.) Both the persistence of low money rates in Japan and a fall in the yen seemed assured — the yen did in fact plunge from a Summer 1995 peak of 80 per dollar to a trough of 127 in March 1997. Thus borrowing yen and investing outside Japan was hugely profitable. Punctuated by the occasional interruption, the proceeds of this "carry trade", as it has become known in market parlance, have poured into the securities and credit markets of the world ever since. In this way low Japanese rates have generated a worldwide bubble in securities prices and credit growth resembling the earlier "bubble economy" in Japan itself.

More generally, whenever the spread between the relevant short and long rates widens, the quantity of short-term funds demanded by the financial sector, consisting of the individuals, firms, and institutions seeking income from interest-rate spreads, enlarges. A wider spread induces such "arbitrageurs" to borrow more at short-term for the purpose of lending more at longer term. Their additional demand for longer-term claims tends to lower long-term rates. A narrowing of the spread, conversely, discourages the lengthening of asset maturities and raises long-term rates. These financial sector reactions explain why short and long rates usually move in the same direction. The opening and folding of the interest rate accordion, the changes in rate levels, and the associated flux in credit extensions and contractions move nominal and real GDP.

As is well documented, the spread between US long-term and short-term interest has been arguably the best (though far from precise) single leading indicator of business downturns (Estrella and Mishkin 1995). A narrowing or, more reliably, inverting of the normally positive spread foretells an impending recession. The financial sector is under restraint. Conversely, a widening spread signals greater credit supply and economic revival (Figure 2).

When interest rate ceilings still prevailed, a rise in short rates beyond certain thresholds impaired or literally cut off the ability of depository institutions to hold and attract deposits. Because many assets held by the institutions were nonmarketable, because the Treasury was legislatively restrained from issuing new longer-dated obligations, because Treasury obligations were "locked in" by having to be valued at least at par on bank balance sheets, because there were no futures and options markets, and so on, long-term bond yields tended to rise much less than short-term rates. The long-term markets simply ceased to function normally. Actual inversion of the yield curve corresponded to near-paralysis of financial intermediaries, since any activity in such conditions produced losses. Recessions followed. But because these began before financial institutions had time and opportunity to become badly overextended, and were immediately accompanied by lower short-term interest rates, there were no serious financial failures.

Since 1982, with deregulation and the growing perfection of the markets, no deep inversion has occurred. This is partly because there has been no draconian tightening of money. But also, in the deregulated environment, rises in short rates are quickly translated into higher long rates, although not necessarily on a one-for-one basis. When the cost of inputs simultaneously rises for all firms in the financial industry, why wouldn't they raise their prices? Since the amount of reserves the monetary authority stands ready to supply at the official short rate is unlimited, the constraint on the economy now operates primarily through the interest elasticity of the demand for credit.

An interesting paradox lurks here. When the authorities raise the short-term rate, to restrain an actually or potentially overheating economy, should they prefer long-term rates to rise a good deal, not at all, or even to decline? The larger the rise in long rates, the more the public's spending decisions will be deterred. On the other hand, the wider the spread between long and short rates, the greater the incentive for the financial sector to continue to borrow at the new short rate and to extend credit, on easier noninterest terms if need be. Should long rates happen to rise more than short rates, the economy may even be stimulated, the predictive power of the long-short differential suggests. Conversely, a fall in long rates might actually be contractionary if it sharply curtails borrowing and lending by the financial sector.

Suppose that demand for credit is elastic to the level of rates, but supply to the long-short differential. Keeping in mind that the supply of funds at the official short rate is theoretically infinite, all sorts of outcomes are possible depending on the (potentially highly variable) shapes of the curves. In actuality, long and short rates move in the same direction most of the time, the long rate moving less (although, of course, with larger effect on the value of long-term assets). An implication is that short-term rate increases may be of little moment until they no longer provoke significantly higher bond yields, presumably because only then have the latter reached a level at which credit demand is highly elastic. If long rates keep rising in step with short, then credit growth may persist substantially unrestrained — until short rates soar high enough to cause default problems.

In today's US, where mutual fund shares have replaced deposits in household portfolios to a considerable extent (Figure 3), stock as well as bond returns may need to be considered. If short-term rates rise but stock prices rise as fast or faster (the cost of capital falls), is policy restrictive? In the Estrella and Mishkin study cited above, stock prices are the next-most-successful predictor to the interest-rate spread, and the two used together dominate all other combinations.

In addition, as pointed out above in relation to the Japanese money rate, central banks cannot afford to focus solely on domestic interest-rate and stock-price levels and differentials, but need to consider (and influence, but how?) their important international permutations.

Central bankers tend to be elasticity optimists, but I have not been a central banker since 1963. In good times, it seems to me, borrowers tend to be insensitive to rising interest rates until they rise enough to create cash flow problems. Then default problems are generated, rendering it difficult to discriminate between the price and the credit-quality consequences of the higher rates. At high rates, lenders perceive higher credit risk and become more reluctant. This is consistent with the observation that, at the onset of recessions, the decline in other rates lags behind the peak in short rates which, ever since creation of the Federal Reserve, has tended to coincide with the business cycle peak (Figure 4). At and immediately after the upper business-cycle turning point, everyone knows that the economy and inflation will soon be declining, yet long-term and loan rates fall late and reluctantly. It must be because the financial sector is inhibited from responding to its improved incentives by its own capital and credit concerns. That is what I found for the pre-deregulation period, and nothing in the subsequent experience suggests any change.

How else to explain the curious result that subtracting a series coincident with the business cycle (short rates) from a lagging one (long rates), produces a leading indicator (the spread)?

In sum, the economic impact of an increase in official short rates is difficult to predict because so much depends on what happens to long rates and the reaction of the financial sector. To the extent that credit demand is inelastic, and large borrowers have hedged themselves against interest rate increases, large increases in rates will be needed to achieve restraint. Large rises in rates mean large drops in asset prices, which in turn render major defaults and serious recessions – and lender-of-last-resort interventions — more likely.

IS THE SAFETY NET SHRINKING OR BROADENING?

The problems of assessing the thrust of monetary policy when the policy instrument is the short-term rate have led all central banks to seek a quantitative intermediate money or credit aggregate to target. However, the deregulation and innovation of recent years have rendered such targets largely useless. They are likely to remain so until there is a return to a more orderly (i.e., regulated) environment. Ironically the most ardent advocates of narrow (as opposed to broad) money definition and targeting also were the most ardent enthusiasts for deregulation — which, step by step, has forced central banks to broaden the definition of money. This in turn has led back to more emphasis on targeting credit and, indeed, national income or price aggregates that are almost impossible for monetary policy to fine tune. In the US, M2, the principal monetary aggregate still being monitored, albeit perfunctorily, now includes eight components in addition to the currency, demand deposits, and travelers checks that defined the original M1 (Anderson et al 1997). None of these eight, it may be noted, are identical to any of the ten components that were added to M1 to arrive at M2 during 1982-1985.

Deregulation has made it more difficult for central banks to maintain control over the quantity of the means of payment as that is perceived by the public. In the financially advanced countries, we have become accustomed to take for granted that checks will be honored regardless of the institution on which they are drawn, and that the total quantity of money can and will be modulated so as to substantially preserve its purchasing power and maintain economic stability. We also assume that certain assets are immediately convertible into universally accepted means of payment at minimal risk and cost. But it is only reluctantly conceded, if at all, that accomplishing this requires a degree of governmental control over the relevant institutions.

Not everyone can be allowed to accept or create checking deposits and, in effect, to print money. The system has to be protected, just as people cannot hook up indiscriminately to the electricity grid, or dump in or draw on the water reservoirs. The club of institutions allowed access, which long consisted exclusively of commercial and central banks, is obliged to accept certain constraints that are costly. If others not subject to such constraints are allowed to mimic the privileges, they will be more profitable and better able to raise capital (Wojnilower 1991). The current tendency, perversely, is not only to let outsiders enjoy the benefits of the club without paying dues, but also, in the name of free markets, to take away from or charge the members for their special privileges such as direct access to central bank credit and payments facilities, governmental deposit insurance, and monopoly over the checking account business.

For the US, the rise of money market mutual funds is probably the most egregious example of this trend. Money market funds are not subject to reserve requirements and other expensive constraints imposed on banks. Nevertheless, they are allowed to offer "deposits" fixed in nominal value and subject to check. Although money market fund balances are not covered by deposit insurance, the public nevertheless assumes that prominent funds are as much within the governmental safety net as are banks falling into the too-large-to-fail category, since the systemic risk from a fund or a bank failure would be identical. (Perhaps even stock index funds are coming to be perceived as quasi-insured.) When outsiders over whom the central bank has no jurisdiction proliferate and flourish, how are the members of the club (the banks) to preserve their profitability, access to capital and, indeed, their lives, except by resigning? Yet the public continues to hold central banks and governments responsible for the integrity of the payments machinery and the currency, as well as for the maintenance of stable prosperity. That is a large order for central banks to accomplish solely through adjustments in the overnight interest rate.

The process illustrates a historical pattern. All societies have restricted the privilege of money creation, in olden times mainly to harvest seigniorage, today to protect the integrity of the payments system and to limit price level and business cycle fluctuation. The private sector tries to circumvent these restrictions by creating means of payment alternative to, or routinely convertible into the officially recognized money. Unless the authorities stamp out these alternatives, or at least refrain from supporting them in times of trouble, the innovations take root and become established.

They become money, much as bank notes and deposits emerged as money in environments in which coins were the only officially recognized legal tender. If the authorities wish to maintain control over the quantity of money, they must somehow bring the innovations under their regulation. The worldwide broadening of money supply concepts in recent years displays this process, although the authorities may not fully appreciate the implications because there has been little occasion for severe monetary restraint. If when money is tightened, it is mainly the growth of the traditional component that is inhibited but not that of the newer alternatives (which not being "taxed" offer the higher returns), then eventually the traditional regulated sector will atrophy and only the free-riding newcomers survive.

One sometimes hears it argued that if the market were left unregulated without a governmental safety net, the need to preserve reputation would inhibit undue risk-taking by agents and intermediaries and make investors more cautious about where they place their funds. This is a curious reading of financial history. At best, perhaps some smaller crises would be self-correcting without severe systemic damage, but the large ones would be cataclysmic.

Even small crises claim many innocent victims and, not least because they often threaten to become big ones, are politically intolerable.

HOW THINGS ARE

With the growing size and scope of markets and transactions, the value of a good reputation is diminishing. No longer is it unusual to see bankrupt firms or countries raising large sums within a few years (sometimes months) after having defaulted. From the standpoint of the individuals who make the markets, the need for a good reputation to attract a steady stream of business is much reduced. Much as with athletic or entertainment stars in a global market, the rewards to be gained from a single major success (like one outstanding season or recording album) often suffice to make the performer rich for life. The temptations to bend ethical standards to score such a deal approach the irresistible.

Reflecting excesses by individual employees, several major institutions have recently incurred colossal losses (Aglietta 1996). Since the environment has been one of easy money and the victims were strongly capitalized, the firms involved did not default or could be absorbed by competitors who assumed their obligations. In times of tight money and wobbly stock markets, such events are much more systemically dangerous. That is when weak credits are forced to default even without fraud coming into play, and also when defensive fraud — fraud for the sake of institutional and personal survival — proliferates.

Economists and regulators stress the need to enforce prompt disclosure of honest information. That is all to the good, but why has the market not compelled firms to make such disclosure? Often investors don't care: few people are thieves, but many or most don't seem to mind doing business with thieves thought to be offering a bargain price. Disclosure does not matter as much as the will and authority of the police to inhibit unacceptable behavior.

So hungry are debt and equity investors these days to place their overflow of funds that credit standards and risk differentials have narrowed to the vanishing point. Huge loans are made on cursory investigation and documentation. The financial sector once again considers itself immune to supervisory restraint. Participants feel secure that political pressures and the great potential for calamity due to market interlinkages will bring prompt lender-of-last-resort support in case of trouble.

In a profound recent analysis, Joseph Bisignano emphasizes that "Technologies subject to increasing returns, which also includes financial intermediary structures, have the property that the resulting market configuration is unpredictable." (Bisignano 1997.) Increasing-returns industries are hard to keep competitive and prone to overexpand. In the financial sector, competitive overexpansion contributes to excessive credit growth and eventually financial-sector defaults that may necessitate lender-of-last-resort intervention.

It is not only the supply side of credit that tends to excess, but the demand side as well. Myopia, optimism, and inclination to gamble are hardwired into humanity and have proved highly resistant to legal and social efforts to contain them. In the financial markets the constraints on these propensities are fewer than elsewhere. As a result, quantities many times the GDP are traded daily. Speculation offers better odds than any other gambling of which I know, and is much more respectable to boot. There can be no doubt that, literally like narcotics, it attracts and creates many addicts. Together these form a crowd and sometimes a mob, albeit the crowd is "virtual", joined mainly by electronics rather than physical proximity. Individuals in crowds take "irrational" actions they would never elect on their own. And everyone knows that it is suicidally irrational to stand in the way of a mob.

There has been no good opportunity to retest my 1980 hypothesis as to the central role of credit crunches — partly because of the stock crash of 1987 and the oil shock of 1990 and partly because world-wide upswings in aggregate demand have been infrequent. But even though credit crunches have not triggered a recession for a long time, disruptions in credit markets have continued to exert strong influence on business conditions. I remain convinced that liquidity "crunches" will occur again, most likely as a result of unexpected bankruptcies. With the regulatory restraints that used to serve as early "circuit breakers" abolished, the burden on lenders of last resort is greater. And with central banks no longer commanding a powerful club of "inside" institutions through which to respond to trouble, future financial embolisms will be more dangerous than the regulatory crunches of the past.

THE FUTURE OF BANKING IN AMERICA

The purpose of the FDIC's study of the future of U.S. banking is to project likely trends in the structure and performance of the banking industry over the next five to ten years and to anticipate the policy issues that will confront the industry and the regulatory community.

This study comes 17 years after the FDIC's last comprehensive consideration of the future of banking. That earlier study, *Mandate for Change*, was undertaken against a background of increased competition for banks, weak profitability, and a reduced market share in commercial lending. The study recommended product and geographic deregulation, with appropriate safety-and-soundness safeguards, to ensure the viability of the banking industry.

Since then, the environment for banking has changed radically. Legislation was enacted to permit both interstate branching and combinations of banks, securities firms, and insurance companies. A generally strong economy, as well as deregulation, led to marked improvements in bank profitability and capital positions. At the same time, however, the deregulation of products and markets intensified competition among banks and between banks and nonbank financial companies. In addition, together with improved information technology, deregulation accelerated the consolidation of the banking industry through mergers and acquisitions and set the stage for the establishment of huge banking organizations of unprecedented size and complexity.

Although the condition of the industry has greatly improved over the past decade or so, banks and the regulatory community will face significant challenges in the years ahead. Competition will continue to be intense, and few banks, if any, will be insulated from its effects. In the view of some observers, rapid consolidation of the banking industry will continue and may adversely affect the availability of credit for small businesses and local economies. Large, complex banking organizations may pose difficult supervisory issues, while the burden of reporting and other regulatory requirements will fall heavily and disproportionately on small banks unless remedial action is taken. Further advances in information technology will permit the development of new products, services, and risk-management techniques but may also pose important competitive and supervisory issues. Nonbank entities will continue to offer bank-like products in competition with banks, raising anew the question of whether banks are still "special" and, more fundamentally, whether banks are sufficiently different from nonbank firms to justify the maintenance of a safety net for banks.

It is useful, therefore, to try to chart the course of the banking industry in the next five to ten years and to consider what policy issues the industry and regulators will face. The authors of this study do not pretend to be clairvoyant. They are mindful of the many financial predictions that were once offered with confidence but turned out to be wrong or premature. This study is perhaps best described as an exercise in strategic thinking. Its approach is to analyze what has happened in the recent past, consider in detail reasons for expecting recent trends to continue or to change, and draw the consequences for bank and regulatory policies. As always, uncertainties abound, and events that may now appear fairly improbable may in fact shape the future. This paper closes with a discussion of a number of such possible events.

The future-of-banking study addresses three broad questions:

1. What changes in the environment facing banking can be expected in the next five to ten years?
2. What are the prospects for different sectors of the banking industry in this anticipated environment? Because the banking industry is not monolithic and different segments of the

industry have, to some degree, different opportunities and vulnerabilities, the study considers separately the prospects for large, complex banking organizations; regional and other midsize banks; community banks; and limited-purpose banks.

3. What policy issues are the industry and regulators likely to face in the years ahead? Separate consideration is given to
   - *Consolidation of the banking industry:* What are the prospects for, and implications of, further consolidation of the banking industry, particularly relating to safety and soundness, market concentration, and small business credit?
   - *Combinations of banking and commerce:* What are the pros and cons of permitting common ownership or control of banks and commercial enterprises? What are the options for regulating such combinations so as to protect the bank safety net and avoid conflicts of interest?
   - *Large-bank supervisory issues:* What are the implications for bank supervision of the growing complexity of large banking organizations?
   - *Governance issues:* Recent corporate scandals have led to efforts to hold corporate directors and managements to a higher standard. What are the likely effects on banking and what should banks do to avoid governance problems?
   - *Financial services regulatory issues:* What should be done, either under existing law or through new legislation, to enhance the effectiveness of the federal financial regulatory system?
   - *Bank liability structure:* What are the implications for supervision and deposit insurance of changes in the structure of bank liabilities?
   - *Economic role of banks:* How does the increased role of nonbank financial institutions and markets affect the rationale for a safety net for banks?

THE ENVIRONMENT FOR BANKING

The future of banking will be shaped, in large part, by the environment—economic, demographic, regulatory, technological, payment- system, and competitive—in which it operates.

Economic Environment

In the decade ahead, a climate of moderate economic growth without severe or long-lasting recessions would be conducive to the strong growth and profitability of the banking industry. In such a climate, bank failures would be few in number and idiosyncratic in nature—typically caused by managerial and internal control weaknesses, excessive risk taking, or fraud, rather than by broader economic forces. Such, at least, has been the pattern of bank failures in most of the years since the inception of the FDIC, with the principal and very large exception of the 1980s and early 1990s. However, the economy is not immune to speculative bubbles like those occurring in the energy, commercial real estate, and agriculture sectors in the 1980s, which were among the important causes of the wave of bank failures during that period, or the more recent bubble in communications technology in the 1990s. Boom-and-bust conditions in markets in which banks participate could once again produce a significant number of failures caused by economic conditions, although the banking industry is stronger than it was on the eve of the 1980s, geographic diversification has reduced the vulnerability of many banks to local economic disturbances, and bank supervision has been strengthened.

Demographic Environment

Among the main demographic trends likely to affect banking in the years ahead are the aging of the population and the continued entry of immigrants. In the next decade or more, the baby boomers (people born during the post–World War II bulge in the birth rate) will retire or approach retirement. There are more than 80 million baby boomers, and they account for 30 percent of the total U.S. population. Life-cycle theory and the available data suggest that they will be engaged in liquidating assets to a greater degree—and will make less use of credit—than younger age groups. Also compared with younger age groups, they will hold a greater proportion of their wealth in liquid assets, including bank deposits. At the same time, baby boomers may be less averse to risk than similar age groups that had experience with the Great Depression. Therefore, the composition of the baby boomers' wealth is likely to be affected not only by their stage in the life cycle but also by their overall motives for saving and their investment experience with equities and other market instruments. Baby boomers will live longer than the preceding generation and may find that their post-retirement incomes will be inadequate to support costs such as health care. Many, though, will inherit wealth from their parents and will need financial services for their retirement planning. Banks will therefore be able to profit by broadening their services to meet baby boomers' financial preferences.

Since 1990, the United States has attracted 9 million immigrants. Of the total U.S. population, 33 million, or 11 percent, are immigrants. Though the number of new immigrants is expected to increase, immigrants as a whole may not supply a proportional amount of funds for bank deposits because of low incomes and lack of legal documentation. In addition, immigrants often send large remittances back to their home countries. Low rates of home ownership and reliance on borrowing from informal sources such as family and friends are other factors likely to keep demand for bank credit low. Immigrants demand fewer mortgage loans because of their lower rate of home ownership and tend to make larger down payments than native-born Americans. Banks now earn service fees for transferring remittances and, in connection with this activity, may be able to provide incentives for immigrants to open bank accounts. Banks are tailoring their products to meet immigrants' unique characteristics—for example, by offering low-fee transaction accounts and flexible mortgage packages. As immigrants reside longer in the United States, their incomes will rise, more of them will buy homes, and they will generally merge into the financial mainstream.

Both baby boomers and immigrants will increase their supply of deposits to banks, but for different reasons. Baby boomers will desire to hold safe and liquid assets when they get older, whereas immigrants will likely become wealthier as they stay longer in the United States. As for the effects of aging baby boomers and immigrants on the demand for bank loans, the two groups tend to offset each other. Immigrants now demand fewer bank loans because of low incomes and a reliance on informal banking, but when they live long enough in the United States, they tend to become home buyers. In the next 10 to 20 years, however, increased loan demand from immigrants may not fully compensate for retiring baby boomers' decreased loan demand.

Regulatory Environment

As in the recent past, future deregulation of bank powers is more likely to start from developments in the marketplace or actions by individual states than from initiatives by Congress or the executive branch. However, Congress and the executive branch may be more receptive to proposals for legislation designed to protect consumers, prevent serious misconduct by bank personnel, or advance national security objectives. The provision of a bank safety net and the existence of regulatory agencies to enforce compliance make banking a politically attractive vehicle for furthering such objectives. The results have been substantial reporting and other regulatory burdens on banks.

These requirements frequently involve fixed costs that tend to be proportionally heavier on small banks. Although, as noted below, we regard community banks as a viable business model, the disproportionate impact of regulatory burden on smaller banks places them at a competitive disadvantage. Excessive regulatory burdens may not only hurt existing banks but may also discourage new entrants, thereby depriving bank customers of the benefits of increased competition from newly established banks. This prospect highlights the importance of reducing reporting burdens wherever possible.

The FDIC established a special task force to reevaluate its examination and supervisory practices in an effort to improve operations and reduce regulatory burden without compromising safety and soundness or undermining important consumer protections. Over the last several years the FDIC has streamlined examinations and procedures with an eye toward better allocating FDIC resources to areas that could ultimately pose greater risks to the insurance funds—areas such as problem banks, large financial institutions, high-risk lending, internal controls, and fraud.

The FDIC is also leading an interagency effort to identify and eliminate restrictions that are outdated, unnecessary, or unduly burdensome. This effort is pursuant to the Economic Growth and Regulatory Paperwork Reduction Act of 1996. Comments are sought from the banking industry about which regulations are the most burdensome and which regulations place the industry at a competitive disadvantage. The agencies have jointly published the first two of a series of notices soliciting comment on regulations in a number of areas and have been conducting outreach sessions with bankers, consumer groups, and community groups. Armed with input from these efforts, the agencies will conduct a comprehensive review of banking regulations and will report to Congress on their findings and on the actions they have taken, or plan to take, about the level of burden. The agencies also expect to send Congress a list of legislative areas for consideration.

Technological Environment

The banking industry is now more dependent on technology than ever before, with annual industry expenditures for technology topping an estimated $30 billion. In recent decades, the focus of large-bank technology developments has shifted. These decades began with a large number of mergers and acquisitions after restrictions on interstate banking and branching were lifted, and the technology component of merging two entities proved to be a challenging task for acquirers. Lessons were learned over time by institutions that experienced numerous rounds of acquisitions. By the late 1990s, Y2K concerns dominated technology planning and, to an extent, restrained the level of mergers and acquisitions. Y2K work also had the effect of benefiting banks by requiring planning for business continuity and disaster recovery. Meanwhile, the world of technology continued to change, with rapid adoption of the Internet and increases in the market capitalization of Internet-related companies. Bankers invested heavily in Internet products and services. More recently, the technology focus of banks has moved to cost cutting, consolidation, and rationalization. Large banks will continue to develop new technologies and adapt to legislative and regulatory changes, such as Basel II and Check 21. Imaging, increased bandwidth, wireless networking, and Web services are innovations likely to have an impressive effect on the use of bank technology. For large banks, security and operational resiliency remain major concerns.

Community banks also depend on technology, but more as users of proven technology than as creators or innovators. By using proven technologies as they become available, community banks now offer a wide variety of products and services, often matching large banks in the scope of their offerings to retail customers. As a result of competitive pressures, even small banks now find it mandatory to have sophisticated, well-functioning technology to support customer service, administration, and financial reporting. But managing technology is a challenge for community banks, and among FDIC-supervised banks, only slightly more than half perform core processing in-house; the remainder outsource this function. Thus, third-party service providers play a critical role in the efficiency and security of technology operations at community banks.

Objective assessments of community bank information technology (IT) operations are available through the examination process and from a survey of FDIC IT examiners. The vast majority of FDIC-supervised banks receive sound composite IT examination ratings. Examiners report that community banks are using technology to provide customers with more and better-quality products and services. Examiners also note vulnerabilities at FDIC-supervised banks in the areas of risk assessment and audit, strategic planning, management of outsourcing, security, and personnel.

Technology will continue to be a major expense, and security will remain a crucial issue for banks of all sizes. Responding to an ever more complex technology environment will be challenging. Nonetheless, proper technology management is within the grasp of every bank and can lead to better customer service, lower operating costs, and a more efficient banking system.

Payment-System Changes

Although the much-heralded checkless society has yet to arrive, major changes are underway in retail noncash payment systems, as the use of checks as a means of payment has declined and electronic forms of payment have increased. After rising for many years, the number of checks used in retail transactions declined from 49.5 billion in 1995 to 42.5 billion in 2000—the latest year for which comparable data are available. Over the same period, the number of retail electronic payments increased from 14.6 billion to 28.9 billion.

Although fewer checks are being written, the number is still very large in absolute terms and in comparison with the number being written in several other countries, some of which have virtually eliminated the use of checks. Therefore, efforts are being made to "electronify" checks early in the process of clearing and settlement by sending the information forward electronically; that process is expected to be faster and less expensive than current methods, which require the physical transportation of large amounts of paper.

Banks will have to adapt their product offerings and pricing as well as their back-office processing to reflect these payment-system changes. Since more electronic transactions are cheaper to process, as is the conversion or truncation (or both) of checks, banks that do not explicitly charge for transaction services on a per-item basis will see a reduction in costs. For banks that have explicit fees for each service (mainly banks that supply cash-management services), it will be necessary to ensure that the profit margins on the electronic transaction services are commensurate with those on the paper transaction services. Banks of all sizes should be able to continue to serve their customers with a mix of capabilities, including ATMs, on- and off-line debit cards, credit cards, and other services.

Bank regulators must be aware of the risk implications of the changes in payment systems and must adapt their approaches accordingly. Operational risk is obviously an important issue. In this regard, the ownership of fund transfer networks has changed dramatically: the number and proportion of networks owned and operated by nonbank entities has increased, whereas those owned by joint ventures of banks have declined. Because the operation of these networks directly affects the risk exposure of banks, the risk-management practices of the network providers may have important implications for the banking industry and the bank regulatory community.

Banks and bank regulators also need to be concerned about the market structure of the network providers, especially those for ATMs, debit cards, and credit cards. Significant consolidation among network providers has already occurred, and any further concentration raises concerns about pricing, quality of service, and product innovation in this segment of the market—one for which bank regulators have no direct responsibility.

Competitive Environment

The shares of debt held by commercial banks and savings institutions as a percentage of the total volume of debt have declined compared with the shares held in earlier decades of the twentieth century.[7] Some observers have interpreted this decline as a sign of competitive weakness or even obsolescence. However, this decline is partly due to the proliferation of channels of financial intermediation, which often involve the issuance of financial instruments to fund other financial instruments rather than the channeling of funds to nonfinancial sectors of the economy—households, businesses, and governments. In this regard, the overall volume of borrowing in credit markets has apparently increased permanently. During the 1980s the volume of borrowing by nonfinancial sectors of the economy rose from 1.3 times annual GDP to nearly 1.9 times annual GDP, an increase reflecting the rising indebtedness of households and nonfinancial businesses, in tandem with deficit spending by the federal government.

The growth of debt in our economy during the 1980s was associated with a decline in the share of domestic nonfinancial borrowing that is directly funded by commercial banks (the share declined from 30 percent in 1974 to a low of 20 percent in 1993). But when debt growth leveled off in the early 1990s, commercial banks' share of this credit-market pie also leveled off, and since the early 1990s it has remained generally stable. The continued need for bank financing on the part of many borrowers reflects their inability—owing to their small size and idiosyncratic risk—to access financial markets directly and cost effectively.

The reduction in banks' share of the credit-market pie reflects a dramatic shift in the way loans are being financed. Specifically, asset securitization (the pooling of loans and their funding by the issuing of securities) has allowed loans that used to be funded by traditional intermediaries, including banks, to be funded in securities markets. The securitization of home mortgages and consumer credit has reduced the extent to which these types of loans are directly funded by commercial banks and has had an even more adverse effect on savings institutions. Nonetheless, commercial banks continue to play a significant role in funding business borrowers. The average share of nonfinancial business borrowing that commercial banks hold on their balance sheets has remained relatively stable for five decades. At the same time, there has been a clear shift in how banks lend—a shift from shorter-term lending to loans secured by business real estate. This shift may reflect banks' continuing comparative advantage in real estate lending, a form of lending less well suited to the standardization necessary for asset securitization.

The savings institution share of total household, business, and government debt has also stabilized in recent years, but at levels much lower than those of earlier post–World War II decades. The reasons for the decline are the liquidation of a substantial portion of the savings and loan industry during the 1980s and early 1990s, the absorption of numerous savings institutions by commercial banks, and the rapid growth of mortgage-backed securities.

Banks' importance relative to capital markets is lower in the United States than in many other countries.

However, some countries are moving closer to the U.S. model as a result of forces that have increased the efficiency of "arms-length" financial markets, including improvements in the processing of information, increases in international trade and capital flows, and political integration. Thus, the lower market share of banks in the United States may be seen as a sign of the advanced development of capital markets and IT in the United States rather than as a sign of terminal weakness in the banking industry.

Of course, market-share data based on balance-sheet totals underestimate the continuing importance of banks in financial markets precisely because they do not include off-balance-sheet activity.

Through backup lines of credit, loan origination, securitization, and other means, banks support lending by other entities and earn fee income. An alternative measure of the importance of banks in the financial system is provided by the bank share of total net income of financial sector firms, which reflects income and expense from both on- and off-balance-sheet activities.

During 1992–2002 net income of publicly traded commercial banks and savings institutions accounted for an average of 44 percent of total profits of all publicly traded financial companies—about the same proportion as in 1985, before the banking crisis of the late 1980s and early 1990s.

Moreover, the net income of the largest individual banks was far greater than that of the largest nonbank financial companies. The ability of the banking industry and the largest individual banks to earn high net income relative to other financial firms is hardly a sign of competitive weakness.

The Environment for Banking: Summary

In general, the environment for banking in the next five to ten years is likely to remain favorable. The economic environment appears conducive to good banking industry performance, assuming that recessions are mild and that we avoid speculative bubbles similar to those that contributed to widespread failures during the 1980s. The banking industry's market share has stabilized, according to a number of measures. Reduced use of checks and increased use of electronic payments are likely to exert downward pressure on costs of the banking system as a whole. Over time, banks will have increased opportunities to serve two growing segments of the population—retired baby boomers and immigrants.

Potential problems in the environment are likely to be associated with inadequate safeguards in the use of technology. Consolidation and increased nonbank ownership of fund transfer networks—especially networks for ATMs, debit cards, and credit cards—may expose banks to new operational risks. Outsourcing certain functions, including moving work offshore, involves political, business-continuity, and security risks. Inadequate IT staffing may make some banks vulnerable to attacks on the software they use, with customers exposed to inconvenience and banks to weakened reputations and weakened competitive positions.

For community banks, in particular, the burden of reporting and other regulatory requirements poses a significant threat to future prosperity. Efforts to address this problem are described above.

PROSPECTS FOR BANKING SECTORS

As is well known, the U.S. banking system is characterized by large differences in the size of institutions; the system includes some of the world's largest banking organizations as well as thousands of relatively small banks. Institutions also differ in the extent to which they are affected by local rather than national economic forces and in the business strategies they have adopted to cope with their environments. Individual banks or groups of banks have, to some extent, different business opportunities, risk exposures, and future prospects, and many of these differences are associated with size. In this study, banks are divided into the following groups:

- Large, complex banking organizations—defined as the top 25 organizations in terms of assets;
- Community banks—defined as institutions with less than $1 billion in assets;
- Regional and other midsize banks—defined as banks that fall between community banks and the top 25 (in other words, banks with assets greater than $1 billion but less than the assets of the smallest of the top 25 organizations—currently about $42 billion); and
- Special-purpose banks—includes credit card banks, subprime lenders, and Internet banks.

Except when specifically noted, "banks" and "banking organizations" refer to independent commercial banks and savings institutions and to the holding companies of such institutions. "Assets" when used to denote the size of different groups of institutions means the assets of commercial banks and savings institutions combined. Asset limits of size groups are adjusted for inflation as measured by the GDP price deflator.

Large, Complex Banking Organizations

Over the past 20 years the structure of the U.S. banking system has changed enormously in response to changes in the legal, regulatory, and financial landscape. At the end of 2003, the 25 largest insured banks and savings institutions held 56 percent of total industry assets, with the 10 largest holding almost 44 percent, up from 19 percent in 1984. For the next 15 banks, the growth has been much less dramatic: the combined assets of the banks ranked 11 through 25 have risen only 2 percentage points, from about 10 percent in 1984 to 12 percent at the end of 2003. Why did these institutions grow to be so large? Has the elimination of restrictions on branching and ownership been the main driving force? Do larger banking organizations enjoy economies of scale? Does management simply want to control ever-larger organizations? Do investors exert pressure to increase asset size, revenues, or net income? To some extent, all of these appear to be true.

The passage of the Riegle-Neal Interstate Banking and Branching Efficiency Act of 1994 undoubtedly helped spur large banks to spread across state lines and to grow. This development helped create large, geographically diversified branch networks that stretch across large regions and even coast-to-coast. The Gramm-Leach-Bliley Financial Services and Modernization Act of 1999 (GLB) allowed the largest banking organizations to engage in a wide variety of financial services, acquiring new sources of noninterest income and further diversifying their earnings. Contributing to these developments were advances in IT that facilitated control of far-distant operations and fostered new products, services, and risk-management techniques.

As these banks have grown, have they gained efficiencies from their growth? The conclusions reached in the economic literature on bank economies of scale are mixed; some studies have found economies of scale and scope, and some have not. With respect to market power, studies of mergers that resulted in high concentrations in local markets did not find significant gains to the acquiring firm. On the other hand, consolidation that leads to geographic diversification seems to be associated with increased profits and reduced risk. Some studies have also concluded that banks may seek growth in an attempt to be regarded by the market as too big to fail. According to this view, the funding costs of a bank would be lower if holders of uninsured deposits, bonds, and other credits assumed they would be protected if the bank failed.

Although the academic literature does not provide conclusive evidence that greater size leads to cost and other advantages, there appears to be continual pressure on bank management from shareholders and market analysts to show growth in both revenue and earnings. Bigness is apparently regarded as advantageous. Nevertheless, the wave of mergers and acquisitions that occurred after enactment of the Riegle-Neal Act and GLB has probably passed. The large number of deals within the recent past partly reflects the backlog created by a restrictive legal environment; in a less-restrictive legal environment, many of the recent mergers and acquisitions would have occurred earlier and over a longer period. Although Riegle-Neal prohibits mergers when the merged bank's domestic deposits would exceed 10 percent of total domestic deposits (or 30 percent of the deposits in any state), only the Bank of America is close to the 10 percent limit (as a result of the recent merger with FleetBoston); other members of the top 25 group are much further from the limit and are not prevented from undertaking mergers by this legal provision. Further mergers among large banks may be expected in the immediate future, although not in the volume experienced after geographic and product deregulation.

Large banking organizations have widely different business strategies. Among the eight largest companies, some have extensive foreign operations, while others are essentially domestic commercial banks. Some have major credit card operations, and others do not. Some have large trading operations and are active in securities markets, while others do not and are not. Some focus on loans to businesses, while others have major consumer operations. Some concentrate on commercial and industrial loans, while a few are very active (or even specialize) in mortgage finance. They also differ in geographic reach within the United States.

With some exceptions, the larger the institution, the more likely it is to engage in a wide range of activities. The smaller institutions are more likely to concentrate on growing their retail and consumer banking franchises, either internally or through mergers, and entering the investment banking business by purchasing smaller brokerage firms or building on a proprietary mutual fund business. At least in the near term, widespread entry into the property and casualty insurance underwriting business is unlikely. Life insurance underwriting and insurance brokerage show more promise, with less risk. Despite the variety of business models, some of the ways in which large banks have changed are similar across all or many of them. They have increased their fee income as a percentage of total income, possibly to reduce their vulnerability to cyclical interest-rate changes. Most of them have increased income from deposit charges, and some have taken advantage of the new powers under GLB to increase trading revenues, investment banking income, and insurance commissions and fees. Much of the noninterest income from new powers is concentrated in the top two or three banks. These banks have also shifted from deposits to collateralized borrowings. Large banks also appear to have been successful in limiting their exposure to credit losses by improving their risk-management practices.

The experience of the eight largest banks during the recent economic recession has been mixed. Four of these banks had fairly consistent returns on book equity over the period, while the other four had large declines in earnings, with one bank experiencing an actual loss in 2000. In no case was the solvency of an organization threatened.

This mixed record may illustrate the advantages and disadvantages of large, complex organizations. In some cases, geographic diversification, international diversification, product diversification, and risk-management practices seem to have paid off well. Although some of the success was undoubtedly due to a very favorable interest-rate environment, loan losses during the period were low. In other cases, there were evident problems in managing large, complex organizations and in managing the process of acquiring and merging organizations. It appears, therefore, that the various strategies for capitalizing on size, geographic diversification, and product diversification can be successful—but that size itself does not guarantee consistent success.

It seems clear that for the immediate future, the large banks will continue to try to grow through internal growth and acquisitions. As these institutions grow and expand the breadth of their products, potential problems of managerial diseconomies and corporate governance may arise. The sheer size and complexity of today's large institutions place a heavy burden on their financial and operational risk-management systems. Undoubtedly many of these problems are being addressed. Permitted single-company exposures are reportedly being reduced at almost all large banks, and exposures are being tracked across business units. Financial risk models are being implemented in response to both the business need for better risk management and a presumption that Basel II will eventually be implemented.

What can be learned from the recent experience of the top 25 banks? The success of the best-performing organizations might argue that large organizations can be efficient and effective. The large losses sustained by the worst performers suggest that the risk of failure in these banks, although very small, is greater than zero. However, the size and diversification of these organizations help them absorb losses.

If larger and larger banks become a reality, how will the FDIC's risk profile be affected? First, if more institutions come up against the 10 percent deposit concentration limit, efforts to raise that limit may be expected over time and may raise concerns about the concentration of economic resources and power. Second, the possible failure of large banks, however unlikely, represents a risk not only to the insurance funds but also to the banking system itself because of the large increases in deposit insurance premiums that might be required. Over the past 19 years the size of the largest banks has grown dramatically compared with the relevant deposit insurance fund. At year-end 1984 the Bank Insurance Fund (BIF) balance was $16.3 billion, and the largest BIF-member bank was about 7 times larger than the BIF. At year-end 1996 the largest single bank was about 9 times greater than the BIF. By the end of 2003 the largest single bank was *almost 19 times* larger than the BIF ($33.8 billion).

Basel II will effectively create a different capital standard for the largest banks. Should the deposit insurance system be changed to isolate small banks from the effects of the failure of large insured institutions? If so, how? How will the FDIC and the regulatory agencies meet the challenges of mitigating the concentration of risk created by these very large and still-growing organizations? Capital adequacy standards and vigilant supervision present the greatest promise. Optimally pricing deposit insurance, creating separate safety-net arrangements for large and small institutions are ideas that deserve discussion and research.

Regional and Other Midsize Banks

For purposes of this study, banks that have assets of more than $1 billion but less than the assets of the smallest of the 25 largest banking organizations (currently about $42 billion) are designated "regional and other midsize" banks. As a group they are heterogeneous, not only in asset size but also in geographic reach. A quarter of them are truly regional in the sense that they have a significant presence in a number of markets, while the remaining three-quarters are sizable banks concentrated in one market—either located in only one state or having more than 60 percent of their deposits in only one market (as measured by metropolitan statistical areas [MSAs]), or both. This study has divided banks in this in-between size group into two subgroups depending on the geographic concentration of their deposits: one subgroup consists of the truly regional banks, and the other consists of the other midsize banks (i.e., those considered to be large local banks rather than regional institutions).

In the past seven years, both subgroups have consistently outperformed community banks in terms of average return on assets (ROA) and have often outperformed the top 25 banks. During the same period the number of regional and other midsize banks increased by 13 percent. In terms of assets, however, the midsize sector lost market share between 1996 and 2003, largely because of the top 25 banks' dramatic growth through mergers and acquisitions.

The regional and other midsize banks may be small enough to avoid any diseconomies that may be associated with managing distant facilities and heterogeneous product lines but large enough to attract qualified employees, diversify their portfolios, and take advantage of IT to offer a wide variety of services and to manage risk. Within this group, banks that are concentrated locally have had somewhat better earnings than those whose offices are dispersed. Whether locally concentrated banks will continue to outperform regionally dispersed banks is uncertain. If economic conditions should significantly worsen in some local markets, banks concentrated in these markets might be hit hard.

Despite the whole group's strong performance, some commentators have predicted the decline or even the disappearance of these banks. This view reflects a judgment that, in order to thrive, a bank needs either the close community ties of a small bank or the geographic scope, marketing power, and product lines of a megabank.

However, it is hard to imagine that one of the best-performing banking sectors is slated for outright disappearance. Like other good performers, regional and other midsize banks have a number of practical options. They may acquire community banks, merge among themselves, or seek to be acquired by larger banks that remain below the 10 percent deposit concentration limit. And rapid growth and mergers among some community banks may augment the number of in-between banks. We expect the number of banks in the regional and other midsize group to remain significant.

Community Banks

Community banks (defined here as institutions with less than $1 billion in aggregate bank and thrift assets) were not swept away by larger banks following product and geographic deregulation, as some observers had expected. Community banks represent about 94 percent of all banks in the United States—nearly the same as their 95 percent share in 1985, when the recent wave of consolidation began. The persistently large number of relatively small banks is characteristic of the U.S. banking system and reflects long-standing public policies based on concern about the concentration of economic power, the desire to maintain local ownership and control, and efforts to protect local banks from competition. In some cases, these considerations had led to a prohibition of branching; for example, in 1985 42 percent of all community banks were located in 12 states that previously had unit banking.

The picture has changed greatly as a result of the banking crisis of the 1980s and geographic deregulation. The number of community banks has declined by 47 percent since 1985, as a result both of failures (in the earlier part of this period) and (more recently and more significantly) of voluntary mergers. Moreover, the community bank shares of total banking industry assets, deposits, and offices have also declined.

Perhaps the most notable feature of the decline in the number of community banks has been its pervasiveness: the number has declined across geographic areas, across both growing and declining markets, and among community bank size groups. The number declined in rural areas, small metropolitan areas, and large metropolitan areas, and, within the latter, in suburban as well as urban areas, with the pace of the declines during the period since 1985 falling within a fairly narrow range. Moreover, in areas that suffered net reductions in population (mostly rural counties), the decline in the number of community banks was comparable to the decline among community banks as a whole.

The number of community banks declined somewhat faster in formerly unit-banking states than in states that had permitted branching. This finding suggests that restrictive branching laws contributed to the establishment of some small banks that could not (or preferred not to) continue as independent entities once branching restrictions were lifted and competition increased. However, the difference in rates of decline was not very large. Among community banks of different sizes, the largest decline was among banks with less than $100 million in assets (where diseconomies of small scale are believed to exist); however, this decline resulted not so much from more mergers or failures as from the fact that numerous small banks grew faster than the rate of inflation and "graduated" to a higher size group. A striking difference between urban and rural areas is in the various cross-cutting forces that ended up reducing the number of community banks. Urban areas had proportionally more mergers and failures than rural areas but also more new institutions, with the result that total net reductions were roughly the same in rural and urban areas. Urban areas are clearly where the action is; urban areas are central in terms of both merger activity and the establishment of de novo banks. The two types of activity are, to some extent, related; dissatisfied customers of a merged bank may be attracted to a new institution, and areas of high population density may be more attractive markets for the establishment of new banks while also containing more attractive merger targets.

The pervasiveness of consolidation among community banks casts doubt on, or provides only weak support for, some familiar explanations of the reduction in the number of community banks. The lifting of branching restrictions in states that previously prohibited branching, diseconomies of small-scale operations, and depopulation and weak local economies all have undoubtedly affected the fortunes of community banks. However, none of these factors seems to have been the main cause of the consolidation among these institutions. In time, these factors may produce further consolidation, although it is difficult to estimate the length of the lags in bank response. These lags may reflect, in part, a lack of interest on the part of potential acquirers in banks located in weak local economies as well as the ability of banks in such areas to perform at a level satisfactory to their owners. In the recent past, at least, the main impetus for consolidation seems to have been individual decisions by shareholders and managers in response to intensified competition.

As noted above, the effect of mergers and failures was dampened somewhat by the establishment of new banks, mostly in areas of high population density. About 1,250 new community banks were established between 1992 and 2003, of which about 100 have been merged and about 1,100 remain as independent organizations. Like other new and young businesses, they exhibit significant risk factors in some cases, but only 4 have failed. If real estate and other markets served by these banks do not experience serious downturns, these institutions will have an opportunity to mature and prosper.

As a result of both a slowdown in mergers and the continued establishment of de novos, the pace of consolidation has slowed considerably in the past few years. In the near term, some further consolidation may be expected. Low returns on equity (resulting partly from higher capital ratios) may lead to consolidation among some institutions, as stockholders seek higher returns through increased leverage at merged institutions. Attracting and retaining qualified employees and management succession will pose challenges for some of these institutions. Dependence on interest income will periodically squeeze margins unless fee income is increased. Regulatory burdens may also contribute to consolidation.

With respect to earnings performance, in recent years the before-tax ROAs have been lower for community banks than for larger banks. However, this gap between community banks and larger banks is narrowed after corporate taxes are taken into account. Community banks hold a larger percentage of their assets in lower-yield, nontaxable municipal bonds. Moreover, about 2,100 community banks were organized as Sub-chapter S corporations as of March 2004 and therefore paid no federal corporate income tax if they met certain conditions. After taxes, community bank ROAs have averaged from 1.0 percent to 1.2 percent in recent years, lower than those of larger banks but a level of profitability that would have been regarded as exceptional in earlier years. As might be expected, community banks located in counties experiencing more rapid growth in either population or real personal income have experienced higher ROAs and net interest margins, although expense ratios are currently similar. These results are hardly surprising; what may be surprising to some is that even in slow-growth areas, the performance of community banks can be considered "satisfactory."

In deposit and loan markets community banks have faced strong competition, not only from within their own ranks but also from larger banks, credit unions, and nonbank competitors. The community bank share of deposits has declined in rural, small metro, suburban, and urban areas, with the largest 25 banking organizations showing a large increase in market share. (These comparisons reflect both internal growth and mergers.) The share held by regional and other midsize banks has also declined, while that of credit unions has remained relatively stable, increasing from 8 to 9 percent since 1994. Within the credit union industry, large institutions (assets over $100 million) have shown an increased share, while small credit unions have lost ground. Leaving aside the very largest banking organizations, credit unions have increased their market share *relative to the smaller banks*, a development that many would attribute to credit unions' tax-exempt status and the expansion of their permissible areas of operation. Not all community banks face credit union competition of the same intensity; credit unions are concentrated in urban areas in the central and eastern states, whereas community banks are located in large numbers in rural, suburban, and urban areas.

After adjustments are made for mergers, small banks have actually shown more rapid growth since the early 1990s than the largest banks. Small banks have paid higher rates, and charged lower fees, than large banks in order to attract deposits. They have also increased their borrowings from Federal Home Loan Banks in order to broaden their sources of funds, as core deposit growth has lagged behind demands for credit. On the lending side, there have been declines in the community bank shares of the increasingly standardized consumer, home mortgage, and unsecured business loan markets—markets that large lenders, using credit-scoring technologies, have penetrated on a nationwide basis. On the other hand, community banks appear to be largely holding their own in real estate lending to businesses and in farm lending. Community banks hold a disproportionately large share of small business and farm loans (real estate and operating loans).

In summary, the number of community banks has been halved since 1985, and these banks' market share has declined relative to the largest banks' market share. On the face of it, the declines in number and market share would seem to suggest that community banks have serious problems. A more detailed examination presents a somewhat more optimistic view. Community banks still represent 94 percent of the total number of banks, not much different from the percentage before the recent wave of consolidation began. Moreover, it is impressive that community banks have been able to register respectable earnings and growth in recent years while facing intensified competition from nonbank financial companies, as well as from other banks after the removal of the branch restrictions that had protected many community banks from competition.

The conclusion we draw is that the community bank is a viable business model. Research suggests that community banks have certain advantages as lenders to small businesses, small farmers, and other informationally opaque borrowers; these advantages are their ability to assess the risks of borrowers who lack long credit histories, their ability to use "soft" data (such as borrower reputations) effectively in risk assessment, and their ability to operate effectively in situations where the proximity of decision makers to customers is important. The proposition that community banks have informational advantages in lending to small business is supported by research suggesting that small banks have higher risk-adjusted returns on business loans than large banks. The willingness of private investors to risk their own money to establish new banks is a powerful market test of the viability of small banks, at least in areas of population density. Moreover, a concentration of de novos in areas where large and distant banks have taken over local institutions suggests, as well, that many customers may be dissatisfied with the more impersonal approach of large banks. Although consumer attitudes may change and larger banks may seek to emulate the personal-service approach of smaller institutions, community banks should continue to be important in the banking industry for the foreseeable future.

Limited-Purpose Banks

Limited-purpose banks are institutions that specialize in a relatively narrow business line. The limited-purpose banks examined in this study are credit card banks, subprime lenders, and Internet-primary banks. Numerically these institutions make up a small share of the banking industry. Yet their unique production functions and product mixes warrant attention.

Although the diversification of risks is widely regarded as desirable, some institutions have chosen to specialize. Focusing on a limited set of activities allows them to develop expertise quickly and become efficient producers. Moreover, technological innovations in the financial services industry, which lead to gains in productivity and economies of scale, may also have promoted specialization.

The credit card banks provide their customers with both convenience and liquidity by offering a product that can be used as a payment device and as an open-end revolving credit. Credit card loans pose unique risks to these lenders, however. In addition to being unsecured, credit card loans do not have a fixed duration, a lack that complicates the measurement and management of interest-rate risk. Moreover, the mass marketing of credit cards may lead to problems of adverse selection, and small average balances on individual accounts may make collection efforts cost ineffective. Despite such risks, credit card banks have managed to offset the effects of potentially greater volatility and risk in income: their average ROAs are considerably higher than those of the industry as a whole. Their high profitability results from high interest rates on credit card loans, securitization, fee income, successful use of technology, and the benefits of scale economies in credit card operations. It is reasonable to expect that credit card banks will continue to prosper. Credit card banks have been undergoing a process of consolidation, and whether further consolidation may be expected depends heavily on whether they have exhausted the benefits of scale economies.

In this study, "subprime lenders" refers to insured institutions that extend credit to borrowers who may have had more limited borrowing opportunities because of their poor or weakened credit histories. Not only can these lenders increase business volume by serving a new customer base, but they can also be profitable by pricing these loans accurately to compensate for greater risk. Although subprime lenders earn interest income higher than the industry average, their lending activity involves greater risk and losses. Moreover, increased scrutiny from regulators on issues such as capital adequacy and predatory lending practices may have effectively eliminated the advantage the insured institutions once enjoyed relative to other financial firms operating in the subprime lending field. In response, subprime lending has tailed off recently, and some participants have withdrawn from the market. On the basis of the evidence to date, it is reasonable to expect bank participation in subprime lending to stay at reduced levels, if it does not decline further. Internet-primary banks are institutions that deliver banking services mainly on-line. By taking advantage of the Internet distribution channel, these institutions offer convenience to their customers. It was once thought that eliminating physical branches and employing fewer employees would enable Internet banks to provide banking services at lower cost, but in reality, Internet banks underperform brick-and-mortar banks. This may reflect limited consumer demand for Internet banking services. These institutions are also at a competitive disadvantage relative to brick-and-mortar banks in lending to small businesses because they lack the means of building long-term relationships with borrowers. The evidence to date indicates that, as a business model, Internet banks have apparently only a modest chance of success, given present customer attitudes and the present state of technology.

Although limited-purpose banks have compiled a mixed record, their activities can be effectively undertaken by larger, more diversified institutions. A number of credit card banks are subsidiaries of large banking companies. On-line banking is offered by numerous institutions that also offer more traditional forms of access. And with appropriate underwriting and capital support, subprime lending can be a useful component of a more diversified portfolio.

Prospects for Banking Sectors: Summary

Individual banks and groups of banks differ greatly in size, strategy, and operating characteristics. They also share some attributes.

Operating in a generally favorable economic environment, banks have responded to intensified competition and the expanded opportunities offered by sweeping legislative and regulatory change. With some exceptions, they have performed at levels of profitability that would have been regarded as extraordinary in earlier years. Assuming effective macroeconomic and regulatory policies, each of the main banking industry sectors—community banks, regional and other midsize banks, and large, complex banking organizations—should prosper in the years immediately ahead.

PUBLIC POLICY ISSUES

Although the banking industry is likely to continue to be healthy, ongoing trends raise a number of public policy issues, mainly related to the increased size and complexity of banking organizations. Chief among the issues that policy makers need to consider are the safety and soundness of banking in an industry dominated by megabanks, and concerns related to bank customers and markets.

The emergence of megabanks has raised the possibility, however remote, that failures could deplete the deposit insurance funds, require large premium increases that place a heavy burden on the remaining banks, disrupt financial markets, and undermine public confidence. Financial and technological risks arise partly from the problems of monitoring and controlling multiple business lines, geographically dispersed operations, and complex corporate structures. Furthermore, the diversification of large banks into new financial areas exposes these institutions to new reputational risks. The involvement of large financial holding companies in recent corporate scandals illustrates this exposure.

The growing importance of large, complex banks also raises issues relating to concentration and competition in individual markets and the availability of credit for borrowers and local markets that were traditionally served by local banks.

The FDIC's approach to analyzing the effects of large banks in those areas and formulating recommendations for possible action rests on three principles:

Banking should evolve primarily in response to the consumer and the marketplace rather than in response to regulation. The strong performance record compiled by the banking industry in recent years amply confirms what banking can achieve when it is allowed to respond to market forces. There are, of course, situations when government action is required to make markets work better. One example is the establishment of deposit insurance and of the bank safety net generally, which has contributed to the prevention of the extreme instability that characterized financial markets during much of the early history of the United States. Legislation and regulation to prevent anticompetitive practices are another example. In both cases, government action was taken to ensure that markets operate safely, fairly, and competitively.

Risks posed by large, complex banks need to be addressed through effective prudential regulation and supervision. Requiring banks to maintain adequate capital is central to an effective regulatory regime. Effective examination, supervision, and enforcement are equally important. Furthermore, regulation and supervision should be backed by market discipline exerted by holders of unprotected bank securities; regulation and supervision should also be backed by sound governance arrangements adopted by the banks themselves. As suggested above, the potential usefulness of a two-tier, large bank/small bank supervisory system needs to be considered.

To help ensure the effectiveness of prudential regulation and supervision, the structure of the bank regulatory system should be reevaluated. In the fragmented bank regulatory system of the United States, the FDIC as the deposit insurance agency has no direct supervisory responsibility for the major risks to which it is exposed. At the same time, state and federal primary regulatory- agencies that are funded by examination fees are increasingly exposed to financial strains arising from the consolidation of the industry. Within present law, or with minimum legislative change, it may be possible to coordinate better the activities of the various banking agencies, reduce the overall cost of regulation and supervision, and help all bank safety-net agencies discharge their responsibilities effectively.

The discussion that follows is based on these principles. It focuses on major public policy issues arising mainly from the consolidation of the banking industry and the consequent emergence of very large and complex banking organizations. The areas covered are the effects of further consolidation, combinations of banking and commerce, large-bank supervisory issues, governance issues, financial service regulatory issues, bank liability structure, and the economic role of banks.

Effects of Consolidation: Safety and Soundness, Competition, and Small Business Credit

After decades of relative stability, the number of banks in the United States has dropped by about one-half from the level of the mid-1980s. More recently, the pace of consolidation has slackened. Although a resumption of the headlong pace that followed geographic deregulation seems unlikely, further mergers and acquisitions can be expected in the period immediately ahead.

As noted above, investors, market analysts, and managers appear to be strongly in favor of mergers as a means of achieving revenue and earnings growth, even though academic studies do not provide conclusive evidence that greater efficiency will be achieved. Some of the anticipated advantages of earlier mergers and acquisitions have failed to materialize, although it is difficult to say how the merger partners would have fared if they had not combined.

Yet we can also expect the number of banks to remain higher than most recent projections by other analysts. In the absence of a new shock to the industry, it seems likely that the U.S. banking industry will retain a structure characterized by the existence of several thousand small institutions, a less-numerous group of regional and other midsize banks, and a handful of extremely large banking organizations.

It seems reasonable, also, to expect that an eventual balance may develop between the number of new-bank startups and charter losses through mergers and acquisitions—with little net change in the number of banking organizations nationwide.

The public policy issues raised by consolidation concern safety and soundness, market concentration and competition, and small business credit.

The effect of consolidation on safety and soundness. The failure of one of the largest U.S. banks is generally regarded as a low-probability event. Very large banks have greater opportunities to diversify, although the resulting reduction in risk may be offset by increased risk taking to enhance profits and by problems in monitoring and controlling increasingly complex and diverse operations.

The much greater size of today's megabanks, compared with their past counterparts, tends to increase the prospect that the failure of such a bank—although unlikely—would seriously affect the banking and financial systems. Depending on the condition of the industry and the general economy, systemic risk could arise from the failure of a bank that is a major player in certain business lines, including payments processing, international operations, derivatives, and major market-clearing functions. If it is concluded that the least-cost resolution of such a bank represents an unacceptable risk to the financial system and if, consequently, the bank regulators act to protect unsecured and uninsured liability holders, the additional cost will be covered by special assessments. These will be based essentially on assets rather than deposits and will be borne more heavily by the largest institutions. Current law contains certain provisions to deal with the special issues posed by size. Among these are the assessment provision of the systemic-risk exception for large-bank failures, the authority for the FDIC to create different premium systems for large and small institutions, and the authority for bank regulators to require more capital based on risk.

Although various options are available, the most direct way to deal with the size of the nation's largest banking organizations is to ensure that they hold sufficient capital to provide a cushion to absorb potential losses. Regulators can accomplish this by establishing minimum regulatory capital requirements in addition to requirements based on the banks' internal risk estimates (as contemplated by Basel II).

Effect of consolidation on market concentration and competition. As a result of the concentration of banking resources, some large banks may be in a position to exert their market power to raise prices of bank services in some markets. Even with the consolidation of the past 15 to 20 years, however, the banking industry is less concentrated than either its nearest competitors among financial industries—the securities and the insurance industries—or many nonfinancial industries. Banking is also less concentrated in the United States than in other developed countries. Moreover, the 10 percent domestic deposit limit inhibits the creation of a banking monopoly through nationwide mergers and acquisitions. Although some large banks may have more influence on the prices of banking services in particular markets than they once had, sizable increases in prices will invite entry by a variety of bank and nonbank firms. Among those entering these markets will be newly established institutions. The entry of new banks is encouraged by the existence of deposit insurance and would be further encouraged if the reporting and other regulatory requirements that currently place heavy burdens on small banks were reduced.

Taking all these factors into account, we foresee that competitive forces are likely to continue dominating banking markets for the foreseeable future.

Effect of consolidation on small business credit. Concern has been expressed about the effect of banking consolidation on the availability of credit for small businesses and small farms. This concern arises because community banks devote proportionally more of their resources to lending to these borrowers than large banks do. Lending to small business has often been "reputational" in nature, requiring the local expertise that is both characteristic of community banks and more favorable to some small business borrowers, such as new or young firms with limited credit histories. Large banks, on the other hand, are likely to focus more on large borrowers and use credit-scoring and other standardized lending methods in underwriting loans. On the basis of the available evidence, the effect of consolidation on small business credit appears to be complex and dependent on numerous factors. For example, it has been argued that as banks get larger, they are better able to diversify their portfolios and therefore increase their lending to all borrowers, including small businesses. New credit-scoring models used by large banks may identify borrowers who were previously not able to obtain credit from small banks. Moreover, whether small business lending increases or decreases may depend on whether the acquiring bank already regards small business lending as an important business line. The effect of consolidation on small business credit availability also depends on whether there are other lenders in the market that can offset a merger-related reduction in lending. These effects seem to differ between rural and urban markets and between already concentrated and more competitive markets.

The effect of consolidation on small business lending will continue to be the subject of research. Although the outcome of such research cannot be predicted in detail, one important consideration is the possibility that consolidation may create opportunities for the remaining community banks. Any reduction in small business lending by large banks should invite increased lending by community banks, while also encouraging the formation of new banks to serve the needs of these borrowers. The presence of a substantial community bank sector and the prospect of new market entrants are potentially important safeguards against the possibility that bank consolidation will make small business credit less available.

Combinations of Banking and Commerce

As is well known, banking consolidation has been accompanied by affiliations of banks and other financial service firms. GLB permitted combinations of commercial banks, securities firms, and insurance companies. Looking ahead, one can expect market forces to push in the direction of more mixing of banking and commerce. The underlying policy issues are whether permitting affiliations among banks and commercial entities serves the public interest and, if such combinations are to occur, what is the appropriate regulatory framework for them. With respect to the first question, there are two dominant views as to the desirability of maintaining a separation between banking and commerce. Proponents of one view argue that the failure to maintain a line of separation—especially in terms of ownership and control of banking organizations—would have potentially serious consequences, ranging from conflicts of interest to an unwarranted expansion of the financial safety net. Proponents of the other view argue that, if adequate safeguards are in place, the benefits from affiliations between banking and commerce can be realized without jeopardy to the federal safety net. Among these safeguards are requirements affecting bank capital and the enforcement of firewalls to protect the corporate separateness of the bank.

With respect to the appropriate regulatory framework, the Federal Reserve Board maintains that supervision of the insured bank's parent and affiliated companies is necessary if the associated risks are to be understood and controlled. The FDIC has long argued that national and state-chartered banks, regardless of size or holding company affiliation, should be able to choose the ownership structure that best suits their business needs if adequate protections are present. Thus, at the heart of the debate is the question of whether the public interest requires federal regulatory oversight of the entire banking organization or just of the bank.

Although the current prohibitions on corporate ownership of banks are sometimes defended on the grounds that banking and commerce have always been separate, the history of U.S. banking reveals no evidence of a long-term separation. Certainly the activities permitted to banks have always been subject to prohibitions, but the prohibitions on affiliations with commercial firms that are currently in effect stem from the Bank Holding Company Act of 1956 and its amendments. Despite these regulations and prohibitions, however, extensive links between banking and commerce have existed and still exist. And the market pressure for more business combinations between banks and commercial firms can be expected to continue. Moreover, the potential risks of allowing banking and commerce to mix—conflicts of interest, concentration of economic power, and expansion of the safety net—can be contained through the use of adequate safeguards and firewalls. Thus, these risks do not appear to justify a separation of banking and commerce.

Does the mixing of banking and commerce constitute good public policy? The evidence suggests that the answer is a qualified yes: with adequate safeguards in place, the careful mixing of banking and commerce can yield benefits without excessive risk. The issue facing policy makers is how these combinations of banking and commerce will be regulated. Specifically, will increasing amounts of commercial activity be subject to umbrella supervision, or will the insured entity be the focus of supervision? Regulators and policy makers should consider what additional powers, if any, are needed for regulators to be able to effectively ensure the corporate separateness of the insured entity, while also ensuring that banks can choose the corporate structure that meets their business needs.

Large-Bank Supervisory Issues

Large, complex banking organizations pose unique challenges to regulators. Traditional methods of examining banks were suited for smaller institutions, and as financial institutions became larger and increasingly complex, bank regulation and supervision had to adapt. The regulatory and supervisory issues raised by the growth of these banking organizations may be considered in the context of the New Basel Capital Accord, or Basel II. As is well known, the new accord rests on three pillars:

Pillar 1: Minimum Capital Requirements

Pillar 2: Supervisory Review Process

Pillar 3: Market Discipline.

Pillar 1 (capital requirements). On June 26 2004, the Basel Committee on Banking Supervision released the framework for the new Basel capital accord. It outlines the minimum requirements for credit, market, and operational risk. The target for implementation of the new accord was year-end 2006, with the most advanced approach available for implementation by year-end 2007. The proposed accord includes two primary changes to the current capital standards. First, it modifies the approach to credit risk; second, it includes explicit capital requirements for operational risk. Most U.S. banks will continue to use the existing risk-based capital rules, but all very large, internationally active banks will be required to adopt the new capital standards and to use the Advanced Internal Ratings-Based (AIRB) approach to credit risk. Under the AIRB approach, the probability of default, loss given default, and exposure at default will be estimated internally by the banks. With respect to operational risk, the new accord proposes that banks using the AIRB approach will also estimate operational risk internally.

As a member of the Basel Committee, the FDIC has three basic goals for Basel II: (1) capital regulations should preserve and maintain minimum capital requirements; (2) the standards should be designed so that they may be implemented and supervised effectively in the real world; and (3) any new standards should not produce substantial adverse unintended consequences. Among such unintended consequences is the possibility that smaller banks will be adversely affected compared with large banks. As noted above, the FDIC also believes that a minimum regulatory capital requirement should be adopted in addition to the requirements based on the banks' internal estimates as contemplated by Basel II. This belief is consistent with the FDIC's principle that a strong capital base not only is necessary for a safe and sound banking industry but also can equip the industry to weather downturns in the economy or the onset of unanticipated events.

Pillar 2 (supervisory review). The supervision of large banks is challenging because of the complexity of these institutions. Four sources of complexity are size, geographic span, business mix, and nontraditional activities. Given the sheer volume of transactions and types of assets, it is difficult to gather, aggregate, and summarize information in a manner that is meaningful for risk management. The wide geographic span of these institutions, including both domestic and foreign operations, may obscure correlations among exposures. More sophisticated products and a wider range of business activities also complicate supervision. As major business units are acquired or sold, the risk profile of the organizations may change considerably. Supervisors will be strongly challenged to develop the expertise necessary for monitoring the activities of large, complex banking organizations, as well as to avoid extending the safety net to nondeposit products.

Pillar 3 (market discipline). Investors in the various securities issued by banks have interests similar to those of supervisors. This similarity of incentives has led to a number of suggestions that supervisors rely on market discipline for information about and control of the riskiness of banks. As also discussed in a later section, there are two critical questions about market discipline. First, do investors know what the bank is doing? Second, can investors control what the bank is doing? Various views have been expressed about whether banks are opaque to the investor, and recent corporate scandals provide grounds for skepticism as to shareholders' ability to control management. The effectiveness of market discipline is likely to remain a subject of further research.

Governance Issues

Failures of corporate governance can cause enormous financial losses, not only to individual corporations and their stockholders but also to society as a whole. One widely quoted estimate of the cost of U. S. corporate governance failures is $40 billion a year, or the equivalent of a $10 a barrel increase in the price of oil. Enron shareholders alone lost $63 billion in Enron's failure. Recent corporate governance scandals have resulted in new legislative, regulatory, and judicial initiatives to counteract perceived corporate governance failings.

Because of their special and important role in society, banks need to be particularly careful about conflicts of interest, or the appearance of them, so as to maintain public confidence. As a result of earlier banking legislation, current bank corporate governance standards are higher than the standards for nonbank enterprises, and most banks to which the Sarbanes-Oxley Act of 2002 applies have little trouble meeting that act's requirements. In fact, many of the provisions of this legislation are derived from bank governance standards; this law introduces nonbanking businesses to standards that banks have been observing for years.

However, the combination of the Sarbanes-Oxley legislation and new stock exchange rules, recent SEC actions and recent court decisions, a new activism on the part of blockholders, and heightened public scrutiny of business behavior has produced a changed corporate governance environment, one that continues to evolve. The major changes in this environment that will affect banks are changing norms of board independence, increased shareholder involvement, and changing and uncertain standards of board accountability. In particular, bank interlocking directorships may run up against the changing norms for board independence. In addition, public dismay over excessive executive compensation is likely to stimulate shareholder scrutiny of boards' compensation policies—and likely to increase the pressure on some boards.

Banks, like other businesses, must be prepared to meet these evolving standards of corporate governance. The most effective way to avoid corporate governance problems is to select a knowledgeable, engaged, and independent board of directors. However, increased commitments of time by board members, increased liability issues, an emphasis on financial expertise, and the trend toward more independent boards are likely to make it more difficult for banks, and other businesses, to recruit board members.

Some observers suggest that banks and other businesses will need to focus on recruiting people who have traditionally not been members of boards in large numbers—women and both younger and older members: for example, more division directors rather than sitting CEOs, and more retired people who have the time and expertise to devote to board membership. In this demanding and changing corporate governance environment, banks and other businesses may need to expand their vision of what constitutes a qualified board member.

Financial Services Regulatory Issues

In the 20 years since the last major study of the federal financial regulatory system, the financial system has continued to evolve and become more complex. Yet, its regulatory system remains rooted in the reforms of the 1930s. Regulation and supervision of large, mutli-product, internationally active financial organizations that span numerous federal financial regulatory agencies pose challenges for a system designed largely to regulate smaller, distinct, locally based organizations Although changes have been made—especially over the past decade—to improve the regulation and supervision of these new financial conglomerates, it is time to take a hard look at the current federal financial regulatory structure.

As the financial services industry grows larger and more complex, the question is increasingly raised as to whether our fragmented, piecemeal system of regulation is up to the task. Since the mid-1980s a number of countries have examined their financial regulatory structures and concluded that changes needed to be made. Internationally, the trend has been to consolidate all—or most—financial services regulation within one agency and to move that function outside the central bank.

Reform of the U. S. financial regulatory structure raises complex issues regarding deposit insurance, the role of the central bank, and the dual banking system. Although many observers would argue that in the absence of a crisis, regulatory restructuring is not a topic that will generate much political interest in the United States, there are issues that will affect how the financial regulatory system is organized and operates regardless of whether full-scale restructuring is desired. Among these issues are funding for the Office of the Comptroller of the Currency and the Office of Thrift Supervision, federal preemption, the resolution of issues that cross functional regulators, and umbrella supervision for all financial conglomerates that own an insured depository institution.

The options outlined in the paper on which this section is based represent possible ways in which reform or restructuring of the federal financial regulatory system could occur. They focus on the least-intrusive, most easily accomplished reforms (those that regulators could undertake themselves or that require little legislative change) to a full-scale restructuring of the federal financial regulatory system. There are valid arguments for taking either approach or even for finding some middle ground, such as a thorough restructuring of the bank regulatory system. Within each option there is room for debate over how regulation might be structured—for example, what entities might be included. The paper is designed to provide background regarding issues that will influence the debate over regulatory restructuring and to provoke thought and discussion about the design of the U. S. federal financial regulatory system.

Bank Liability Structure

Growth in core deposits (total deposits less time deposits in denominations of more than $100,000) has failed to keep pace with the corresponding growth in bank assets. There may be many reasons, either singly or in some combination, for this phenomenon. The supply of core deposits may be growing at a slower rate than bank assets, banks may be increasingly using alternative funding sources that have lower costs, and some alternative sources may offer risk reducing features. As all of these explanations are likely to be true, the mix between core deposits and alternative funding sources will continue to change. This prospect suggests continued reliance on wholesale funding sources (such as Federal Home Loan Bank advances and brokered deposits) and efforts to expand other nondeposit sources of funds.

These changes in liability structure raise several issues for banking regulators. The one that has received most attention recently is market discipline—particularly for large, complex banking organizations. The research to date shows that unprotected investors monitor bank performance and respond to changes in risk exposure. Supervisors play an important role in ensuring that markets have accurate data on banks, since troubled banks otherwise may overstate capital. The evidence is weaker on the ability of markets to encourage banks to reduce their risk exposure when trouble arises. And for the very largest banks, market discipline may be diminished by the perceptions of market participants that such banks are too big to fail—that is, the perception that uninsured depositors and other creditors would be protected if the institution failed. In the future, more emphasis should be put on disclosing information to the markets as well as on increasing the use of market data to inform and enhance the supervisory process. Another issue raised by banks' heavier reliance on wholesale funding sources and rate-sensitive deposits for funding is liquidity risk exposure, which has increased. Regulators have responded by updating their examiner guidance on liquidity risk. It may also be worthwhile to seek better ways to measure liquidity risk and better ways to handle the operational challenges associated with liquidity failures.

A third issue concerns the assessment base, and a fourth concerns depositor preference. To the extent that asset growth is funded by nondeposit liabilities, the exposure of the FDIC tends to increase without any increase in the assessment base on which premiums are calculated. (The assessment base is essentially the amount of domestic deposits after certain adjustments.) In the past, various proposals were advanced to expand the assessment base. And changes in the liability structure have highlighted the importance of domestic depositor preference when banks fail. Some observers have questioned the cost savings attributed to the present priority provision and have pointed to the provision's potential effects if a multinational banking organization were to fail. In light of changes in the structure of bank liabilities, it may be useful to consider the advisability of revising the assessment base to ensure that premiums are properly aligned with the risks to which the FDIC is exposed, and the advisability of reviewing the effects of the present system of domestic depositor preference.

The Economic Role of Banks

Historically, banks have been regarded as a special class of intermediary because they perform four unique functions: (1) they issue transaction accounts that have universal acceptability and are available at par on demand, (2) they fund idiosyncratic (and illiquid) loans with liquid liabilities, (3) they serve as backup sources of liquidity, and (4) they play a key role in the transmission of monetary policy. Consequently, policy makers have maintained a government safety net that protects and regulates the banking industry to ensure that it operates with minimal disruption. Yet, over the past quarter of a century, revolutionary advances in IT and telecommunications have combined with the economic and political forces of globalization and deregulation to fundamentally alter the operations of financial intermediaries (both bank and nonbank) and the markets in which they operate. One result of these changes is that financial markets are much more complete, efficient, and competitive today than they were 25 years ago. This development has led some observers to argue that banks are no longer unique among financial institutions and therefore do not merit the current level of government protection or regulation.

This study concludes, however, that banks have not lost their importance as financial intermediaries and that they have in fact evolved to meet the challenges and demands of the new world of finance. Banks, for example, are still at the center of the payments system. Indeed, virtually every financial transaction that involves a net transfer of wealth is still eventually settled through the banking system. Banks also continue to play an important role in the transmission of monetary policy. And despite signs of disintermediation and what some see as a decline in the relative importance of banks, banks continue to serve as the primary sources of credit to important segments of the economy (such as small businesses and small farms).

Moreover, as the capital markets have become more developed, banks have evolved to provide important behind-the-scenes support to much of the intermediation activity that occurs elsewhere. For example, almost all commercial paper issues are backed by bank-issued stand-by letters of credit that enhance the paper's credit rating and increase its liquidity. In securitizations, banks are involved in originations, servicing, and monitoring and in the provision of credit enhancements. In this respect, banks remain an important player in the intermediation process even though they are no longer the primary lender or the direct source of the loaned funds. Finally and perhaps most importantly, as has been demonstrated repeatedly during a number of financial panics and crises in the United States over the last three decades, banks play an essential role as emergency sources of liquidity to the rest of the financial system and to the broader economy as well. Indeed, several studies have shown that banks may in fact have a comparative advantage in providing liquidity on demand.

In conclusion, ample evidence is available to support the position that banks (and the business of banking) are not fading away. Rather, in the more complex, sophisticated, and volatile financial world of the twenty-first century, banks' importance may actually be growing.

CONCLUDING COMMENTS

This study views banking as a strong, competitive industry that continues to serve useful economic purposes. Within the banking industry, we conclude that each of the three main sectors—community banks, regional and other midsize banks, and the largest banking organizations—has favorable prospects for the years immediately ahead, even though the number of institutions is likely to decline further. What could materially diminish these relatively favorable prospects?

With respect to community banks, a number of competitive and regulatory developments could diminish their market role and viability. One possibility is that credit-scoring and other financial technology used by large banks and nonbank financial companies could advance to the point that it would supplant the relationship lending practiced by community banks in financing local credit needs, including those of small businesses and small farms. And large banks might adopt organizational structures more conducive to reputational lending—for example, by giving branch managers more authority. The consequences might be analogous to the results in home mortgage lending, where a nationwide market has much diminished the role once played by local portfolio lenders. Given the heterogeneous nature of small business loans and the organizational problems of controlling the activities of far-flung branch systems, this result does not seem likely in the time frame of this study—five to ten years—but it cannot be ruled out completely or indefinitely.

The burden of reporting and other regulatory requirements could also threaten the prospects for community banks. Although the banking industry as a whole is a politically attractive vehicle for implementing various nonbanking political and social programs, the fixed costs of such requirements fall particularly heavily on smaller banks. The resulting regulatory burden could have effects analogous to those of earlier regulations that weakened the ability of banks to compete with credit unions and other nonbank institutions not subject to similar burdens.

Community banks that lack adequate IT staffs are also exposed to the possibility of attacks on the software products they use. In addition to the direct losses they might suffer, the inconvenience to their customers and the damage to their reputations could be a serious competitive disadvantage.

For large banks, the principal issues are the risks associated with size and diversity—the very features that are these banks' main strengths. Problems identifying and mitigating correlated risks, reputational risks arising from potential conflicts of interest and lapses in governance, and operational risks associated with IT systems are among the most prominent of the risks faced by large banks.

For all banks, the possibility of economic bubbles in markets where banks participate, like the bubbles in energy, agriculture, and real estate markets during the 1980s, cannot be entirely discounted. This is particularly so as economic and financial decision making related to banking is increasingly in the hands of those who have experienced nothing but profits. We consider these and similar possibilities to be low-probability, high-impact events within the five- to ten-year horizon of this study. In many cases these possibilities are being addressed by bank management and bank supervisory agencies. Nevertheless, it is important to keep them in mind as a cautionary accompaniment to the relatively favorable picture of banking painted in this study.

At the same time, important policy issues will continue to command the attention of bankers and bank regulators. The consolidation of the banking industry highlights the challenges of supervising large, complex banking organizations. The possibility of large-bank failures poses risks not only to the deposit insurance funds but also to the banking system itself. Market forces are likely to push for more business combinations of banks and commercial firms, raising again the issue of how best to regulate such combinations. The existing regulatory structure appears to be increasingly out of alignment with the rapidly changing financial products and markets. The nature of the safety net itself may need to be reexamined to ensure that it effectively accommodates an industry characterized by a few megabanks alongside thousands of community banks. These difficult issues are likely to be prominent in discussions of the future of banking in the years ahead.

Chapter

13

Market Discipline Prior to Bank Failure

INTRODUCTION

Banking deregulation or re-regulation has been an ongoing process since the 1970s. Many of the restrictions placed on banking as a result of banking panics in the 1920s have been either lifted or modified. Geographic barriers and many product restrictions have been eased. Financial market globalization, product innovations, new technologies, and consolidation, along with regulatory changes, are causing banks and bank supervisors to reconsider how they do business. Supervisors must balance their need for information with the burden imposed on the regulated entities.

The objective is to minimize regulatory burden without compromising the safety and soundness of the banking organization. This can be achieved by increasing market discipline and the use of market information. Market discipline may be enhanced by increasing the incentives for debt holders to monitor bank management – thus complimenting the work of bank supervision. Debt holders can provide bank management with incentives to limit their risky activities by demanding a larger risk premium on bond spreads. In addition, the use of market information in bank supervision can potentially allow bank supervisors to spend less of their scarce resources collecting information from bank management.

Previous studies have examined the role of debt holders in disciplining bank management and have shown that pricing in the debt market is sensitive to the risk profile of the issuing banking firms [Flannery and Sorescu (1996) and Jagtiani, Kaufman, and Lemieux (2000)]. However, the literature sheds little light on whether debt holders can effectively monitor banking firms during the period prior to bank failure. Since the federal safety net subsidy is most critical and market discipline is most needed during the period prior to failure, we focus on the pricing of bank bonds during the twelve quarters prior to failure. Understanding the pricing behavior of banking firms' publicly traded debt during the period prior to failure is a critical element of maintaining the stability of the financial system.

This paper may be considered an extension of two earlier studies by Jagtiani, Kaufman, and Lemieux (2000) and Flannery and Sorescu (1996), which examine the pricing of bank holding company (BHC) bonds during the post-FDICIA period (1992-1997) and pre-FDICIA period (1986-1991), respectively. Both studies find some degree of market discipline in the market for bonds issued by BHCs. However, there has been no study that investigates pricing behavior when banking organizations are facing financial difficulties — our paper fills this gap in the literature. Our results provide implications for proposals that (1) attempt to utilize debt holders to compliment bank supervision, (2) advocate the use of bond spreads in the supervisory process, and 3) advocate increased disclosure to enhance market discipline [see Evanoff (1993) and Haubrich (1998)]. The rest of the paper is organized as follows. Section II describes the data and presents summary statistics of the data.

The Data

Our sample consists of banks that failed during the period 1980 to 1995, whose parent bank holding company had publicly traded bonds outstanding during the recent quarters prior to failure. We started with 185 failed banks (104 BHCs) during the sample period. Several of the failed banks were associated with the same

BHCs.1 Most of the banks on our initial list were eliminated because of the lack of bond data. None of the banks in our sample had outstanding publicly-traded debt, and the parent BHCs of only five of these failed banks did. Our final sample includes those five failed banks whose parent BHCs had outstanding bonds as of their fail date. These banks are Continental Bank, MBank, Southeast Bank N.A., Bank of New England, and Maine Savings Bank. Their parent BHCs are Continental Illinois Corp., MCorp, Southeast Bank Corp., Bank of New England Corp., and One Bancorp, respectively. All of the bonds in our sample are straight bonds, which are not convertible, callable, or puttable. Bonds issued by Continental and MCorp are senior notes, and the rest are subordinated notes. Of all the outstanding bonds of these five BHCs, we selected the bond that had the most price observations. Our sample period varies, depending on when the bond was issued and the fail date. For each banking organization, the sample period starts either twelve quarters prior to failure or when the bond was first traded in the secondary market. All of the prices (end-of quarter) used in this paper are secondary market prices collected from the *Moody's Bond Record* and *Standard and Poor's Bond Guide.* Historical Treasury yields, which are used in calculating bond spreads, are taken from the Federal Reserve Statistical Release H.15 Selected Interest Rates when not available from the Bloomberg. The accounting risk characteristics of the BHCs are collected from the quarterly Y-9 Reports. Moody's historical bond ratings are collected from the monthly *Moody's Bond Record.* BOPEC ratings (given by bank regulators) are collected from the National Examination Database (NED). In addition to the limitation on bond data, our study is also limited by availability of the accounting and rating information. As a result, our sample observations are significantly reduced in the analysis that involves insured deposits, bad loans, or BOPEC rating.

Market capitalization for BHCs is calculated using share prices times the number of shares outstanding as reported in the *Standard and Poor's Stock Guide.* Continental Bank and Southeast Bank are the primary subsidiaries of their parent BHCs, comprising approximately

95 percent of their parent BHC's assets. Bank of New England and MBank are 66 percent and 39 percent, respectively, of their parent BHC's assets. Unlike the rest of the sample, Maine Savings Bank is only a small fraction (about 4 percent) of One Bancorp, which is the smallest BHC in the sample.

The Empirical Methodology

Following Jagtiani *et al.* (2000), we examine the relationship between bond spreads and risk characteristics of the issuing BHCs. Six different credit risk measures are specified in the model: (1) bad loans to total assets; (2) return on assets; (3) percent of insured to total deposits; (4) leverage ratio; (5) bank regulators' ratings; and (6) Moody's bond rating. In addition, a number of control variables are specified in the model, including asset size, a dummy variable that differentiates senior debt from subordinated debt, and dummy variables identifying each of the sample banks in the fixed-effect equation, as shown in equations (1), (1)', (2), and (3) below. In order to avoid multicollinearity, the intercept, asset size (*LOGTA*), and class of debt dummy (*DUMSUB*) are excluded from the estimation in equation (1)' when the bank dummies (*DUMConti*, *DUMSE*, *DUMNE*, *DUMOne*, and *DUMMCorp*) are included in the model. The dependent variable (*SPREAD*) is calculated by subtracting the estimated yield on U.S. Treasury securities with the same term to maturity from the yield on the observed BHC bond. The Treasury yield is obtained from yield curves as of each quarter-end estimated by a straight-line extrapolation from quarter-end market yields reported by Bloomberg for 3, 6, and 9- month and 1, 2, and 3-year to maturity.

BADLOAN is the ratio of the sum of non-performing and defaulted bank loans plus other real estate owned, which represents collateral obtained through foreclosure, to total on-balancesheet assets (consolidated across all subsidiary banks). Non-performing loans include loans past due over ninety days that may be accruing or non-accruing. The larger the *BADLOAN* ratio is, the greater the likelihood of loss, and the larger the bond spread; therefore, a positive coefficient is expected. *ROA* is the ratio of the BHC's annualized quarterly net income to its quarter-end, on-balance-sheet assets. The more profitable the BHC is, the less likely it is to default, and the smaller the bond spread; therefore, a negative coefficient is expected. *MKTLEV* is the leverage ratio measured by the BHC's ratio of book value of liabilities to the market value of common stock plus the book value of perpetual preferred stocks. This is also the definition used in Jagtiani *et al.* (2000) and Flannery and Sorescu (1996). The higher the leverage is, the more likely bondholders will incur losses, and the larger the bond spreads; thus, a positive coefficient is expected.

MOODY is a cardinalized credit rating for the sampled bonds assigned by Moody's as of the end of quarter. The cardinalization is based on Ronn and Verma (1987), ranging from 1 to 9 (see the Appendix). The larger numerical ratings indicate poorer credit quality, so a positive coefficient is expected. Below-investment grade bonds are assigned a number larger than 4.6 *BOPEC* is the regulator's credit rating assigned to BHCs based on the examination results performed by the Federal Reserve. The ratings range from a high of 1 to a low of 5 and are assigned for each of the components (B=Bank, O=Others, P=Parent, E=Earnings, and C=Capital) as well as a composite overall rating. This rating system was adopted in 1982; however, the ratings are available on the NED much later. These ratings are not available for Continental, which failed in 1984; therefore, Continental is dropped when BOPEC ratings are included in the analysis.

The BOPEC rating for Bank of New England was not available until December 1987. Unlike Moody's ratings, which may be adjusted continuously, BOPEC is assigned approximately every twelve to eighteen months. In addition, BOPEC ratings are not assigned on the same date across the sampled BHCs. BOPEC ratings are subject to an aging problem, which has been recognized in previous studies. Following previous studies, we attempt to deal with this problem by taking into account the amount of time that has passed since the rating was assigned. This is particularly important for those banking firms whose BOPEC was downgraded. Thus, our measure of the BOPEC rating is a weighted-average of the rating that was assigned immediately prior to and immediately after the associated observation date. The weight is time, and more weight is given to the rating that is closer to the relevant date.

In addition to the aging problem, the overall composite BOPEC ratings tend to vary little across our sample BHCs. This may be due to the deteriorating financial condition of the banking organization in our sample. It is important to point out that these *composite* BOPEC ratings are relatively subjective, and are not obtained through a mathematical formula based on the individual components (B,O,P,E,C). Unlike the composite rating, the rating of the individual components tends to vary significantly across failed banks, reflecting the varying condition of the components across these banks, and through time. Our measure of BOPEC is an average of each *component's* weighted-average rating.

Several control variables are included in the model. *LOGTA* is the log of total consolidated assets. *DUMSUB* is a dummy variable which is equal to one for subordinated debt (Bank of New England Corp., Southeast Bank Corp., and One Bancorp) and zero for senior debt (Continental Illinois Corp. and MCorp). Finally, *DUMConti*, *DUMSE*, *DUMNE*, *DUMMCorp*, and *DUMOne* are bank dummies, which take the value of one for Continental, Southeast, Bank of New England, MCorp, and One Bancorp, respectively, and zero otherwise.

The Empirical Results

BHCs with more bad loans (*BADLOAN*) and BHCs that are less profitable (*PROFIT*) are required to pay a larger spread. *DUMSUB* is significantly positive, as expected, indicating that subordinated notes are subject to a larger risk premium than senior notes. Comparing this estimation with our analysis of healthy BHCs in Jagtiani *et al.* (2000), we find that increases in profitability seem to be more important (larger negative coefficient) in the pricing of healthy BHC bonds than troubled BHC bonds. In addition, the coefficients of *DUMSUB* suggest that the priority of claims in the event of failure is much more important as serious financial problems become apparent. In terms of leverage ratio, *MKTLEV* is not significant. We have also examined the various interactive terms of *MKTLEV* with bad loans and profitability, but they are also not significant. The results suggest that the market does not view leverage to be important in determining the spread for BHC bonds during the period prior to failure. However, Jagtiani *et al.* (2000) find that, under normal financial conditions, *less-capitalized* banks are penalized more than *better-capitalized* ones for each additional unit of increased risk as measured by these ratios. Our accounting risk factors overall explain about 66 percent of the variation in spread during this stress period. The results suggest that there is strong market discipline in the market for BHC bonds during the period prior to failure.

The intercept, asset size, and *DUMSUB*, which are included in column (1), are not included here to avoid multicollinearity. When individual bank variations are considered, the results remain consistent with those reported in column (1). The coefficients of *BADLOAN* and *PROFIT* remain unchanged in terms of sign and magnitude, although the significance of *PROFIT* declines from the 1 percent level to 11 percent. Overall, the general results hold that BHCs with more bad loans and BHCs that are less profitable pay a larger bond spread. *MOODY* and *BOPEC*, along with the firmspecific dummies, explain approximately 73 percent and 64 percent, respectively, of the variation in spreads across firms and through time. It is interesting that, unlike in the *MOODY* equation, only the *DUMNE* variable is significant in the *BOPEC* equation, implying that regulators' ratings capture bank-specific characteristics more completely than the ratings assigned by credit rating agencies.

The results here are consistent with Jagtiani *et al.* (2000), which examines the pricing of BHC bonds under normal financial conditions. Comparing these results with Jagtiani *et al.* (2000) suggests that, at the BHC level, market discipline is strong when it is most needed; i.e., when the subsidiary bank is in real financial difficulties. Bond spreads range widely from under 1 percent to extremely large spreads prior to failure — just under 20 percent for MCorp. and 30 percent for Southeast. For Bank of New England, the spread was about 70 percent two quarters prior to failure, and up to 100 percent just before its failure. In contrast, Jagtiani *et al.* (2000) report a very small range of bond spreads (less than 1 percent) in the normal environment.

It is obvious that the market penalizes the banks by charging dramatically larger spreads starting approximately five or six quarters prior to failure, particularly for Bank of New England Corp., MCorp, and Southeast Bank Corp. The spread did not change very much for One Bancorp, probably because its failed subsidiary bank, Maine Savings Bank, was only a small fraction of the overall BHC (about 4 percent of the BHC's assets). In the case of Continental Illinois Corp., the spread also did not increase much, although the failed bank was about 65 percent of the BHC's assets. This is quite unusual, and may be explained by the fact that the market and the credit rating agencies at that time seemed to believe that actions taken by Continental Bank's management to restructure its liabilities would resolve the bank's financial problems. The Moody's rating for Continental Illinois Corp. did not deteriorate as much as the other sampled BHCs. The rating on Continental's bonds remained at A2 until the bank actually failed, compared with Caa and Ca for other sample BHCs. In general, the credit ratings fell below investment grade around eight quarters prior to failure.

Overall, our results in this section provide important policy implications for bank supervision. First, since BHC bonds are priced according to risk, requiring banking organizations to issue debt in greater volume and frequency will likely enhance market discipline in the banking system, due to the increased oversight of bank management by concerned bondholders. Second, since spreads on BHC bonds rise sharply as the subsidiary banks' financial condition deteriorates, regulators may be able to augment supervisory information with market information on spreads on publicly traded debt issued by banking organizations.

In addition, our results in conjunction with Berger and Davies (1998) highlight the importance of market disclosure to effective market discipline. Berger and Davies (1998) find that bank examinations produce valuable private information, particularly when the examinations result in rating downgrades, suggesting that the information may reach the market through loan quality data released to the public during the examination process. Consistent with Berger and Davies (1998), our examination of the timing of published reports of negative financial information and the timing of market reaction in each of these failures further demonstrates the importance of mechanisms that ensure accurate and timely financial disclosure to effective market discipline. Specifically, we find that the change in bond spreads was preceded by disclosure of negative financial information, which occurred during the regulatory examinations in four out of five cases, with the exception of MCorp.

Conclusions

This paper examines the pricing of bonds issued by the parent BHCs of failed banks. Our findings indicate that BHC bonds are priced according to risk in the period where the federal safety net subsidy is most critical (prior to the failure of its subsidiary bank). Bond spreads start rising as early as six quarters prior to failure, as the issuing firm's financial condition and credit rating deteriorate. While previous studies of bond spreads for healthy BHCs find spreads range several basis points across BHCs, we find that spreads for troubled banking organizations are many times those of healthy BHCs. The results of this study concur with Jagtiani, Kaufman, and Lemieux (2000) and Flannery and Sorescu (1996), indicating that proposals that attempt to increase market discipline by increasing subordinated debt would be effective (at the BHC level). Requiring BHCs to issue publicly traded debt in greater volume and frequency will likely enhance market discipline in the banking system when it is most needed — when a banking organization's financial condition deteriorates. Our results also highlight the importance of market disclosure in effective market discipline. Efforts to increase accurate market disclosure in a timely fashion will improve the ability of the market to correctly price bank risk and effectively enhance market discipline.

Bibliography

Bandow, Doug, and Ian Vasquez: *Perpetuating Poverty: The World Bank, the IMF, and the Developing World*, Washington, DC: Cato Institute, 1994.

Bhuleshkar, Vasant: *Indian Economy in the World Setting*, Bombay, Himalaya, 1988.

Bouman, F.J.A.: *Small, Short and Unsecured: Informal Rural Finance in India*, Delhi, Oxford University Press, 1989.

Edminster, R.O.: *Financial Institutions, Markets and Management*, McGraw Hill, New York 1986.

Edwards, S.: *Capital Controls, Exchange Rate and Monetary Policy in the World Economy*, Cambridge, Cambridge University Press, 1995.

Goodhart, Charles: *The Evolution of Central Banks*, The MIT Press, Cambridge, 1988.

Guhan, S.: *The World Bank's Lending in South Asia*, Washington, Brookings Institution, 1995.

Hauft, Ottomar: *Distribution of Stock of Money*, Effingham, London, 1892.

Jha, N.K.: *Bank Finance and Green Revolution in India*, Amar Prakashan, Delhi, 1985.

Le Prestre, Philippe: *The World Bank and the Environmental Challenge*, London, Associated University Presses, 1989.

Magliveras, Konstantinos D. *Banks, Fraud and Crime*, Lloyd's of London Press, London, 2000.

Probyn, Mr. : *Indian Coinage and Currency*, Effingham Wilson, London, 1897.

Ranade, Sudhanshu: *Rural Banking Adrift*, Bombay, Jaico Publishing House, 1984.

Ritter, L.S., Silber, W.L.: *Principles of Money, Banking and Financial Markets*,Basic Books, New York, 1977.

Index